TURNER IN THE NORTH

TURNER IN THE NORTH

A TOUR THROUGH DERBYSHIRE, YORKSHIRE, DURHAM, NORTHUMBERLAND, THE SCOTTISH BORDERS,
THE LAKE DISTRICT, LANCASHIRE AND LINCOLNSHIRE
IN THE YEAR 1797

David Hill

Yale University Press
New Haven and London

2 4 6 8 10 9 7 5 3

First published on the occasion of the exhibition
Turner in the North of England 1797
Tate Gallery, London 22 October 1996–16 February 1997
Harewood House, Yorkshire 15 March–8 June 1997

Set in Sabon by SX Composing DTP, Rayleigh, Essex
Designed by Kate Gallimore and Sally Salvesen
Printed in Spain by KSG Elkar

Library of Congress Cataloging-in-Publication Data
Hill, David, 1953–
Turner in the North : a tour through Derbyshire, Yorkshire, Durham, Northumberland, the Scottish Borders, the Lake District, Lancashire, and Lincolnshire in the year 1797 / David Hill.

Includes bibliographical references and index.
ISBN 0-300-06942-1 (hardcover: alk. paper).
ISBN 0-300-06944-8 (pbk.: alk. paper)
1. Turner, J. M. W. (Joseph Mallord William), 1775-1851 —
Notebooks, sketchbooks, etc.   2. England, Northern, in art.
I. Title.
NC242.T9H55   1996
741'.092   dc20   96-21635
                                                                    CIP

FRONT COVER: *Norham Castle, Sunrise*,
Cecil Higgins Art Gallery, Bedford
BACK COVER: *Norham Cast, Sunrise*; detail of Pl.132
HALF-TITLE PAGE: *Harewood Castle from the east*; detail of Pl. 233.
FRONTISPIECE: *Harewood House fom the south*; detail of Pl. 224.

Contents

Preface and Acknowledgements

This book is published on the occasion of the exhibition, *Turner in the North of England, 1797*, at the Tate Gallery, London, 22 October 1996 – 16 February 1997, and Harewood House, near Leeds, Yorkshire, 15 March – 8 June 1997. Both book and exhibition celebrate the bicentenary of one of the most important tours of Turner's career. It is appropriate that the exhibition should have a London and a Yorkshire showing, for Turner was born in London and lived all his life there, yet the scenery of Yorkshire and the north of England was amongst the most important landscapes in the world to him. The venues are doubly appropriate, for the Tate Gallery is custodian of the largest collection of Turner's work in the world, most of it Turner's own bequest, and Harewood House, the home of the Earl of Harewood, provided the principal motive for Turner's first visit to the north. The son of the first Earl, Edward Lascelles invited Turner to Yorkshire to make a series of views of the house, and this provided a springboard for Turner to make a tour across the north of more than 1000 miles. Both Lascelles and his father bought work from Turner, and Harewood still houses much of the work that Turner made for them. Some part of this is normally on display at the house, which is open to the public from March to November and offers a full range of visitor facilities. The Tate Gallery is one of the world's great museums, and offers a permanent display of Turner's oil paintings, and regular changing exhibitions of his works on paper.

I seem to have had most of the fun in this enterprise. The exhibition arrangements have been handled by Carolyn Kerr, Exhibitions Officer, and Ian Warrell, Assistant Keeper in the Turner Collection at the Tate Gallery, and Ann Sumner, Senior Curator at Harewood House. It has been a pleasure and privilege to work with them. Both have given their time and expertise with great generosity. Ian Warrell's contribution particularly has been above and beyond the call of duty, and I am grateful to him for reading my manuscript and suggesting innumerable improvements and amendments. In addition to this, I have most flagrantly employed, and probably abused, the principle that many hands make light work. Turner covered an enormous amount of ground on this tour, and I have called upon the local and expert knowledge of very many individuals, and many more have assisted in one way or another with the exhibition. Let not their number, or alphabetical ordering, diminish my gratitude to anyone: John Adams, John Arnold (Durham Cathedral), S.C. Band (Derbyshire Local Studies Library), Mrs D.M. Barker, Graham Bartlett (National Meteorological Library), Simon Bergin (English Heritage), Ron Bewley (Bamburgh), Sally Bird (Northumberland Heritage), George Bott, Peter Brears, Judy Brevis (English Heritage), Rev. Stuart Brindley (All Saints, Rotherham), Ann Brown (Old Dronfield Society), Mike Davies-Shiel, Hugh Dixon (National Trust), Christopher Dorman-O'Gowan, Rita Freedman (York City Archivist), Richard Green (York City Art Gallery), Jenny Hess (Historic Scotland), Canon Higham (Peterborough Cathedral), Evelyn Joll, John Kington (University of East Anglia), G.A. Knight (Lincolnshire Archives), Rev. Robert Lambie (Ripon Cathedral), Vicky Martin (English Heritage), Samantha Middleton (Bowes Museum), Corinne Miller (Leeds City Art Gallery), Deirdre Mortimer (York Minster Library), Patrick Noon (Yale Center for British Art), Rachel Pollock (Wordsworth Trust), David Posnett (Leger Galleries), A.W. Potter (Royal Academy), Geoff Preece (Doncaster Museum and Art Gallery), Ruth Rattenbury (Tate Gallery), Marion Roussie (Beaverbrook Art Gallery), Eric Shanes, David Sherlock (English Heritage), Sherri Steel (York Castle Museum), Martin Stray (Harrogate Library), Terry Suthers (Harewood), Mr. & Mrs. R.M. Taylforth, D.J. Taylor (Scunthorpe Museums), Penny Thompson (Rochdale Art Gallery), Paul Truelove, Jean Tuck, Antonino Vella (Wakefield Art Gallery), Jane Wallis (Derby Museum and Art Gallery), Henry Wemyss (Sotheby's), Andrew White (Lancaster Museum), Stephen Wildman (Birmingham City Art Gallery), Sally Wilks (Harewood), Ann Woolsey (Rhode Island School of Design, Museum of Art), Andrew Wyld (Agnew's), Lord Yarborough, Bob Yardley and Ed Yardley, together with the many curators and private owners who have made photographs available for reproduction, and works available for exhibition. With regard to the last I should say that as the book goes to press, the exact composition of the exhibition is not yet finalised, and a supplementary list of the exhibition will be available at each venue. In many cases, however, Turner's work will prove too fragile to travel to the exhibition. I have nevertheless attempted to be as comprehensive as possible in the book.

Finally I must mention the postman who, in the middle of January, tried to deliver a letter of mine to the custodian at Dunstanburgh Castle. Dunstanburgh is one of the most remote sites on the tour, has no road access, and is a walk of at least two miles from the nearest village. The letter came back to me with a message written on the envelope: 'Gates Locked, No Letter Box'.

1. Self Portrait, *c*.1798. The artist at about the time of his north of England tour.
Oil on canvas, 745 x 585 mm, Tate Gallery, London (B&J 25).

I   ROUGH-HEWN MATTER

TURNER IN THE NORTH, 1797

Introduction

Even by Turner's own estimation, his journey through the north of England in 1797 was one of the most important tours of his career, and marked the origin of his success. In 1831 when he travelled again through the north country, as his coach toiled up the steep hill past Norham Castle, he suddenly rose from his seat and made a low bow to the ruins. Understandably puzzled by this behaviour, a fellow passenger enquired as to its meaning. Turner explained that some years earlier he had painted Norham. The picture 'took', he said, and from that day on for the rest of his career he always had more commissions than he could execute.[1]

At that time he was fifty-six years of age and at the peak of his career. He had been Professor of Perspective at the Royal Academy for twenty-four years, had travelled over all of mainland Britain and much of Europe besides, his work was the most admired, discussed and controversial highlight of any exhibition, he enjoyed a considerable fortune and the company of many of the most illustrious figures of his age. He was working now on a series of illustrations for the life and work of Sir Walter Scott, and had spent the last few days as Sir Walter's guest at Abbotsford. It was quite an achievement for the son of a Covent Garden hairdresser.

The picture that Turner remembered was *Norham Castle on the Tweed, Summer's morn* (Pl. 129), exhibited at the Royal Academy in 1798. When he visited Norham the previous summer, he was twenty-two but this was by no means the first tour he had made. He had already explored the Thames Valley, Kent, the Isle of Wight, south Wales and the Midlands, but it was by far the most extensive, and the first to take him into the remoter country of Britain. Norham Castle, overlooking the river Tweed and the borderlands of Scotland was the most northerly point that he reached on this tour, and the point at which he penetrated most deeply into what William Gilpin memorably described as the 'rough-hewn matter' of northern scenery. As Turner acknowledged, it was also the point at which in many ways he discovered himself and his future direction as a painter of landscape.

Ruskin dramatised the moment vividly:

And at last fortune wills that the lad's true life shall begin; and one summer's evening. after various wonderful stage-coach experiences on the north road, which gave him a love of stage-coaches ever after, he finds himself sitting alone among the Yorkshire hills. For the first time, the silence of Nature round him, her freedom sealed to him, her glory opened to him. Peace at last; no roll of cart-wheel, nor mutter of sullen voices in the back shop; but curlew-cry in space of heaven, and welling of bell-toned streamlet by its shadowy rock. Freedom at last. Dead-wall, dark railing, fenced field, gated garden, all passed away like the dream of a prisoner; and behold, far as foot or eye can race or range, the moor and cloud. Loveliness at last. It is here then, among these deserted vales! Not among men. Those pale, poverty-struck, or cruel faces – that multitudinous, marred humanity – are not the only things that God has made. Here is something He has made which no one has marred. Pride of purple rocks, and river pools of blue, and tender wilderness of glittering trees, and misty lights of evening on immeasurable hills.[2]

In the northern landscape perhaps things really do exist in a state of greater primordial intensity. The spaces are bigger, the relief more imposing, the weather wilder, the rock more rugged, the wind fresher and the roads muddier. It is certainly a country that reminds us of our physical being. Although Ruskin's account is fanciful in many respects, not least as we shall see with respect to the human dimension, it seems to contain an essential truth: that in the north Turner discovered a quality of experience which was new, and to which he devoted himself thereafter. Until 1797 he was essentially a painter of architecture, but from this point he was increasingly concerned with landscape and the matter of which the world is made: rock, air, water, mist, and light; with the stuff with which it is clothed, and with the energy of the processes that bring this material to life.

The principal documents of the tour are two large, leather-bound sketchbooks in the Turner Bequest at the Tate Gallery in London. The first, the *North of England* sketchbook (TB XXXIV) is inscribed on the cover: 'Derbyshire, Yorkshire, Durham, Northumberland, Tweedale Scotd, Lincolnshire, Northamptonshire' and contains ninety-three drawings, eight in watercolour. The second, the *Tweed and Lakes* sketchbook (TB XXXV) inscribed 'Yorkshire, Tweed, Lakes of Cumberland – Westmorland, Lancashire, York' and contains eighty-nine drawings, eleven in watercolour. Together with various loose drawings, some obviously detached from the sketchbooks, and some made on separate sheets (*see* Part VII The Sketchbooks), he made more than 200 sketches, most of extraordinary detail, care and beauty.

The general framework of the tour is recorded in the *North of England* sketchbook, except for the Lake District where he worked exclusively in the larger *Tweed and Lakes* book. It is easy to see from the numbers of sketches, and from the occasions when he worked in the larger sketchbook, which sites detained him longest. The most important are Kirkstall Abbey, Ripon Cathedral, Fountains Abbey, Durham, Melrose Abbey, the Lake District, York and Harewood House. As we shall see, the level of interest on site was not reflected exactly by the subjects which were developed into finished work. This is partly a result of other people's interests, in that patrons leafed through the sketchbooks and made their own selections. It is also the result of Turner's own interests changing after the tour, and probably because of it. It is also an indication that the response to landscape is not the same in memory as it is in fact, and it is abundantly clear from the sketchbooks and the finished results of this tour that Turner was concerned equally with both. His sketches were made as much as a means to achieving a high quality of experience on site, as for the sake of any work that might have resulted from them.

Turner's route in outline was a huge lopsided figure of eight. We do not know exactly when he left London but this was probably at the end of June after the Royal Academy exhibition closed.[3] His first sketches were made at Wingfield Manor a few miles north of Derby. After this he travelled up the eastern side of the country taking in many of the greatest castles and abbeys in Yorkshire, Durham and Northumberland. At Berwick he turned west down the Tweed valley to Jedburgh and from there took a coach to Keswick. He spent a couple of weeks in the Lakes, working his way south to Furness and Ulverston. He crossed the sands of Morecambe Bay to Lancaster and from there coached to York before visiting Harewood House. From Harewood he travelled across east Yorkshire, crossed the Humber estuary to Brocklesby Hall, not far from Grimsby, and finally made a wide sweep through the market towns of Lincolnshire before returning to London via Peterborough. In total he must have covered over 1000 miles, and taken somewhere in the region of eight weeks. The weather in the north was fairly good in July, for in that month Johnson Grant made a tour through Derbyshire and Yorkshire to the Lakes, and his account of the journey published the following year[4] reports settled conditions throughout, it being particularly hot on the 14th, except for a thunderstorm at Keswick on the morning of the 17th and two wet and dreary days at Ullswater on the 19th and 20th. The first half of Turner's itinerary as far as Melrose and Jedburgh, which must have occupied most of July, seems also to indicate good weather, apart from the suggestion of recent rain at Dronfield in Derbyshire, and of a thunderstorm at Warkworth in Northumberland. The sketches in the Lake District, probably made in the first week or so of August indicate mainly wet and misty conditions, however, and it seems that the weather broke up badly thereafter, for *The Times* agricultural report published on 5 September paints a dismal picture describing 'the corn harvests throughout the land [as]. . . generally unpromising, scarce a district but has suffered severely by the Blight, or mildew; and the incessant rains have added to the calamity. . .oats and barley have suffered much from the severity of the weather. . . Hay suffered by the rains.' He was back in London in September for we know that he made a short trip into Surrey during that month.[5] Retracing the route, or visiting only a few of the sites, will demonstrate vividly what a mammoth undertaking this was, how great the distances involved, how varied the scenery, and how unfailingly sustained was Turner's commitment and enthusiasm.

Turner and Edward Lascelles of Harewood

The basic purpose of Turner's journey to the north seems to have been to visit Harewood House, the home of the Lascelles family, situated between Leeds and Harrogate. He had struck up an association with Edward Lascelles, eldest son of Lord Harewood, by early 1797 for in May Lascelles paid three guineas for a watercolour.[6] This is identifiable as the *Interior of Westminster Abbey* exhibited at the Royal Academy in 1796.[7] On the basis of his obvious capabilities as an architectural draughtsman Lascelles invited Turner to paint a series of views of the family home in Yorkshire (p.152). This marked the beginning of an association which was to last ten years, during which time Turner rose from comparative obscurity to unmitigated succes, and in so doing played a major part in revolutionising the possibilities of the watercolour medium. In both cases Lascelles's patronage can be seen to have acted as a vital catalyst.

Edward's father had inherited Harewood in 1795 and the portrait painter John Hoppner was one of the first artists to visit the family at their new seat. On 14 November Joseph Farington reported: 'Hoppner has been at Mr Lascelles at Harewood House in Yorkshire. Lord Harewood left Mr Lascelles £30,000 a year and £200,000 in money. – Hoppner says they are very good people. – He went with young Mr Lascelles, who has a taste for the arts, & has practiced a little, several excursions to see remarkable places. Bolton Bridge is a very picturesque spot.'[8] Farington further observed on 25 January 1796 that 'Young Mr Lascelles of Harewood House is reckoned very like the Prince of Wales. – The Prince is not pleased at it. He calls Lascelles the Pretender. Making a remark on a portrait painting of him by Hoppner he desired an alteration, at present said He "It is more like the Pretender." At Brighton the Prince has been struck on the shoulder familiarly with a "Ha Lascelles how is it?" To which He has returned a marked look of disapprobation.' The portrait painted of Lascelles by Hoppner in 1797 (Pl. 2) gives us some idea of his character and style. The Pretender spent most of his time at the family's London house in Hanover Square, enjoying a generous allowance from his father, indulging in every luxury of his age, including warm baths at Harley Street, truffles, Schweppes soda water and losing considerable sums at cards, and exercised his taste for the arts in subscriptions to the opera and theatre, fine china and furniture.[9] He also collected pictures. His taste however in this last department was adventurous in the extreme. His preference was for the work of young, up-and-coming *avant-garde* artists, and over a period of about fifteen years he was instrumental in establishing the careers of Turner, Thomas Girtin, John Varley, John Sell Cotman, William Havell, Augustus Wall Callcott and Peter de Wint, who between them transformed the art of watercolour from being a modest and dignified drawing room practice, to one capable of dealing with matters of profundity on terms that rivalled oils.[10] He had a good eye, and all his artists became famous. This might in part have been because of their association with him, and certainly because of the work that he encouraged. In any case it meant that in virtually every instance the works that he bought were bargains. From paying three guineas for Turner's *Interior of Westminster Abbey*, within ten years he would have to pay more than twenty times that sum for a comparable piece.

Lascelles was probably introduced to Turner by Viscount Malden, later Earl of Essex, of Cassiobury Park near Watford. Lascelles was a frequent visitor to Cassiobury and would no doubt have seen the early work of both Turner and Girtin that his friend had collected. Most particularly about 1795, Malden commissioned Turner to make five watercolours of the family's property at Hampton Court, Herefordshire.[11] The series represents one of Turner's most important early essays in country house portraiture, and would have provided an obvious model for the series he was later to do of Harewood. In the event Turner made considerable advances on the prototype, developing a grandeur of scale, solidity of handling, saturation of colour and ambition of imaginative content that makes the earlier works seem positively slight.

2. John Hoppner, Portrait of Edward Lascelles (1764–1814), 1797. A major early patron of Turner. His commission to visit Harewood provided the opportunity for Turner to make his tour of the North of England. Oil on canvas, 898 x 696 mm, Harewood House .

Viscount Malden seems to have found his young artists in an informal Academy run by Dr Thomas Monro who had a house not far from Cassiobury at Bushey in Hertfordshire. Over the years Monro had built up a collection of work by eighteenth-century landscape painters, and he put this and drawings that he borrowed from artist friends at the disposal of his young tyros, bringing them together in the evening at his London house, setting them to work copying items from the collection, and rewarding their endeavours with payment of a few shillings per evening and a supper of oysters. This copying work might seem tedious by today's standards, but through this process the students learned the most intimate details and techniques of all the best established artists in their field. None could have been given a better foundation for their subsequent careers.

Over the years Monro encouraged a succession of young artists in this way including Turner and Girtin, Cotman, John and Cornelius Varley, Louis Francia, William Henry Hunt and Peter de Wint, and in this way collected a large number of lesser works by these artists. His collection was sold at Christie's over five days in late June and early July 1833, and the sale included thousands of items, many apparently doubtfully attributed. Turner himself bought four lots on the second day, and his agent bought another five on his behalf. The authorship of many of these has posed problems for scholars ever since. Most of the drawings bought by Turner were listed by A.J. Finberg in his *Inventory of the Turner Bequest*, 1909, in an 'Appendix of Doubtful and Other drawings' where he suggested that many of the pencil drawings and watercolours were in fact by Girtin and not by Dayes or Turner himself as the sale attributions or later scholars might have suggested. With some exceptions this has been supported by Andrew Wilton in the most recent serious study of the problem.[12] The drawings are mostly of Alpine or Italian subjects, and in many instances copied from the work of John Robert Cozens, but besides these is a sufficient number of north of England subjects to suggest that despite difficulties of attribution, Turner had ample opportunity from this source to derive some idea of the north before he set out.[13]

Many of the artists who 'graduated' from Monro's Academy were taken up by Lascelles, and he doubtless took a close interest in the kind of work that they did there. Girtin even had the opportunity to pass on the benefit of his instruction to his patron for there is a record of a payment to Girtin for lessons,[14] and an album of Lascelles's work, mostly monochromatic but nevertheless quite impressive watercolours very much in the style of the Monro circle, survives in the library at Harewood.[15] In the event he came to admire Girtin's work even more than that of Turner, contending in 1799 that Turner 'finished too much' and 'effected his purposes by industry'. Girtin, he thought, had the greater 'genius'.[16] His support for Turner continued undiminished, however, and he bought work beyond the completion of the Harewood series, including two highly developed products of the north of England tour, *Kirkstall Abbey, Yorkshire* (Pl. 39) and *Norham Castle on the Tweed, Summer's morn* (Pl. 130), and also two of the most spectacular watercolours following Turner's election as Royal Academician in 1802, *Lake Geneva*, now in America,[17] one of the results of his first tour to the Alps in 1802, and *Pembroke-castle, Clearing up of a thunder-storm*, exhibited at the Academy in 1806.[18] The Harewood series itself represents one of the most important groups of work from his early career, but the further significance of Turner's association with Lascelles is that it presented the artist with a motive to make his tour of the north of England in the first place. For it was on the basis of this tour that his future direction as a landscape painter was determined.

Sources and Precursors

How Turner planned his route, decided which sites to visit, or determined his approach to his subjects, we do not know, but judging from the sheer number of sites, the thoroughness with which he studied them, and the fact that he seems to have missed very little that would not have required a considerable detour to include, he must have invested considerable effort in his preparation.[19] He had already painted small watercolours of *Wakefield* (Pl. 19), *Sheffield*[20] and *Carlisle*[21] for the *Copper-Plate Magazine*, and although the engravings of these were published between October 1797 and August 1798, they are all compositions that obviously predate the tour of 1797, and were probably based on sketches by other artists.[22]

Girtin was clearly Turner's most most immediate source of information about the north. Quite apart from the Monro circle work that seems attributable to him, Girtin had a considerable knowledge of north of England subjects through his apprenticeship to one of the leading topographical artists of the time, Edward Dayes. Dayes seems to have travelled in the north several times, and to have been particularly well grounded in its subjects through his association with the antiquarian James Moore, who travelled extensively making sketches and had Dayes work these up into finished watercolours. One of the results of this arrangement was the publication in 1792 of a series of *Monastic Remains and Ancient Castles in England and Wales*, and in the same year Moore travelled in the north and to Scotland to gather material for *Twenty-Five views in the Southern Part of Scotland* published in 1794. Dayes became something of an expert on northern subjects and his journal of a tour through Derbyshire and Yorkshire was published posthumously in 1805. Turner was one of the subscribers to this edition. In Dayes's studio Girtin worked on numerous northern subjects,[23] and he would certainly have been able to transmit this to Turner, even if Turner did not make enquiries directly of Dayes himself.

In 1796 Girtin put this grounding in north of England subjects to good effect by himself making an extensive tour of Yorkshire, Durham and Northumberland and the Scottish borders. The immediate results of this tour, two watercolours of Jedburgh, two of Lindisfarne Priory and four of York, were hanging on the walls of the Academy exhibition of 1797 even as Turner made his own preparations for departure. We have only a partial record of Girtin's itinerary but it included many of the sites that Turner visited in 1797. He visited Ripon, Fountains, York, Richmond and Egglestone in Yorkshire; Durham; Tynemouth, Warkworth, Dunstanburgh, Bamburgh and Lindisfarne in Northumberland; and Kelso, Dryburgh, Melrose and Jedburgh in the Scottish borders. In many cases (cf. e.g. Part III, Lindisfarne, Jedburgh, and Part V, York) there are extremely close comparisons between his compositions and Turner's, and it seems highly likely that Girtin showed Turner his sketches and the work that he was developing from them, and gave freely of whatever advice and information he could supply. The exact picture of what Girtin did in 1796 is somewhat clouded by the fact that the north of England became a major subject in his œuvre, and it has not yet proved possible to establish anything like a firm chronology for his work. He returned a number of times up to his death in 1802, largely through his close association with Harewood where it is said that a room was kept permanently reserved for his use.[24] The picture is further complicated by the fact that Turner seems to have reciprocated Girtin's help, and put his own sketches at his friend's disposal, and there are some cases (cf. e.g. Part II, Kirkstall, and Part V, York) where Girtin seems to have made work based directly on Turner's example.

Another source of information for both Girtin and Turner was the very fine watercolourist Thomas Hearne. Hearne perhaps did as much as anyone of his generation to record north of England subjects, and to bring them before the public. In 1777 and 1778 he visited the gentleman amateur and connoisseur Sir George Beaumont in the Lake District, and with him made two tours, the first year to Northumberland, Durham and Yorkshire, and the second year to Scotland returning through the Borders, Northumberland, Durham and Yorkshire. From the sketches made on these visits he developed numerous watercolours, many of which were engraved from 1778 in a very high quality and much admired publication, *The Antiquities of Great Britain*. By the time the volume was completed in 1786, it consisted of fifty-two plates, thirty-seven of which derived from his tours with Beaumont. Girtin studied these closely and copied the subjects of Kelso, Ripon, Barnard Castle and Melrose. Hearne was also a favourite of Dr Monro. In 1795 he told Farington that he 'considered Hearne as superior to everybody in drawing',[25] and it seems very likely that both Girtin and Turner studied his work in the evenings at Monro's Academy. It is possibly coincidence that in 1797 Turner sketched some of the same subjects as Hearne, but there can be no doubt that he was much influenced by the older artist's example. Hearne was one of the most sensitive, intelligent, knowledgeable and skilled artists of his generation, and although there have been some attempts recently to bring him the widespread attention that he deserves,[26] his audience remains relatively restricted. Very few artists managed his understanding of architecture, and fewer still his ability to bring his subjects to life with telling detail,[27] thoughtful effects of light and intelligent construction. Turner built his own art on essentially the same foundations, and although he went on to develop a much richer and altogether more dramatic style which somewhat eclipsed the older man's work – in 1807 Viscount Malden, by then Earl of Essex, told Farington that he could not 'be brought to relish Hearne's drawings; but think[s] them cold and tame imitations. Turner has lately made drawings.. which have an effect which pleases. . .'[28] – he

never forgot that the essential quality of Hearne's work stemmed from the knowledge that underpinned it. By the time that Turner and Girtin made their tours of the north of England, Hearne was busy on a second series of the *Antiquities* begun in 1796, and it is likely that both young men sought his advice and recommendations. A touching proof of their association is that at Girtin's funeral in 1802, Hearne was, with Turner, one of the mourners.

Turner's tour to the north was made at the end of a century in which the general consciousness of Britain and its contents increased dramatically. As travel became quicker, more practical and even, occasionally, more comfortable, so increasing numbers of tourists took to the roads to discover Britain for themselves. Route finding was made simpler by the publication from 1675 of John Ogilby's road books, and by the increasing availability of maps, and by an explosion in the publication of journals, histories and guides. The quantity of such literature increased dramatically as the eighteenth century progressed. It is perhaps dangerous to generalise over the contents of this literature, as most travellers incorporated a complex range of interests into their individual responses, but a number of general themes might be defined: the state of the country in terms of standards of living, manufacture and agriculture; science including flora, fauna, geology and natural curiosities; history and antiquities; and scenic experience and description. Of these the last was much the latest to develop, but by the end of the eighteenth century was by far the most dominant.

A number of writers were particularly influential in widening awareness of the north of England. In his *Tour through the Whole Island of Great Britain* published in parts between 1724 and 1727, Daniel Defoe drew a lively picture of a human landscape teeming with towns and villages, their inhabitants devoted to trade, commerce and industry. His bold, and no doubt true, statement that 'Liverpoole is one of the wonders of Britain'[29] gives a clear signal as to where his interests lay. He was fascinated by the machinations of the Leeds cloth market in which up to £20,000 worth of goods could be traded in an hour in whispers,[30] but of the north country outside the towns he had little to say apart from how desolate it all seemed. Travelling across the Pennines from Rochdale to Halifax he was caught in snow, and struggled, up dale and down, for what seemed an eternity, his sight straining for some hint of a Christian country.[31] He perhaps had good cause for complaint, it being August. Travelling from Harewood to Ripon he 'went directly north over a continued waste of black, ill-looking, desolate moor, over which travellers are guided. . . by posts set up for fear of bogs and holes.'[32] On another occasion journeying north from the 'rich, populous and fruitful' landscape of Lancashire, he could find little else worth his comment. Windermere had some interesting fish in it, but Westmorland was a country noteworthy only for being the 'wildest, most barren and frightful of any that I have passed over.'[33] Scenery meant nothing to him, and there is little evidence that his attitude was not anything but entirely reflective of its time. The book proved immensely popular as a guide and went through nine editions to 1778. It is perhaps indicative that tastes had changed by then, the ninth edition was the last until 1927.

Antiquarian histories were another popular form and enjoyed particular vogue during the eighteenth century. There were numerous examples specialising in the north of England including Ralph Thoresby's *Ducatus Leodiensis* on the area of Leeds (1715), Francis Drake's *Eboracum* on York (1736), John Wallis's *History and Antiquities of Northumberland* (1770), Thomas West's *Antiquities of Furness* (1774), Joseph Nicholson and Richard Burn's, *History of Cumberland and Westmorland* (1777), and William Hutchinson's *History of County Durham* (1785). Some of these, such as Thomas Gent's histories of York (1730) and Ripon (1733), and Ely Hargrove's *History of Knaresborough*, first published in 1775, were pocket-sized and functioned more as guides, but most tended to be published for a select subscription of gentlemen in such a luxurious format as to have never enjoyed much more than limited circulation.

The interest in antiquities, and a consciousness of England's history, was nevertheless strong , and a market developed for illustrations of these sites in the form of engravings, many produced as adjuncts to the histories or as freestanding publications. One of the earliest and most comprehensive undertakings in this area was Samuel and Nathaniel Buck's *Antiquities; or Venerable Remains of above Four Hundred Castles, Monasteries, Palaces &c &c in England and Wales* which was published by subscription in seventeen annual parts between 1726 and 1742, and amounted in total to 422 plates. The series included virtually every antiquarian site of significance in the country, but the Buck brothers toured the north in 1719–20 and gave prominence to northern subjects early in the series, twenty-four Yorkshire subjects being issued in 1726. The grand compendium of antiquities came very much into fashion after the late 1770s. In 1774 the Bucks' series was reissued and in 1773 Francis Grose began publication of his *Antiquities of England and Wales* which continued to 1787, and was afterwards issued in a number of editions up to 1798. In 1778 Thomas Hearne began publishing his high quality plates of *Antiquities of Great Britain*. This amounted to a volume of fifty-two plates by 1786 including many north of England subjects. In 1778 George Kearsley began publishing the *Virtuosi's Museum* which amounted to 150 views published in 1781[34] and again by Boydell in 1782–3, mostly of the work of Paul Sandby, but which contained comparatively few northern subjects. By no means the last or best of these compendiums was Henry Boswell's *Historical descriptions of picturesque views of the antiquities of England and Wales*, published in 1786, containing hundreds of small and somewhat old-fashioned views of castles and abbeys including numerous northern subjects. By itself, this might not have been of any very great importance were it not for the fact that as a schoolboy of thirteen or fourteen Turner hand-coloured a copy for a friend of his uncle in Brentford. The copy survives in Chiswick Public Library and one can have no doubt that Turner's experience of this in his formative years had a decisive effect

on the plan of his life. Over the next forty years or so he managed to visit a large proportion of the sites it contained.

By the time that the Bucks' *Antiquities* was reissued in 1774, the style of the plates must have begun to seem rather old-fashioned. As the new generation of artists, particularly Paul Sandby and Thomas Hearne, began to tackle this sort of subject, they began to develop much greater pictorial interest. The scenes were increasingly brought to life by the introduction of figures, dramatic effects of light and weather, a sense of the landscape in which the subjects were set, greater representational skill and detail, and mood and atmosphere creating a sense of imaginative content. In the background to this process was a developing sense of landscape as subject matter with the capacity to convey richness of meaning and association. Seventeenth-century painters in Italy such as Claude Lorrain, Salvator Rosa, Nicolas Poussin and Gaspard Dughet, together with Dutch and Flemish painters such as Rubens, Rembrandt, Bakhuyzen, Ruisdael, Berchem, Cuyp and many others found their way into British collections and these works began to inform responses to native scenery. British artists, most notably Richard Wilson adopted these frameworks, and many began by the middle years of the eighteenth century to apply these possibilities to the depiction of specific British subject-matter. It was a slow and sporadic process to begin with, and artists such as Thomas Smith of Derby who published a *Book of Landscapes* in 1751 which included a view of High Force in Teesdale[35] – exceptionally remote subject matter for that date – and a series of *Views of Windermere, Thirlmere and Derwentwater* in 1761,[36] or William Bellers who issued a series of Lake District subjects in 1752-3,[37] were exceptional at that time. British artists were swelled in number by foreigners such as Balthazzar Nebot, John Baptiste Claude Chatelain, François Vivares or the Dane Nicholas Dall, who from the 1760s made something of a speciality of northern England subjects, exhibiting a view of the spectacular but somewhat off-the-beaten-track Kilnsey Crag in Wharfedale at the Society of Artists as early as 1766. In the early 1770s he made a series of four paintings of Yorkshire subjects, Harewood Castle, Aysgarth Falls, Knaresborough Castle and Richmond Castle as part of the original decorative scheme for the saloon of the newly-built Harewood House, and Turner would have seen these in 1797 when planning his own paintings of *Plompton Rocks* (Pls 236, 237) to join them.

Even though three of Dall's four Harewood paintings are antiquarian subjects, his emphasis is definitely on their interest as part of a scenic experience of the country, and it was the north of England, and particularly the Lake District, which was to provide much of the subject-matter for the first widespread popularisation of pure landscape. In 1783 Samuel Middiman began publication of a series of fifty-three plates of *Select Views in Great Britain engraved by S. Middiman from pictures by the most eminent artists with Descriptions* which continued to 1787 and included work by George Barret, Francis Wheatley and John Warwick Smith.[38] When the complete series was reissued in 1813 Middiman claimed that it was 'one of the first to have created a taste for the sublime scenery of Great Britain. The Lakes and Mountains of Westmorland, Cumberland and Lancashire, now the general resort of the Tourist and the admiration of the painter, were but little noticed at the time of the publication of the early numbers.'[39] Perhaps he had failed to market the work properly, for the Lake District was by that time frequently visited and its scenery enjoyed. Thomas Hearne, as we have already seen was there in 1777 and 1778 and made many watercolours of Lakes subjects thereafter. While there he enjoyed the company of his fellow-artist Joseph Farington, a north countryman born at Leigh in Lancashire, and who enjoyed a long career in London art society becoming one of the central characters around whom Royal Academy society revolved. His diaries recording the day to day comings, goings and gossip of this society have secured him lasting fame, and we have heard from him already several times in this respect, but he was also a competent, and sometimes impressive artist with a particular specialism in north of England subjects. He was resident at Keswick from 1776 to 1781 collecting material for regular Lake District exhibits at the Royal Academy over the next few years, and for a series of twenty superbly engraved *Views in the Lakes &c in Cumberland and Westmorland*, published like Hearne's *Antiquities* with text in both English and French between 1784 and 1789. He made regular tours to the north of England and would have been a major authority on the subject. It is perhaps unfortunate that Turner did not get to know him personally until after his own tour in 1797, for they seem to have first met just before the Academy exhibition of 1798 opened, when Turner was putting the finishing touches to his own north of England exhibits. Farington records that he 'found Turner there touching his pictures. . . seemed modest and sensible'.[40] It seems hard to imagine, however, that Turner would not have already been familiar with Farington's work.

Landscape sensibility dawned equally slowly in topographical literature. In Defoe the only flashes of description occur when the landscape imposed itself on him inconveniently, and few travel writers before the 1780s made description of scenery much of a priority. Some exceptions prove the rule, and many of the most outstanding of these, like the artists, developed their responses in the Lake District. Among the best-known were John Dalton, who in 1755 published a *Descriptive Poem Adressed to Two Young Ladies [&c]* describing the scenery around Derwentwater,[41] John Brown who in 1767 published a *Description of the Lake and Vale of Keswick*[42] and Thomas Gray whose journal of his tour through the Lakes and the Craven Dales of north-west Yorkshire in 1769, first published in 1775[43] became a benchmark by which other scenic description was to be judged. It is significant that both Brown and Gray make reference to artists, Brown famously to the 'Beauty, Horror and Immensity' of Derwentwater requiring 'the united powers of Claude, Salvator and Poussin' to do it full justice,[44] and Gray to more contemporary work, noting that Vivares, Smith of Derby and Bellers had preceded him at Malham and Gordale in Yorkshire.[45] Dalton's model was more literary, being very much in the style of the most powerful influence on eighteenth century appreciation of landscape, that of James Thomson, whose poem *The Seasons* was first published in parts in the late 1720s, and thereafter complete in 1730 and in dozens of editions right down to the nineteenth century. Few poets have treated the description of nature so vividly or so copiously, and although his descriptions are rarely of specific sites or places, it is perhaps significant for our purposes, and more particularly for Turner who read Thomson avidly, that the poet hailed from the Tweed valley, and although most of his life was spent in the south, might well be seen to have derived much of his experience of landscape from his childhood in the north.

Apart from his subject-matter, Gray's most important contribution to landscape sensibility was that his response was essentially, although frequently exaggeratedly, *felt*. It was the capacity of scenes to stir his emotions that he communicated most vividly. Neither Gray nor Brown nor Dalton achieved a very wide audience among tourists in their original publications, however, until they were included as appendices to the second edition of Thomas West's *Guide to the Lakes* in 1780.[46] The very title of 'guide' suggests that it was conceived for use in the field, and its main purpose was to direct its users to outstanding vantage points from which they might enjoy the landscape as scenery. He directs the eye from object to object in the scene, giving the names of mountains and islands, and drawing attention to any particular forms or features in view. No-one had written anything quite like it before. The most popular published tours of the time, books such as Arthur Young's *Six Month Tour through the North of England* published in 1770,[47] or Thomas Pennant's *Tour in Scotland and Voyage to the Hebrides in 1772* published in 1774,[48] which included a comprehensive itinerary through the Lakes, Northumberland, Durham and Yorkshire, although both illustrated, show relatively little concern for scenery as such. West was concerned with little else, and his *Guide* quickly became one of the best-selling books of the time and had run to nine editions by 1799, little more than twenty years after first being published. It is interesting to note that in 1797 William Gell made a tour to the Lakes,[49] and mentions, probably as a typical framework of references West, Grose, Byrne and Gray as his sources.

The other great scenographic text of the 1780s was William Gilpin's *Observations, Relative chiefly to Picturesque Beauty made in the year 1772 on several parts of England, particularly. . . the mountains and lakes of Cumberland and Westmorland* published in 1786.[50] This, too, went through several editions, but had a much less straightforward purpose than simply describing and encouraging the experience and enjoyment of scenery. Gilpin had visited the Lakes in 1772 and his manuscript embellished with prints and watercolours survives in the Bodleian Library in Oxford. His observations include flashes of brilliantly vivid descriptive prose, but his main purpose was to develop a theory and process which might be applied to the raw material of observation, and thereby transmute it into the proper and pleasing forms of art. In the north of England, as he conceived it:

> . . . it cannot be supposed that every scene, which these countries present, is correctly picturesque. In such immense bodies of rough-hewn matter, many irregularities, many deformities, must exist, which a practised eye would wish to correct. Mountains are sometimes crouded – their sides are often bare, when contrast requires them to be wooded – promontories form the water-boundary into acute angles – and bays are contracted into narrow points, instead of swelling into ample bosoms. In all these cases, the imagination is apt to whisper, What glorious scenes might here be made, if these stubborn materials could yield to the judicious hand of art. And to say the truth, we are sometimes tempted to let the imagination loose among them. By the force of this creative power an intervening hill may be turned aside; and a distance produced. – This ill-shaped mountain may be pared, and formed into a better line. . .[51]

Though Gilpin evidently delighted in touring, his theory held uncultured perception in low esteem, and he argued himself out of enjoyment of simple experience. His book was popular, but his pedantry ridiculed, and the *Observations* might best be understood as an entertaining attempt to swim against the tide. From the generalised ideals of Italianate painting, late eighteenth century taste was already learning to delight in the specific particularities of reality.

Turner's tour of 1797 draws all these strands together. Through Derbyshire, Yorkshire and Durham, his subject is mostly the old stones of the antiquarians, in scholarly and deep felt response to a succession of ancient houses, churches, castles and abbeys. Gradually in the borderlands of Northumberland and the Tweed valley this subject-matter expands to include the broader sweep of their setting and a sense of his own and their exposure to the elements under broad skies, battered by waves on wide sea strands and bold headlands, or suffused by the sun in quiet inland valleys. From this he graduates to the dissolving forms of the Lake District, where elemental energies transmute from rock and lake to rain-laden clouds on the shoulders of dark fells. Then suddenly he is back in the bustling space of modern life, studying the new form of Harewood House in its ordered estate, and the hubbub of York streets and the market towns of Lincolnshire. These themes overlap a little, but the tour nevertheless gives a sense of Turner moving through every aspect of the framework of subject-matter and response that had been established in the eighteenth century. It is slightly frustrating therefore, not to have been able to make direct connections between Turner and any of the literature that was available to him, with the notable exception of Thomson's *Seasons*. He does not for example seem to have used West's *Guide*, or at least if he did, he studiously avoided sketching from any of his recommended viewpoints, nor Gilpin, nor Pennant, nor even Gray. The same is true, with the exception of Girtin, and perhaps Thomas Smith of Derby (*see* Part II, Kirkstall) for the artists. He probably learned of potential subject-matter from a wide variety of sources, but in selecting viewpoints he seems to have followed very much his own direction.

Turner, however, differs from most of his predecessors in one important respect. Though many different kinds of persons made journeys in the eighteenth century – journalists, professional tradesmen, artists, family groups, gentlemen and clerics, travel for personal pleasure and interest was still so expensive as to be beyond the means of all but the rich. Tourism for someone of Turner's class was very much a privilege. He clearly felt lucky to be able to go forth and participate in the experience and spectacle of the world and he seized the opportunity tenaciously. His sense of good fortune in being able to do so never once wavered throughout his life.

II OLD STONE

Journey North;

Derbyshire, Yorkshire, Durham

Kirkstall Abbey, detail of Pl. 24

One morning at the end of June 1797, a young man of twenty-two was among the throng of passengers in the courtyard of a north London coaching inn. He was embarking on a tour of at least two months through some wild country in possibly wild weather, which would involve him in every mode of conveyance including horse-riding, boating and walking besides coaching. He would not have been heavily encumbered for he would at various times have to carry all his belongings on his back. An umbrella would have been useful, a warm and weatherproof coat and hat essential, and shirts, breeches, linen, stout boots and shaving kit a minimum besides. He was also carrying some equipment which marked him out from the average traveller: pencils, brushes, paints and two large folio sketchbooks, expensively bound in full calf-leather covers fitted with brass clasps. His fellow-travellers would have had no particular reason to notice, except for the fact that little escaped his attention, but the young man with keen eye and somewhat withdrawn disposition, was setting out to become one of the greatest of all painters of landscape.

En route for Derbyshire he probably took one of the fast Great North Road coaches to Stamford, which would have taken a full day, slept over night, and the next day pressed on via Leicester towards his first site, Wingfield Manor, about seventeen miles north of Derby. Interesting as Wingfield might be, this route seems something of a detour from Turner's main purpose. His sketches on the tour start properly in the Don Valley in Yorkshire, and he could have travelled conveniently to Doncaster straight up the great north road. His detour into Derbyshire seems to want some explanation and it may be that he visited Sir George Beaumont who lived at Coleorton between Leicester and Derby.[1] Sir George was one of the leading experts on north of England subjects, having travelled with the watercolourist Thomas Hearne in the late 1770s, and he would have been well-equipped to give Turner advice. We can have no doubt that Turner took advice wherever he could, and that he was well prepared for his journey. In the event none of his sources could have felt their time wasted. Few can have invested as much energy and commitment in a tour as Turner did in his journey to the north in 1797.

Wingfield Manor
Derbyshire

Derby 17 m s. Chesterfield 11 m N. Immediately s. of South Wingfield village. English Heritage, open April – October, admission charge. Viewpoint to NW accessible by public footpath from village.

Wingfield stands on a small hill above the Amber valley. Its jumble of towers, gables, chimneys, courtyards and halls was built for Ralph, Lord Cromwell in the middle of the fifteenth century, and when completed was one of the largest courtyard palaces in Britain. In the sixteenth century it was owned by the Earl of Shrewsbury who used it to house Mary, Queen of Scots, and in the seventeenth century was an important garrison during the Civil War. In 1644 following a siege against 200 Royalist soldiers, the house was made mostly uninhabitable. During the eighteenth century the Halton family occupied the great hall, but following the completion of a new house nearer the village in about 1780 the remains were left to moulder except for part used as a farmhouse.[2]

One visitor from about the same time as Turner was John Byng. On 19 June 1790 he found the place deserted but secured the services of a local guide:

> He deplored the late desertion and desolation of this place: within these ten years it was (in part) genteely inhabited, and since that by a gardener, till within this twelvemonth; but the present owner, Mr Halton, has demolish'd this grandeur to help build his little meanness, having lately torn up the flooring of the fine old vaulted cellars, and strip'd off the lead that roof'd the hall. – This hall (of which I have a print) is yet glazed, and in it are coats of arms, stags horns, and some stain'd glass (*out of reach*); and in another room a ruined spinnet, from which (as a *true* antiquary) I *brought-away* some of the jacks: amongst many apartments, long fallen in, is sprung up good timber. My guide (the best that cou'd be) made the most pertinent remarks; led me into every corner; and then around the grand outside. Spake of the siege it sustain'd in the civil wars; shew'd every rent in the walls as if made by cannon balls. . . In its present state, from shade, situation, and remains, it is one of the most curious, and well-worth seeing bits of antiquity in the kingdom.[3]

3. Wingfield Manor, Derbyshire, inner courtyard, 1797.
Pencil and watercolour, 230 x 270 mm, 'North Of England' sketchbook, Tate Gallery, London, TB XXXIV 1.

4. Wingfield Manor, Derbyshire, inner courtyard. Turner appears to have shifted viewpoint while making this sketch in order to include as much detail as possible.
Photograph, the author.

The publication of *A History of the Manor and Manor-house of South Wingfield in Derbyshire* by T. Blore in 1793 suggests that the house was gaining celebrity, but few images of the house have yet been collated, and Turner's sketches of the site stand as important historical records. His first (Pl.3) was taken in the inner courtyard, recording the south porch, roofless great hall, and gable of the great chamber to the left (Pl.4). Visitors to the site will find it entertainingly difficult to find a single viewpoint which gives the buildings exactly as recorded in the sketch, and the rather strange perspective of the

two end gables of the great hall (parallel in fact), suggests that he shifted viewpoint at least once. His objective, as always, was to include all the characteristic and important features in view, and even though this is by no means the most detailed sketch that he was to make on the tour, there is already a customary sense of care and method in his work. He finished the sketch with some delicate washes of colour and by the end of this tour no-one can have been more familiar with the play of light on old stone, whether basking in the sun, or glimmering in cool rain.

He completed his work at Wingfield by taking the view from the NW (Pls 5, 6), from the lane running down to the new house. Thus in his first two sketches of the tour, the balance of his interests is in evidence. Firstly those of the antiquarian draughtsman he was as he set out, and secondly those of the landscape painter he was to become. Turner's landscape furthermore was not just scenery, but a place in which lives were lived. In the foreground is a woman carrying a child, standing back from the road, as a heavily loaded haywain rumbles up the hill, no doubt to deliver its load to one of the village barns behind us.

5. Wingfield Manor, from the north-west.
Photograph, the author.

6. Wingfield Manor from the north west, 1797. Turner's sketches frequently include figures. He was always interested in the human dimension of his landscapes.
Pencil, 230 x 270 mm, 'North Of England' sketchbook, Tate Gallery, London, TB XXXIV 2.

Dronfield
Derbyshire

Approx 17 m N of Wingfield Manor via Chesterfield. Rotherham 12m NE via Sheffield (6m N). Church of St John the Baptist. For details of services and access apply to the rector. Close approximation to Turner's view from road nearby to SE.

Dronfield lies midway between Chesterfield and Sheffield, and its old inns, particularly the early seventeenth century Green Dragon near the church, provided a convenient halt for coaches, and Turner seems to have taken advantage of the break in journey to sketch the impressive church[4] (Pls 7, 8). St John the Baptist was begun in the early twelfth century and much enlarged in the fourteenth and fifteenth centuries when the parish enjoyed a peak of prosperity. After that Dronfield slipped into relative obscurity until the industrial revolution, and in 1795 was deemed to be remarkable only for its quietness and neatness, for the 'finest spring water in the kingdom [which] issues abundantly from the rocks and winds in serpentine directions, almost through every part', and for the fact that an elm tree four and a half feet high was growing out of the north wall of the chancel.[5] The tree

7. Dronfield, Church of St John the Baptist, 1797. The volume of water in the stream suggests recent rain.
Pencil, 230 x 270 mm, 'North Of England' sketchbook, Tate Gallery, London, TB XXXIV 3.

8. Dronfield, Church of St. John the Baptist.
Photograph, the author.

seems to have been removed by the time of Turner's visit, but he made a considerable feature of the water, contrasting the geometry of the village with the uneven road and rickety structures around. In fact the village's surroundings have hardly a solid line in them, as if the whole landscape is about to slide away from under the buildings, as eager to flow away as the stream. The contrast of structures and the flow of time was to become a major theme of the tour. Perhaps this was partly a result of the weather. To judge from the stream at Dronfield, Turner must recently have encountered rain. This was to be a pleasure enjoyed on many more occasions on this tour.

Conisbrough Yorkshire

Between Rotherham (approx 6m SW) and Doncaster (6m NE). Castle managed by Ivanhoe Trust in association with English Heritage. Visitor Centre, admission charge. Turner's viewpoint by river at Burcroft (N), where mill site presently (1996) awaiting redevelopment.

It is six miles from Rotherham to Conisbrough through 'a country of much beauty, hill, dale and wood', much of which is as pleasant today as when Viscount Torrington described it in 1789.[8] Conisbrough is one of the most ancient settlements in the area, having roots in Saxon times, and its remarkable castle was built by Hamelin Plantagenet, brother of Henry II, in the decades after 1180.[9] The limestone walls of its geometric tower can seem starkly white at one time, pink, silver, yellow or blue at another. Coming on it by surprise you might be forgiven for thinking that Xanadu had materialised in the midst of this otherwise unremarkable Don valley village. It is a sight to inspire the wildest speculation as to its origins. Edward Dayes thought it must be Roman, but was prepared to consider possible Phoenician or even Phrygian influences in its design.[10] Not long after that Conisbrough attained world fame by being adopted by Sir Walter Scott as the Saxon fortress site of his novel *Ivanhoe*.

The sun catches the walls most strikingly when seen from the south (Pl. 11), but Dayes and also Turner on the evidence of his sketch (Pl. 12), thought that the best view was from the river Don to the north. This viewpoint had additional interest, however, for at Burcroft was another of Walker's iron foundries (*see* Rotherham), and Turner incorporated the mill buildings and lock into his drawing.[11] This particular foundry supplied most of the guns for the great ship *Victory*,[12] a fact that Turner might well have known, and in which he would most certainly have been interested. It seems possible that Turner even went to see the manufacturing process at work, for a loose page possibly associated with this tour (Pl. 13),[13] shows the interior of a foundry, with a large cannon in the foreground, no doubt recently cast, and waiting its turn on some gun carriage or perhaps on the decks of a man-of-war destined for Trafalgar.

11. Conisbrough Castle from the south east.
Photograph, the author.

12. Conisbrough Castle from the north, 1797. From near the river, with Walker's iron foundry in the foreground.
Pencil, 230 x 270 mm, 'North Of England' sketchbook, Tate Gallery, London, TB XXXIV 4.

13. Cannon foundry, 1797? Possibly the interior of Walker's foundry at Rotherham or Conisbrough.
Pencil and watercolour, 247 x 347 mm, Tate Gallery, London, TB XXXIII B.

Doncaster
Yorkshire

Conisbrough 6m SE, Pontefract 12m NW. Turner's viewpoints both altered. St George's church rebuilt 1854-8, view from WSW near railway station, but obscured by modern development except from railway.

Doncaster today is more a place of transit than of destination, but was not always thus. In 1724–6 Daniel Defoe described it as 'a noble, large, spacious town, exceeding populous, and a great manufacturing town, principally for knitting; also as its stands upon the great northern post-road, it is very full of great inns.'[14] In 1792 Viscount Torrington reported that 'Doncaster looks well in approach; and is a well-built, well-paved, wide-streeted town', although his inn, *The Angel*, was somewhat less than 'great'. . . 'nasty, insolent, and with city stabling. . . a sad room. . . I could not eat of what they brought. . . I long'd to be able to kick the landlord.'[15] Perhaps Turner fared better, for the temper of his sketch (Pl. 14) from the banks of the Don, imputes a settled atmosphere to the town with its medieval buildings gathered around the great church, chimneys smoking from dozens of hearths, and row-boats and barges tied up at the shore.[16]

St George's church was built in the late twelfth century, and added to over the next 300 years, and was famous for the scale of its crossing tower.[17] Inside Turner sketched the crossing from the south chancel (Pl. 15)

with its intersecting arches, old paving and jumble of monuments.[18] One of Turner's recurrent interests on this tour was that of continuity versus change. His subjects here as elsewhere suggest a world in which time passed slowly. It was not to remain so at Doncaster. In 1853 the old church suffered a fire and had to be rebuilt, with the result that Turner's sketches, particularly that of the interior, are quite important historical records. Shortly after came the Great Northern Railway bringing industry, expansion and large-scale redevelopment. Thousands of people now come through Doncaster every day, but few actually visit. Turner's sketches of Doncaster express a more leisurely pace, especially in the river boats which apart from walking probably represented the slowest mode of travel imaginable. The irony in this is that Turner was one of the first representatives of the new world, always on the move. He was hardly ever in a place to which he belonged. It is probably appropriate that the best place now from which to see his view is from the windows of a train.

14. Doncaster, St George's church from the river, 1797. The church was rebuilt following a fire in 1853. The view is now largely obscured by modern development.
Pencil, 230 x 270 mm, 'North Of England' sketchbook, Tate Gallery, London, TB XXXIV 5.

15. Doncaster, interior of St George's church, 1797. The nave and crossing from the south chancel.
Pencil, 230 x 270 mm, 'North Of England' sketchbook, Tate Gallery, London, TB XXXIV 6.

Pontefract
Yorkshire

Doncaster 12m SE. Wakefield, 8m W. All Saints Church 1m NE of town centre. Turner's viewpoints freely accessible around church.

Turner spent much time on this tour studying old stones. Pontefract is a town of major historical importance and was described by Edward Dayes in 1805 as 'a handsome borough-town pleasantly situated on the side of a hill. The inhabitants are gay and genteel.'[19] It had formerly boasted one of the largest castles in Britain. Richard II was killed there, and it played a central role in the Civil War, but as a result of the latter, the castle was flattened and in 1797 there was little for Turner to see.[20] All Saints church, ruined during a seige of 1644, did survive, however, to provide testimony to Pontefract's history, and Turner made three sketches of its remains. In his sketch of the south side of the church, with the castle hill beyond to the left (Pl. 16), we see a group of figures in the sheltered angle of the porch where the morning sun is gathered. Turner's interest in old stones was not only antiquarian. Old stone has also basked in the sun, chilled

16. Pontefract, All Saints church, south side, 1797. Turner made a mistake with the placement of the south gable top right.
Pencil, 230 x 270 mm, 'North Of England' sketchbook, Tate Gallery, London, TB XXXIV 7.

17. Pontefract, All Saints church, west end, 1797. The church was ruined in the seige of Pontefract Castle in 1644.
Pencil, 230 x 270 mm, 'North Of England' sketchbook, Tate Gallery, London, TB XXXIV 8.

18. Pontefract, All Saints Church, west end.
Photograph, the author.

in the rain, and bears the visible signs of having been acted upon by nature. For the possessor of the new metropolitan sensibility this was important, it represented contact with reality.

He also sketched views of the chancel (*NOE* 9) and of the west end (Pl. 17). In all these he exercised particular care in observation. The very activity of sketching, the time it consumed and the engagement with the subject that it engendered, were all ways of making that contact with reality more intense. This engagement was not entirely passive. In the sketches from the south and west he has changed viewpoints mid-drawing to clarify or include detail. Nor was this process entirely free of error. In the south view we can see that Turner initially misplaced the gable of the south transept, and ended up with it higher up and further to the right than he had expected.[21]

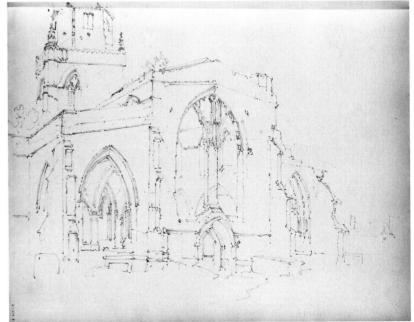

Wakefield
Yorkshire

Pontefract 8m E. Kirkstall, via Leeds 13m NW. Bridge to S. of town centre, Turner's viewpoint freely accessible S. end of bridge. Footpath by river downstream ½m to viewpoint towards Heath Hall from near junction of canal and river. Services in chapel, first and third Sundays each month, 3.00 pm.

In 1805 Edward Dayes described Wakefield as: 'One of the most opulent and genteel of the clothing towns in Yorkshire. It is situated on the banks of the navigable river Calder; and having greatly improved in trade, of late years, the inhabitants have been enabled to ornament it with many respectable houses. The streets are clean, and the walk on each side is flagged. The great object of curiosity here, is the bridge, and the beautiful *Chapel* which stands on it. . . On the front are remains of some curious sculpture, in compartments.'[22] Nor was Dayes alone in being impressed. Only a few weeks before Turner, on 8 July, J. Grant visited Wakefield and called it 'one of the prettiest little towns in England.'[23]

Turner was familiar with Wakefield even before his visit in 1797 for about four years earlier he made a watercolour which was engraved in the *Copper-Plate Magazine* (Pl. 19).[24] Although quite an attractive composition of the view of the bridge and town from downstream, the details are so vague as to suggest that the design was based on someone else's information.[25] Probably because of this, he sought out the same subject (Pl. 20) in 1797, to study closely from a nearer viewpoint (*NOE* 10), and also made a detailed study of the ornamented front with its 'curious sculpture in compartments' (*T&L* 1A),[26] together with a sketch of Heath Old Hall, from a viewpoint a short distance downstream (TB XXXVI Q).

St Mary's chapel was built with the bridge in 1342, shortly after the parish church (now cathedral)[27] of All Saints was completed, and it must have seemed particularly vital in blessing visitors to the city when the Black Death ravaged the area in 1349-50, hardly before the mortar had dried. It is thus over a hundred years older than the chapel at Rotherham which Turner had already sketched, and of even greater architectural significance with its ornate front. Perhaps this greater significance was reflected in its superior fate, serving when Turner visited as a library, rather than as a gaol as at Rotherham.

19. *Wakefield Bridge and Chapel*, 1798. Published in the 'Copper Plate Magazine', 1 June 1798. Based on an untraced watercolour, probably painted some years before the tour of 1797.
Engraving, author's collection.

20. Wakefield Bridge and Chapel.
Photograph, the author.

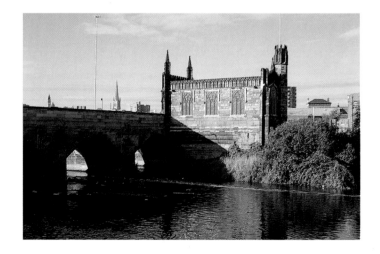

The subject was the first so far in Turner's itinerary to be developed into a finished picture (Pl. 21).[28] He took full advantage of the opportunity to demonstrate the extent to which his knowledge and ability had increased since the earlier composition. His technical and dramatic advance is self-evident, but there are other features which suggest the development of a pictorial intelligence of subtle power. Firstly the chapel occupies a central rectangle dividing the composition almost exactly into thirds on both the horizontal and vertical axis.[29] Secondly he gave careful thought to the lighting of his composition, setting the sun to the left, shining across the bridge. The device

21. Wakefield Bridge and Chapel, c.1797-8. The effect of light raking across the chapel supports is worth consideration. Watercolour, 260 x 434 mm., British Museum, London, 1910–2–12–283, (W.241).

is dramatic, giving him the opportunity to create strong diagonal shadows which throw the structure into sharp relief, but also elucidatory, in that it allowed him to highlight an interesting feature of the architecture. He had noticed the inventive way in which the chapel was corbelled out from the bridge arches, and used the light to draw attention to this. The flat gable wall of the building beyond gives a straight edge to its shadow, but the same angle of light traces a much more complicated path across the chapel masonry. Such matters would never have occured to a lesser artist. Turner must surely have hoped that these features would be noticed.

Kirkstall Abbey
Yorkshire

Three miles west of Leeds centre.Wakefield 13m S. via LeedsKnaresborough 18m. N. via Harewood and Harrogate. Free access to exterior viewpoints all year, daylight access to cloisters only. Abbey House Museum nearby.

Kirkstall Abbey was begun in 1152 on a wide fertile sweep of the river Aire to the west of the small village of Leeds.[30] In 1797 it remained a country setting, but today is submerged in urban sprawl, blackened by pollution and menaced by a busy road. The effect of the road is mitigated a little by the parkland it cuts through however, and the buildings stand substantially to their full height, so that Kirkstall can still remind us how beautiful a site the Cistercians chose to develop. It was, moreover, one of the most celebrated sites that Turner had yet visited, having been frequently portrayed in the eighteenth century.[31] The eleven sketches he made here equal in number the entire output of the tour so far, and must represent two or even three days sustained work.

He began under cover, making sketches in the dormitory undercroft (*NOE* 10a) and chapter house (Pl. 22). The former collapsed in 1825, but the latter is preserved

22. Kirkstall Abbey, Chapter House, 1797.
Pencil, 230 x 270 mm, 'North Of England' sketchbook, Tate Gallery, London, TB XXXIV 11.

23. Kirkstall Abbey, Chapter House.
Photograph, the author.

perfectly (Pl. 23). This might seem a somewhat obtuse way of him first engaging with the site, but perhaps the weather was wet. Turner would, however, have had a powerful motive for seeking out this kind of interior subject. At the 1797 exhibition of the Royal Academy a watercolour of similar material, the *Trancept of Ewenny Priory, Glamorganshire*, was described by a reviewer as 'one of the grandest drawings he had ever seen, and equal to the best pictures of Rembrandt.'[32] Clearly there was a taste for such things, and the drawing of the undercroft was developed into a finished watercolour (Pl. 24), exhibited at the Royal Academy in 1798 under the erroneous title of *Refectory of Kirkstall Abbey, Yorkshire*.[33] Turner's memory was of a wet season, if we might take the pool of water and the cattle sheltering indoors as our guide.

It is worth considering the amount of time that Turner

24. *Refectory of Kirkstall Abbey, Yorkshire*, exh. R.A., 1798, no.346.
Actually shows the dormitory undercroft (collapsed 1825).
Watercolour, 448 x 651 mm, Sir John Soane's Museum, London, (W.234).

expended in the study of his subject-matter. Even the slightest of his sketches must represent fifteen to thirty minutes work, most are more highly wrought and must have occupied him for up to an hour, and the large elaborate sketches in the *Tweed and Lakes* sketchbook might have taken anything up to two or more. The sum total of over two hundred sketches made on this tour reflects a huge amount of work, of astonishingly sustained intensity. Few artists can ever have been so absorbed in their work, or have possessed such dedicated drive and concentration. It is perhaps appropriate that he should have begun his work at Kirkstall with these interior subjects, for they record on a metaphoric level the artist's own immersion in his material. Likewise the quiet rumination of the cattle represents the contemplative nature of the artist, and in one striking detail in the dormitory watercolour (Pl. 24), of the silhouette of a cow's head cast on to the wall to the right, we might see a representation of the artist's projection of himself into his material.

Kirkstall stood even more substantially to its full height than today until 27 January 1779 when half the crossing tower collapsed, bringing down a considerable part of the nave and north transept. The debris lay still uncleared when Turner visited eighteen years later. He made the destruction a major focus of his attention and devoted three highly detailed sketches to it (Pls 26, 27,

25. Kirkstall Abbey, crossing, choir and north transept from nave, moonrise, *c*.1800? A poetic composition based on Pl. 26, the pair to a composition of Bolton Abbey, Pl. 205.
Watercolour, 210 x 292 mm, Tate Gallery, London, TB CXXI H.

26. Kirkstall Abbey, crossing, choir and north transept from nave, 1797.
Part of the tower collapsed in 1779. The debris lies uncleared in the foreground.
Pencil, 270 x 230 mm, 'North Of England' sketchbook, Tate Gallery, London, TB XXXIV 12.

27. Kirkstall Abbey, south aisle from crossing, 1797.
The basis (in reverse) of a study for a figure composition (Pl. 28).
Pencil and watercolour, 370 x 274 mm, 'Tweed And Lakes' sketchbook, Tate Gallery, London, TB XXXV 81.

28. Peasant figures among ruins
(a composition based on Kirkstall Abbey), *c*.1805-7?
Pen and ink and wash, 254 x 187 mm, Tate Gallery, London, TB LXX R.

29. Kirkstall Abbey, north aisle and crossing, 1797. The foreground cart was presumably crushed when the tower collapsed. The remaining structure seems alarmingly unsafe.
Pencil, 370 x 274 mm, 'Tweed And Lakes' sketchbook, Tate Gallery, London, TB XXXV 2.

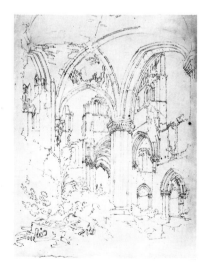

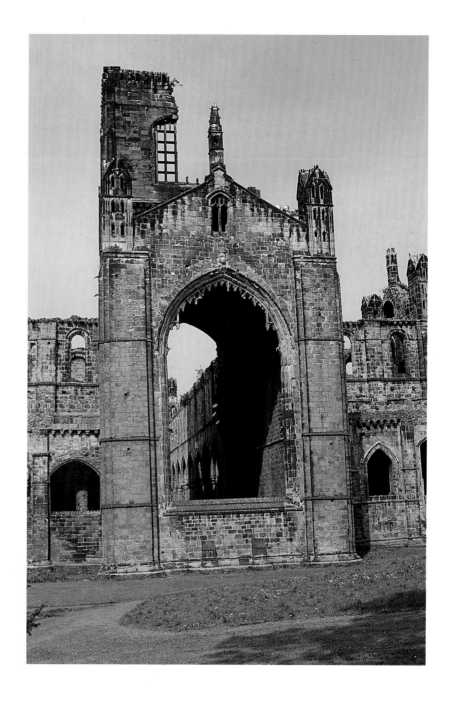

30. Kirkstall Abbey, east end, haymakers, 1797.
Pencil, 270 x 230 mm, 'North Of England' sketchbook, Tate Gallery,
London, TB XXXIV 14.

31. Kirkstall Abbey, east end.
Photograph, the author.

29). In the foreground of one (Pl. 29) lies a hay cart flattened no doubt in the fall, and contributing picturesquely to the sense of decay. Given the decrepitude of the vaults above, one might wonder about the wisdom of Turner, or the two ladies beyond, having entered into the ruins at all. The modern visitor today will be reassured that the walls have since been rebuilt and the tower buttressed. Some time later he sketched out a rough colour study for a watercolour of the crossing (Pl. 25), at the same time as another of Bolton Abbey (q.v., Pl. 205) from the same sketchbook, but both remained no more than ideas. The loose relationship of these studies to fact might suggest a date of about 1807 when he was developing compositions for his series of mezzotints, the *Liber Studiorum* which included a version of the dormitory undercroft of Kirkstall published on 11 February 1812 as *The Crypt of*

32. Kirkstall Abbey, west front, 1797. Close study will reveal that Turner got himself into all manner of difficulties with this drawing.
Pencil, 370 x 274 mm, 'Tweed And Lakes' sketchbook, Tate Gallery, London, TB XXXV 3.

33. Kirkstall Abbey, west front.
Photograph, the author.

Kirkstall Abbey.[34] The images in this series tend to the generic or poetic rather than the specific, and it is possible that it was at this time that he also developed a design for a figure composition (Pl. 28) based on his watercolour sketch of the nave (Pl. 27).[35]

Outside Turner sketched the east front (Pls 30, 31) with haymakers at work with a wain that had escaped the fall. He also made two sketches of the west front. The first, of the whole west range (*NOE* 13), shows cattle and wagons to the right and reminds us that the principal function of Kirkstall at this time was as a working farm. The second (Pl. 32) is a detailed study of the west front with its Norman portal and carved windows. Comparison with the subject (Pl.33) is entertaining. It will be noticed that Turner has shifted viewpoints more

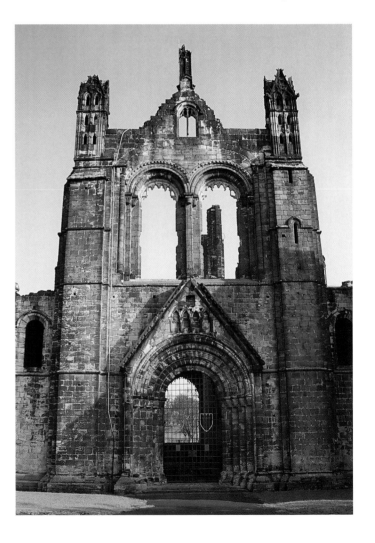

than once to bring in the detail of the nave and tower at the same time. It will also be noticed that Turner's drawing is full of discrepancies. The left side of the portal is much thicker than the right. He has recorded only four bands of decoration, when there are in fact five. The porch and arches are lopsided. The blind arches above the portal have failed to fit the space. He has got into trouble with the arch under the gable window. These problems are worth noting for they remind us of the difficulties of the task, and the thought and planning required to achieve any kind of serviceable result. Turner is commonly thought to have had little care for accuracy of this kind, but nothing could be further from the truth. He struggled doggedly with the task, for on the basis of the fullest knowledge of his subject, his art gained its fullest power and meaning.

It has already been claimed that Turner set out on this tour an architectural draughtsman, and returned from it a painter of landscape, and his last two sketches of Kirkstall show him pulling back from the architecture to depict the abbey in its setting. From the top of Kirkstall Hill, on the old Leeds to Bradford road, he took his most panoramic view of the tour so far (Pl. 34), sweeping across the valley from Kirkstall village at the bottom left to the abbey at the right, and tracing the course of the river to the smoke rising from Kirkstall forge in the left

34. Kirkstall Abbey from Kirkstall Hill, 1797. With smoke rising from Kirkstall Forge in the left distance.
Pencil, 230 x 270 mm, 'North Of England' sketchbook, Tate Gallery, London, TB XXXIV 15.

35. Thomas Girtin, Kirkstall Abbey from Kirkstall Hill, 1800. Possibly based on Turner's sketch?
Watercolour, British Museum, London, 1855–2–14–53.

36. Kirkstall Abbey from Kirkstall Hill.
Photograph, the author.

middle distance. Comparison with the site today (Pl. 36) reveals the extent of development in the two centuries since. Turner never developed a finished picture of the scene but his friend Thomas Girtin painted the view in about 1800 (Pl. 35). The relationship is interesting, for Girtin's watercolour seems perhaps to relate more closely to Turner's sketch than to the site itself. He seems to have forgotten the weir altogether, and places the barn that appears below it in Turner's sketch mistakenly on the river's edge. The farm in the centre foreground of Turner's sketch reappears in the foreground of Girtin's

37. Thomas Smith of Derby, Kirkstall Abbey, 1747. Turner's lighting effect (Pl. 39) is suspiciously close.
Engraving by Francois Vivares published 15 January 1747.

38. *Kirkstall Abbey, on the River Aire*, *c*.1824. Turner's final depiction of the site, with the dazzling intensity of colour typical of his middle age.
Watercolour, 160 x 225 mm, Tate Gallery, London, TB CCXIII M (W.741).

picture but the precise details recorded carefully by Turner are simplified or ignored. Girtin seems to distil the main dramatic features, the sweep of the valley, the placement of the abbey, and the smoking chimneys of the forge in the distance. No sketch of Girtin's survives, and it is tempting to wonder whether their friendship might not have been close enough for Turner to have lent Girtin the sketch to work from.

Turner's last sketch of the site was from the weir to the south-east, and this gave rise to one of the most striking results of the whole tour (Pl. 39). The viewpoint recalls an earlier well-known view by Thomas Smith of Derby engraved in 1747 (Pl. 37). The relationship is suspiciously close, right down to the lighting effect and tree in the left foreground. Smith is relatively obscure today, but his modernity is striking when compared with most mid-eighteenth-century landscapists. It seems highly probable that Turner was influenced by this source, and the relationship reminds us of another aspect of Turner's genius: his willingness to learn from whatever source he could find. Kirkstall remained a favourite subject of Turner's and he returned in 1808 and 1824.[36] On the last visit he returned to the same viewpoint to develop his final depiction of the site (Pl. 38). He was by that time established as the leading landscape painter of his generation, and had been commissioned to make views for a series of engravings called *Rivers of England*. As he developed the later work in his now dazzlingly atmospheric colour, it is impossible to imagine that he would not have remembered taking some of his first mature steps in landscape here, nearly thirty years before.

39. Kirkstall Abbey, Yorkshire, *c*.1798. Painted for Edward Lascelles of Harewood.
Watercolour, 514 x 749 mm, Fitzwilliam Museum, Cambridge (W.224).

Ripon
Yorkshire

Ripon 14m N via Ripley. Fountains Abbey 3m W. Richmond 21m N via Catterick. Ripon Cathedral open every day. Near approximations to Turner's views to SW by River Skell, and to NW by Ure bridge accessible by road and footpath.

Ripon and Fountains Abbey are highlights of any visit to Yorkshire, and both were frequently visited and depicted in the eighteenth century.[41] Turner presumably put up at one of the inns in the town, and used it as a base for his explorations in the vicinity, probably staying for at least three days. He began by finding a general view of the cathedral from the south-west (Pl. 44), with the Ripon canal in the foreground and the river Skell to the right. The exact view has been obscured today by modern development, but a close approximation (Pl. 43) can be found by the Skell not far from the Water Rat public house.

Ripon Cathedral has been the mother-church of the Diocese of Ripon since 1836, but the title of Minster by which Turner would have known it is an indication of an antiquity that stretches back to Saxon times, *Minster* being an Anglo-Saxon word for an evangelical centre. The first church was built by St Wilfred in the seventh century and swept away in the Danish invasions two

43. Ripon Cathedral from the River Skell.
Photograph, the author.

44. Ripon Cathedral from the south east, by Ripon canal, 1797.
Pencil, 230 x 270 mm, 'North Of England' sketchbook, Tate Gallery, London, TB XXXIV 19.

hundred years later. Since that time the church has been repeatedly demolished and rebuilt so that the present building incorporates some feature of almost every major phase from the Saxon crypt to the present day.[42]

Besides his sketch from the south-east, Turner also surveyed the town from the north by the Ure bridge (Pl. 47) and the north-east from the riverbank (TB XXXVI E). In the town he sketched the view down Kirkgate to the west front of the cathedral (Pl. 48). The sketch is interesting for how well Kirkgate seems to retain its character, even though much has been altered, and for the evidence it shows, at the end of the street, for a gate to the cathedral precincts, now long since disappeared. Within these precincts he sketched the great west front dating from about 1220 (Pl. 45). The view is perfectly preserved (Pl. 46), although close comparison will again reveal numerous small discrepancies, some no doubt the result of sub-

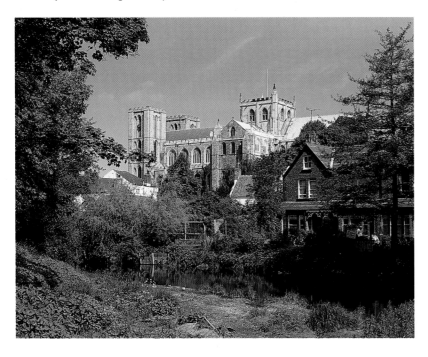

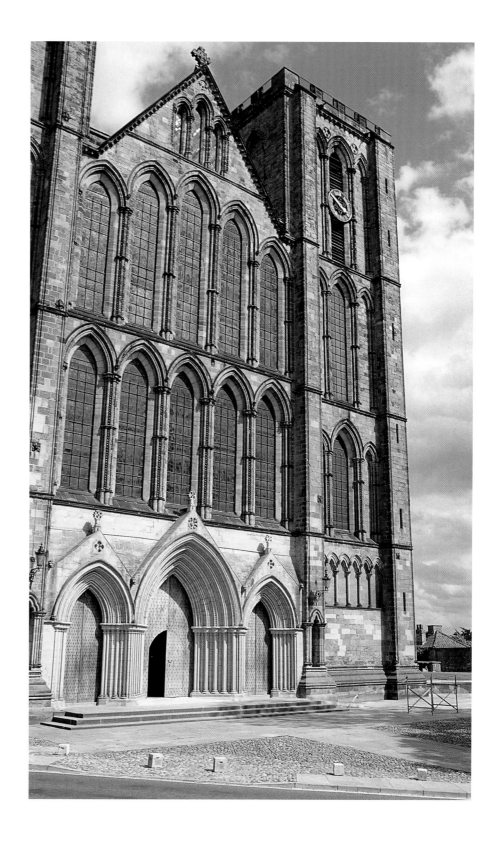

45. Ripon Cathedral, west front, 1797.
A model of economic, but rapt observation.
Pencil, 270 x 230 mm, 'North Of England' sketchbook, Tate Gallery,
London, TB XXXIV 20.

46. Ripon Cathedral, west front.
Photograph, the author.

sequent restoration. Most striking of all, however, is Turner's sense of proportion and of the organising principles of the architecture, which enables him to use just sufficient detail to represent the whole. Even in spite of the economies, the drawing gives a powerful sense of absorption, as if the very act of looking was the end in itself.

Inside the cathedral he made two of the most complete and highly wrought drawings of the whole tour. The first (*T&L 5*) records the crossing and nave from the north transept, and the second (Pl. 50) records the crossing and choir screen (Pl. 49) from a bench at the base of the column at the junction of transept and north aisle. With such a complex subject it is hard not to be impressed by the skill with which he has managed the perspective and placement of detail. Even for as accomplished an artist as Turner there must have been two hours work in this sketch alone. In the centre he has counted and recorded every niche and ornament of the choir screen even allowing his interest to spill into the space of the left-hand column of the chancel arch. The slippage denotes his absorption. The sketch is not just an exemplar of his

47. Ripon, Ure Bridge and Cathedral from the north, 1797. Pencil, 206 x 267 mm, Tate Gallery, London, TB XXXVI D.

48. Ripon Cathedral from Kirkgate, 1797. Note the now-disappeared gateway to the cathedral precincts at the end of the street. Pencil, 274 x 370 mm, 'Tweed And Lakes' sketchbook, Tate Gallery, London, TB XXXV 8.

skill, although one scholar described it 'as perfect as human handicraft can be'[43] but it is palpably an exercise in meditation. The artist rapt in his subject and oblivious to all else. Turner was clearly by this point fully immersed in the work he had set himself on this tour and had already stored up a large amount of information and experience. Another artist might well have gone home at this point, justifiably well-satisfied with what they had already achieved. It is worth reflecting how far he had yet to travel, and how much work there was yet in front of him.

Turner revisited Ripon in 1816 when he was collecting subjects for illustrations to Thomas Dunham Whitaker's *General History of the County of York*.[44] On this later occasion he made several studies of the Cathedral[45] and returned to the Ure bridge to resketch the view taken in 1797. It seems probable that he was intending to develop this into a finished composition for engraving, but in the event the project was curtailed by Whitaker's death, and the opportunity was denied him to utilise the material he so obviously enjoyed gathering at Ripon.

49. Ripon Cathedral, Choir and south transept.
Photograph, the author.

50. Ripon Cathedral,
Choir and south transept from north transept, 1797.
Described by one scholar 'as perfect as human handicraft can be.'
Pencil, 370 x 274 mm, 'Tweed And Lakes' sketchbook, Tate Gallery,
London, TB XXXV 6.

Fountains Abbey
Yorkshire

Three miles W of Ripon. Richmond 21m N via Catterick. National Trust, open all year, visitor centre, admission charge.

Two days after Christmas 1132, Archbishop Thurstan of York led thirteen monks who had been staying at his palace in Ripon to land by the river Skell on which they were to found the new abbey of Fountains. It was a site well able to satisfy their demands for more rigorous privation which had led to them being forcibly expelled from their previous house, St Mary's in York. Over succeeding centuries this sanctuary became one of the largest and most powerful corporations in Britain, controlling land and trade from coast to coast. From the thirteenth to the fifteenth century, there was hardly any sphere of economic activity in the north, with which the monks of Fountains were not in some way concerned.[46]

In the early years of the eighteenth century John Aislabie made the ruins a feature of his gardens at Studley, and laid out ponds, lakes, grottos, waterfalls, temples, statues and promenades to create a fantasy garden which stretched nearly the whole length of the Skell valley from Fountains to Ripon. By 1732 it was already described as 'The Wonder of the North', and was frequently depicted thereafter in paintings and engravings.[47]

Turner's interest was focused on the abbey and he began his sketches by taking a view of the east end with its soaring columns and arches piling up to the great east window and Abbot Huby's tower (Pls 51, 52), the latter completed only a few years before the abbey was dissolved by Henry VIII. Below the east window we can see a group of Aislabie's gardeners, no doubt enjoying (as were the women at Pontefract) some warmth from the morning sun, gathered in the sheltered angle of the buttress.

His second sketch (Pl. 53) comes to terms even more closely with the architecture, moving inside the chapel of the nine altars to sketch the view across the presbytery to Huby's tower. Visitors today will enjoy finding the column base that Turner utilised as a seat. On a summer's afternoon it will be discovered that the seat is a perfect sun-trap, and an indisputably pleasant place to sit and meditate upon the architecture with the stone warm

51. 'East End of Fountains Abby', 1797. With a group of gardeners sitting in the sheltered angle of the buttress beneath the great east window.
Pencil, 274 x 370 mm, 'Tweed And Lakes' sketchbook, Tate Gallery, London, TB XXXV 7.

52. Fountains Abbey, east end. Photograph, the author.

against one's back. It is the same experience that the gardeners are enjoying in the first sketch.

Turner's sketches trace out a full day at the site, from the morning spent sketching the east front through the afternoon sat in the chapel of the nine altars, to a final sketch made in the evening by the river Skell (*NOE* 89). This last he chose to develop into a finished watercolour which he exhibited at the Royal Academy of 1798 as *The dormitory and transept of Fountain's Abbey – Evening* (Pl. 54).[48] As with Kirkstall (q.v.), Turner's identification of the subject was wrong. In fact he shows the cellarium and lay brothers' dormitory crossing the river Skell, with the end wall of the refectory to the right. It is interesting, however, that he found his way to this subject at all, for

36

even today it is an obscure spot, overgrown, damp and difficult to reach. An explanation, however, is to be found in the two figures on the river-bank near the centre of the composition. One is sketching in a large volume such as that used by Turner on this very occasion, and the other carries a fishing rod. Fishing rivalled painting in Turner's interests, and it seems very likely that it was trout as much as art that initially attracted him to the spot. Anyone who knew Fountains might well with justification have thought the viewpoint strange, but Turner seems to have invited his audience to consider that very point. Perhaps, he might be leading us to conclude, because it was not artistic motives that had taken him to this spot, he was able to enjoy an experience that would never have come the way of someone searching merely for views.

Turner revisited Fountains in 1816 when collecting material for his illustrations to the *General History of the County of York*. He clearly intended at least one finished watercolour for the series, and made several new sketches, even going so far as to make sketch plans of the ruins.[49] One finished watercolour resulted, a view to the base of Abbot Huby's Tower from the south transept, which was not in the event engraved, and it is interesting that one of Aislabies gardeners, possibly one of those sitting in the sunshine in his sketch of the east end in 1797, found his way into this, sweeping up fallen leaves in the crossing.

53. Fountains Abbey, Choir and Huby's tower from the chapel of nine altars, 1797. The viewpoint is a perfect suntrap on a summer's afternoon.
Pencil and watercolour, 370 x 274 mm, 'Tweed And Lakes' sketchbook, Tate Gallery, London, TB XXXV 80.

54. *The dormitory and transept of Fountain's Abbey – Evening*, exh. R.A. 1798, no.435. The figures, one
sketching and one fishing, suggest that Turner's motives for visiting this viewpoint were not entirely artistic.
Watercolour, 456 x 610 mm, York City Art Gallery (W.238).

Richmond
Yorkshire

21m N from Ripon via Catterick.[50] Egglestone Abbey/ Barnard Castle 15m NW. Castle English Heritage, open daily all year, admission charge. Turner's viewpoint W of castle on river-bank above Green Bridge freely accessible by public footpath, although view somewhat impeded by trees.

Richmond is the quintessential northern town with its great Norman castle, river, bridges, mills, waterfalls, churches and spacious market place.[51] In his two sketches, one from downstream near St Martin's (*NOE* 26), and another from the west just upstream of Green Bridge (*T&L* 9, Pl. 55), he managed to incorporate almost every one of these elements, and capture a sense of the geographic situation of the town on its bluff above the river Swale.[52]

If Turner on this tour developed his sketching practice into an art of meditation in its own right, in so doing he also empowered the work in his studio. The richer the experience, the richer the material with which he had to work. In the case of Richmond we are particularly fortunate that two unfinished works survive which allow us to see something of the process whereby he transmuted his experience into art.

55. Richmond Bridge and Castle.
Photograph, the author.

56. Colour-beginning, Richmond Bridge and Castle, *c.*1816-18. A study for a watercolour intended for T.D.Whitaker's *History of Yorkshire*.
Watercolour, 390 x 485 mm, Tate Gallery, London, TB CXCVII H.

In the first (Pl. 57),[53] painted a couple of years after the tour,[54] he sets the time at sunrise, with the castle *contre-jour* revealing itself reluctantly to the day. His depiction of this effect is paradoxically only made possible by information and knowledge, since in order to paint the castle indistinctly, he needed to know exactly what underlay that indistinctness. Out of this he has constructed an essence of light and colour and pigment, forming itself in primordial swathes and wraiths of matter, at a time of day when creation might seem as much a product of poetry as of physics.

Turner returned to Richmond in 1816 to make illustrations for a Thomas Dunham Whitaker's, *History of Richmondshire*, and sketched a number of new views which resulted in finished watercolours.[55] Although he did not resketch the view taken in 1797, he nevertheless chose it as one of the subjects to be developed for, although no finished work was actually completed, he did begin one, and the sheet as it was left off (Pl. 56), shows the extent to which Turner had by then developed his practice into an act of almost primordial creation.

57. Richmond Bridge and Castle, sunrise, 1798-9.
Watercolour, 412 x 540 mm, Tate Gallery, London, TB XXXVI V.

Easby Abbey
Yorkshire

1m SE of Richmond. English Heritage, open all year, admission free.

Turner would most likely have walked the pleasant mile of footpath downstream from Richmond to find St Agatha's Abbey, as today, in almost as sequestered a setting as at its foundation in 1155.[56] He made three sketches at the site, one a detailed study of the north range (*NOE* 24), another a study of the view from downstream (*NOE* 25),[57] and the third a view from near the mill upstream (Pl. 59), with the guest's solar leaning precariously away from the rest of the building. The last seems to be a page from the *Tweed and Lakes* sketchbook,[58] which Turner worked up in watercolour to a high level of finish, possibly on the spot.

He used the view from downstream as the basis of a large finished watercolour (Pl. 58). Although the viewpoint is now almost completely obscured by trees, enough can be discovered to reveal that Turner selected a very narrow angle of view from quite a considerable distance, no doubt in order to obtain a view which united the ruins with the river. As a result it appears that he was on the opposite bank, but in fact the river swings sharply to the left in the foreground. The distance was too great for him to be entirely sure about the architectural detail with the result that there are numerous inaccuracies particularly around the angle between the great hall and the solar to the right of centre. Nevertheless he recalled a plausible effect of evening light shining on the wall of the great hall, and cattle coming down to the river to drink.

He revisited the site in 1816 in connection with Whitaker's *History of Yorkshire*, and was then able to correct the deficiencies of his earlier observation and develop a second watercolour of the view (Pl. 61). The later composition was developed through an elaborate colour-beginning (Pl. 60) in which he worked out the elemental structure. Once again personal experience was his theme. A milkmaid sitting against the wall of the great hall enjoys the sun on her face, while a farmer brings his horses down to the river to drink. This experience also led to knowledge, and Turner's portrayal of the light reflecting from the moisture-laden air, as seen against

58. St Agatha's Abbey, Easby, from the River Swale, *c*.1797–1800. A large early watercolour, possibly originally intended for exhibition.
Watercolour, 629 x 889 mm, Whitworth Art Gallery, Manchester (W.273).

what would otherwise be the evenly shaded wall of the solar, has a formal and intellectual subtlety which distinguishes his work from all others. As in his earlier sketch at the site (Pl. 59), he makes an important feature of the solar breaking away from the rest of the building, by this time juxtaposing the vertical reflection of a duck's wing against the far-from-vertical reflection of the solar. It is also worth remarking that the mallard was also a kind of autograph, being a pun on his own given name of Mallord.

59. St Agatha's Abbey, Easby, Yorkshire, 1797. The view from immediately upstream of the abbey.
Possibly a page from the 'Tweed and Lakes' sketchbook.
Watercolour, 270 x 371 mm, British Museum, London, 1958–7–12–406 (W.274).

60. Colour-beginning, St Agatha's Abbey, Easby, *c*.1818. A study for the finished watercolour Pl. 61.
Watercolour, 393 x 504 mm, Tate Gallery, London, TB CCLXIII 360.

61. *St Agatha's Abbey, Easby, Yorkshire, c.*1818. One of the most beautiful and subtle of Turner's
finished watercolours for Whitaker's History of Yorkshire.
Watercolour, 288 x 415 mm, British Museum, London, 1915–3–13–48 (W.561).

Egglestone Abbey
Durham

Richmond 15m SE. Barnard Castle 1½ m NW. English Heritage, open all year, admission charge. Turner's viewpoints from road on opposite side of Tees, and from near packhorse bridge over Thorsgill (N).

Egglestone Abbey stands in the modern county of Durham, but in Turner's day was in Yorkshire facing Durham across the river. The abbey was founded in 1195 by a colony of monks from St Agatha's at Easby.[59] The site had all they needed, timber and stone for building, a fall of water for a mill, and a stream bringing fresh water for domestic consumption. As at Easby Turner would have found the site little developed beyond the buildings that the monks erected.

His sketches include views from the bridge over Thorsgill (*NOE* 28) and from the opposite side of the river (Pl. 62), together with a quick memorandum of the presbytery and canon's dormitory (*NOE* 90 verso).[60] His subject in the second was as much the mill as the abbey ruins. It seems to have been a somewhat delapidated affair, but would have been of considerable interest to Turner the artist since it was then in use as a paper mill. A fourth sketch belonging to this sequence possibly shows the interior of the mill (*NOE* 90).[61] The owner was James Cooke, who lived there with his wife Elizabeth who continued to work it after his death until 1809, when her son Henry took over. He ran the mill with his wife Hannah until they moved to Richmond in 1830. Turner resketched the site in 1816 in connection with Whitaker's *Richmondshire*, when he noted that some building work was taking place.[62] This was possibly rebuilding after a fire in a drying loft in 1809, or has more recently been suggested, an extension to the Cookes' house. This would have been quite a pressing requirement, given that they were then in the process of raising no fewer than seven children.[63]

The subject provided Turner with one of the most interesting compositions of his *History of Yorkshire* series (Pl. 63). The scene is full of quiet activity that projects a sense of belonging to the site, and might be interpreted as a projection of Turner's own desires, as a representative of a new metropolitan identity, constantly on the move, lacking the roots of those he depicted. His viewpoint on the opposite side of the river to the mill

62. Egglestone Abbey and Mill, 1797. The mill was a paper mill owned by the Cooke family. Pencil, 230 x 270 mm, 'North Of England' sketchbook, Tate Gallery, London, TB XXXIV 27.

might be further interpreted as representing a sense of detachment, the alienation of an observer merely passing by. It seems from Turner's pictorial account that the inhabitants of Egglestone enjoyed a good life, at least as it is embodied in the male figure, presumably Henry Cooke, who fishes in the river outside the mill. Perhaps the same cannot be said for the woman, presumably Hannah, who is at work cutting and preparing felts for the paper mill, in between, no doubt, looking after her brood of children.

65. *Egglestone Abbey, near Barnard Castle, c.*1818.
The mill owner and his wife on the riverbank by the mill?
Watercolour, 286 x 419 mm, Private Collection (W.565).

Barnard Castle
Durham

Richmond 15m SE. Durham 21m NE. Castle, English Heritage, open all year, admission charge. Circuit of Turner's viewpoints described below.

Barnard Castle was begun shortly after 1093 by Guy de Baliol, who came over with William the Conqueror, and from whose son, Bernard, it took its name. Its strategic importance guarding an important crossing of the Tees was such that it was fought over by warlords, kings and bishops and frequently changed hands. Occupants included Hugh de Baliol who entertained King John there in 1216, and was besieged by Alexander of Scotland. His son John founded Balliol College at Oxford, and his son in turn, another John, become King of Scotland in 1292.[64] In 1797 the bridge marked the boundary between Durham and Yorkshire and the castle might have appeared to have been designed to superintend access from the larger county. Shortly after Turner's visit, Walter Scott ensured its fame to the present day by making it the setting for his epic poem *Marmion*.[65]

Turner made two sketches (Pls 65, 66), and both viewpoints are easy of access. A footpath runs down to the river from the castle gate and a short walk up the river leads to a bridge which offers a good view of the castle (Pl. 67). Over the bridge paths lead by the side of the road downstream past the bridge to Turner's other viewpoint (Pl. 64), and the circuit can be completed by continuing downstream, crossing the footbridge by the mill, and returning to the castle via the buttercross and market square.

Turner clearly felt in no hurry to complete his work at Barnard Castle, and both sketches are highly wrought and full of detail. That from downstream (Pl. 65)[66] is exceptionally sharp and careful, especially in the jumble of buildings on the Durham bank. These have since disappeared, but one can have no doubt that humble as they were, Turner recorded every window and gable faithfully, fitting together each element with almost obsessive pleasure. Even given the huge distance he had yet to cover, he seems to have had no sense at all of any urgency to move on.

On the contrary, he seems happy enough to put down roots. In his other sketch (Pl. 66),[67] with fewer buildings to entertain him, he applied himself to tracing the exact forms

64. Barnard Castle from downstream.
Photograph, the author.

of the rock outcrops and even the shrubbery growing on the slopes. He revisited the same site in 1816 in connection with *Whitaker's History of Yorkshire*,[68] and again in 1831[69] when he was making studies for an illustrated edition of the work of Sir Walter Scott, and the sketches from the later visits reveal that the chapel on the bridge had by that time disappeared. His only finished watercolour of the site was painted in the later 1820s for his series *Picturesque Views in England and Wales* (Pl. 68),[70] but despite the later sketches, he set the scene at the time of his first visit, including the bridge chapel of his first visit, at the dawn of his career as a painter of landscape.

65. Barnard Castle and Bridge, from downstream, 1797. Turner was prepared to invest remarkable care
into even the humblest features of his compositions.
Pencil, 230 x 270 mm, 'North Of England' sketchbook, Tate Gallery, London, TB XXXIV 30.

66. *left* Barnard Castle and Bridge, from upstream, 1797.
Pencil, 230 x 270 mm, 'North Of England' sketchbook, Tate Gallery, London, TBXXXIV 29.

67. *left* Barnard Castle from upstream.
Photograph, the author.

68. *above* Barnard Castle, Durham, *c.*1825. Set at the time of his first visit, even though he had returned in 1816.
Watercolour, 292 x 419 mm, Yale Center for British Art, New Haven, USA (W.793).

Durham
County Durham

From Barnard Castle 21m SW. Tynemouth (via Finchale 4m N)[71] 21m NNE. Cathedral open all year. Turner's viewpoints all readily identifiable in cathedral, or on riverbanks by footpath from Framwellgate to Elvet bridges.

By the time Turner arrived at Durham he was three hundred miles from London and must have been on the road about three weeks. It would have been an appropriate place for him to spend some time and rest. The Norman cathedral, castle and old town on its narrow peninsular bounded by the river Wear would have afforded both amenity and interest.[72] From the seven sketches in the *Tweed and Lakes* sketchbook and one in the *North of England* sketchbook it would seem that he spent three or four days there, but did anything but rest. He took views near Framwellgate Bridge (Pls 69, 70), Prebend's Bridge (Pls 77, 78), and Elvet Bridge (Pls 75, 76), and made studies of the interior of the cathedral (Pls 71–4).

Turner developed a number of studio works from his sketches. One of the first must have been the view of the castle and cathedral from below Framwellgate Bridge (Pl.

69. Durham, Framwellgate Bridge and Cathedral from downstream.
Photograph, the author.

70).[73] The subject was chosen from the *Tweed and Lakes* sketchbook by John Hoppner in 1798,[74] it seems as a gift to elicit his support in the forthcoming election for a new Associate of the Royal Academy. The watercolour proved too popular for its own good, and has been faded by exposure to sunlight. The resulting golden colouration seems somewhat ironic, given that Hoppner advised Turner that his pictures tended too much to the brown, and that Turner specifically attended to this deficiency on this tour by colouring as much as he could from nature.[75]

Inside the cathedral he sketched the view of the crossing and nave from the south transept (Pl. 71), the crossing and north transept from the south aisle (Pl. 72), and the nave from the south aisle (*T&L* 13). The second was developed into a large watercolour (Pl. 73), presumably intended for exhibition. The information in the sketch was not, however, transcribed directly. Instead he imagined a viewpoint one bay further west than that of the sketch to create a more extended view down the south aisle as well as over the crossing. The greater the distance in the watercolour, the more the architecture seems to dissolve into light, and in order to further develop this effect he also straightened the line of the aisle and removed the arch guarding the entrance to the choir from the south transept. Thus he created an unimpeded view right down the south side to two tiny figures suspended like mites in a shaft of sunlight. At the opposite side two further figures balance the composition, picked out on the otherwise shaded floor of the north transept. He was able to construct perfectly the foreground column, missing from the sketch, from his understanding of the way in which the architecture worked, alternating clustered columns with decorated drums, and the result marks perhaps the culminating point in his depiction of this kind of subject. One is forced to wonder quite what prevented it being exhibited at the Academy. He did, however, use his third sketch for a slightly less grand composition, a presently-untraced watercolour[76] of the view of the nave from the south aisle, actually from the same viewpoint as

70. Durham Cathedral from the river, *c*.1798.
Made as a present for his friend and supporter, John Hoppner.
Watercolour, 305 x 407 mm, Royal Academy, London (W.249).

71. Durham Cathedral, crossing, nave and north transept from the south transept, 1797.
Pencil, 370 x 274 mm, 'Tweed And Lakes' sketchbook, Tate Gallery, London, TB XXXV 10.

72. Durham Cathedral, crossing and north transept from the south aisle, 1797. A composite view made
from two viewpoints, used as the basis of the watercolour Pl. 73.
Pencil, 370 x 274 mm, 'Tweed And Lakes' sketchbook, Tate Gallery, London, TB XXXV 12.

73. Durham Cathedral, crossing and north transept from the south aisle, *c*.1797. Adding together information from two sketches, *see* Pls 72, 74. Tombs of John and Ralph, Lords Neville in foreground.
Watercolour, 758 x 580 mm, Tate Gallery, London, TB XXXVI G.

74. Durham Cathedral – interior, 1802. A view from the south aisle of the nave, looking west, engraved from an untraced watercolour (W.276) and published in T.Warton's 'Essays on Gothic Architecture', 1802.
Engraving, British Library, London.

75. Durham, Elvet Bridge from downstream, 1797.
Pencil, 230 x 270 mm, 'North Of England' sketchbook, Tate Gallery, London, TB XXXIV 31.

76. Durham, Cathedral, Castle and Elvet Bridge from upstream, 1797
Pencil, 274 x 370 mm, 'Tweed And Lakes' sketchbook, Tate Gallery, London, TB XXXV 14.

77. Durham Cathedral from Prebend's Bridge.
Photograph, the author.

he made an important, if comparatively rushed, series of sketches,[79] but it was the mid-1830s before he finally came round to using his material. When he did, it was for one of the last and greatest of his watercolours in the series *Picturesque Views in England and Wales* (Pl. 78). The scene is neither as the eye, still less as the camera would see it, but perhaps all the more representative of the site because of that.[80] Framwellgate bridge, the weir and mill are in their customary relationship, but the cathedral appears as it would from opposite the mill. Turner's purpose seems to have been to imitate memory more than strict visual fact. The mind would remember the most dramatic elements of the site, but not necessarily their strict relationship. It would certainly remember evening sunlight lifting from the river and bathing the town in pink and gold and transmute it into memories of poetic and emotional effect. The purpose of Turner's art was to discover the mental truth of a site, as perceived by a living rather than mechanical imagination.

his larger watercolour, but looking north-west instead of north-east, which was engraved for Warton's *Essays on Gothic Archictecture*, published in 1802 (Pl. 74).

He completed his survey of Durham with sketches of Elvet Bridge (Pls 75, 76), a picturesque jumble of shops and houses dating back to the thirteenth century.[77] His major intention at Durham, however, seems to have been to develop a composition including the cathedral, castle, mill, weir and Framwellgate bridge from near the relatively recently-built Prebend's Bridge, dating from about the time of his birth, 1772–7 (Pl. 77).[78] From the order in which the sketches occur (*T&L* 11, 89) they would seem to represent his first intention for a view of the city. He revisited the subject in 1801 on his way to Scotland when

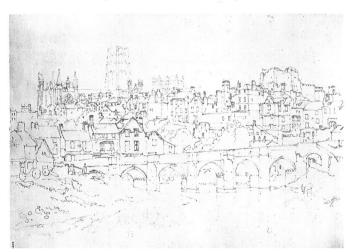

78. *Durham Cathedral, c.*1835.
Watercolour, 295 x 442 mm, National Galleries of Scotland, Edinburgh (W.873).

III   BORDERLAND

Northumberland and the Tweed Valley

Turner probably crossed the Tyne from South to North Shields, and in Northumberland entered into a district more windswept and remote than any he had travelled through before. He followed the coast with its craggy promontories and wide sandy beaches as far north as Berwick, and then turned west through the borderlands of the Tweed valley. In this country, battered on one side by the sea, and bounded on the other by bleak moorland, his work became imbued with a new sense of exposure and space. From these subjects he derived some of the most compelling images of his career.

81. Tynemouth Priory across Prior's Haven, 1797.
Pencil and watercolour, 230 x 270 mm, 'North Of England' sketchbook, Tate Gallery,
London, TB XXXIV 35.

83. Tynemouth Priory across Prior's Haven, 1797
Pencil and watercolour, 198 x 276 mm, Tate Gallery, London, TB XXXIII T.

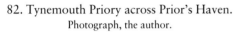

82. Tynemouth Priory across Prior's Haven.
Photograph, the author.

84. *Tynemouth Priory, Northumberland, c.1822.* The boats blithely steer
across each other's paths despite the cautionary lessons offered by the wreck.
Watercolour, 159 x 241 mm, Blackburn Art Gallery (W.545).

85. *Tynemouth, Northumberland, c.*1829.
The epic struggle of salvagers was Turner's most common theme on the Northumberland coast.
Watercolour, 280 x 407 mm, destroyed by fire, February 1962 (W.827).

Bothal
Northumberland

18m N Tynemouth. 12m S Warkworth. Bothal castle is a private residence with no public admittance. Turner's viewoints are freely accessible from village street, N of church, looking to castle gateway, and by river (public footpath by side of castle). Church open only for services or by arrangement.

Bothal was built in 1343 and is one of Northumberland's least-known castles (Pl. 87). With its model village and Norman church of St Andrew it survives in a quiet backwater apparently unvisited by anything of the modern world.[7] Even in Turner's day Bothal was off the beaten track,[8] and it is testimony to the thoroughness of his preparation that he found it at all. He made two sketches at the site.[9] The first (Pl. 88) records the view from the north down the village street to the gateway keep of the

86. Bothal, figures on a bridge, 1797.
Pencil, 270 x 230 mm, 'North Of England' sketchbook, Tate Gallery, London, TB XXXIV 36.

87. Bothal Castle.
Photograph, the author.

castle, surmounted by sculpted figures as at Alnwick (q.v.), with the squat church to the left and cottages to the right. The castle and village were extensively modernised in the 1830s and it is instructive to compare the impoverished cottages and muddy road in the sketch with their spruce successors today. His second sketch (Pl. 86) is unique for the tour in being a figure composition. Taken from near the river Wansbeck looking north to the church tower, it shows two young men and a small dog standing on a rustic bridge. One plays a tin whistle, but the sound serves only to create an impression of quiet. The idea of hearing its notes makes us think of the other sounds with which it would compete, the babbling of the stream below the bridge, or birdsong, or the rustling of leaves in the branches.

88. Bothal Castle and church from the north, 1797.
Pencil, 230 x 270 mm, 'North Of England' sketchbook, Tate Gallery, London, TB XXXIV 37.

Warkworth
Northumberland

Bothal 12m s. Alnwick 6m N. Warkworth Castle, English Heritage, open all year, visitor facilities, admission charge. Turner's views readily accessible by road or footpath.

Warkworth is a small town clustered around a large castle on a promontory looped round by the river Coquet. The picturesque town grew up between an early Saxon fort and the river and increased dramatically in significance after 1332 when the Percy family took possession of the castle. They controlled a large part of Northumberland and their power was expressed in the massive cruciform keep they built in the early fifteenth century. The new building would have been residence to the most famous of the Percies, Harry Hotspur, son of the first Earl of Northumberland and prominent supporter of, and later conspirator against, Henry IV. Three of the scenes of Shakespeare's *Henry IV, Part I* are set at Warkworth.[10]

Turner made five sketches. His first was taken from the east bank of the river (Pl. 89),[11] with numerous boats lying by the shore. Their prominence suggests that

89. Warkworth Castle from the south east, river Coquet in foreground, 1797.
Pencil, 230 x 270 mm, 'North Of England' sketchbook, Tate Gallery, London, TB XXXIV 38.

90. Warkworth Castle from upstream.
Photograph, the author.

Turner might well have hired a boat to cross the river, and to examine the views of the castle from the water. There would have been a plentiful supply of potential carriers since Warkworth was a famous spot for netting salmon. All but one of his sketches are taken from the river, and all include boats.

His next sketch has hitherto escaped notice, but close examination of the following page of the *North of England* sketchbook (Pl. 92) reveals a faint view of the castle from the north-west,[12] abandoned at a preliminary stage and subsequently drawn over. The sketch Turner made over this beginning is a view of the interior of the castle keep, stronger, but little more detailed than the drawing it effaced. One commentator has wondered that Turner made this sketch at all,[13] given that the subject without lamplight would have been extremely dark. The same commentator suggested that Turner might have

91. *Warkworth Castle, Northumberland – Thunderstorm approaching at sunset*, exh. R.A., 1799. no. 434.
The whereabouts of the thunderstorm is worth consideration in relation to the direction of wind.
Watercolour, 521 x 749 mm, Victoria and Albert Museum, London (W.256).

been taking shelter from a Northumberland squall. This would also account for the early abandonment of the first effort and a hasty retreat indoors to while away time with the second. The gloom inside might also explain why he failed to find a new page of his sketchbook to draw on. Conditions cleared up enough for him to finish his survey however with two detailed sketches, one of the castle and town from the fortified medieval bridge (Pls 93, 94),[14] with St Lawrence's church visible through the right hand arch, and another (*NOE* 40) of the castle from the west (Pl. 90)[15].

The last was developed into a major watercolour exhibited at the Royal Academy in 1799 under the title *Warkworth Castle, Thunderstorm approaching at Sunset* (Pl. 91). It would be typical of Turner for this storm to be the recollection of one which drove him indoors. The storm at present lurks innocuously behind the castle, and would seem to pose no threat since the direction of the smoke blowing up the bank would suggest that it was passing away. But Turner knew that the ground winds in a thunderstorm travel in the opposite direction to that of the storm, as they are sucked into the great anvil of the advancing cloud.[16] It is perhaps the kind of knowledge that a countryman or meteorologist would possess, but not that of the average painter or exhibition-goer. Turner is drawing attention to his knowledge as a man of nature, one who had spent almost as much time exposed to the elements as the two salmon netters in the boat on

the river. No doubt their activity would have been lent some urgency if they could see the clouds building up behind the castle.

When he exhibited the picture at the Academy he further extended the imaginative dimension by quoting some lines from James Thomson's famous poem: *The Seasons*:[17]

> Behold slow settling o'er the lurid grove,
> Unusual darkness broods; and growing, gains
> The full possession of the sky; and on yon baleful cloud
> A redd'ning gleam, a magazine of fate
> Ferment
> (*Summer*, 1103–5/1111–3)

The passage described the sudden onset of a summer afternoon thunderstorm, but set it in an extended work which catalogued a lifetime's experience of nature and all the knowledge and wisdom that the poet had derived from that experience. In equating his own task with Thomson's, Turner was making a bold claim. He was asking to be seen as more than an architectural draughtsman, and more even than as a painter of landscape. He was declaring himself to be as dedicated to the celebration of nature as the poet had been.

92. Warkworth Castle, interior of keep looking out towards the gateway, 1797. A first sketch of the castle from the north west was abondoned at an early stage and drawn over. Perhaps Turner was driven indoors by a thunderstorm.
Pencil, 230 x 270 mm, 'North Of England' sketchbook, Tate Gallery, London, TB XXXIV 39.

93. Warkworth Castle and Bridge.
Photograph, the author.

94. Warkworth Castle and bridge from north, 1797.
Pencil, 230 x 270 mm, 'North Of England' sketchbook, Tate Gallery, London, TB XXXIV 41.

Alnwick
Northumberland

Warkworth 6m SE. Dunstanburgh 8m NE. Alnwick Castle, the home of the Duke of Northumberland, open daily Easter–mid October, visitor facilities, admission charge. Exact viewpoints of abbey gateway and castle on private land, but that of church readily accessible by road.

In medieval times Alnwick was the second town of Northumberland, a busy market centre on the Great North Road, and an important defensive site, controlling the only bridge over the Aln for miles. It is fortunate in having lost little of its character since Turner's time. It was a Celtic site, acquired a Norman bridge and castle, and like Warkworth became a major seat of the Percy family, Earls of Northumberland.[18] The major medieval developments, abbey, castle, church and bridge (though the latter was replaced by John Adam in 1773) are to the north, largely disassociated from the rest of the town which grew up around the market square. This should be borne in mind by anyone planning to walk around Turner's viewpoints.

He made three sketches. The first is of the fourteenth-century gateway of Alnwick Abbey (Pl. 95),[19] which stands in a private field to the north of Canongate bridge, but can be seen adequately from the road. Of the twelfth-century abbey nothing else remains standing. His second sketch (Pl. 96) was of St Michael's church, built on a

95. Alnwick Abbey Gateway, 1797. The gateway, to the north west of St Michael's church, is all that remains of the once-prosperous abbey complex.
Pencil, 270 x 230 mm, 'North Of England' sketchbook, Tate Gallery, London, TB XXXIV 42.

96. Alnwick, St Michael's Church, 1797. The well in the foreground has now disappeared.
Pencil, 270 x 230 mm, 'North Of England' sketchbook, Tate Gallery, London, TB XXXIV 43.

97. Alnwick Castle and Bridge. Photograph, the author.

mound overlooking the Aln on the northern edge of the town. The mound evidently caused the builders some trouble, for the tower seems to have had tendency to slip away and needed ludicrously large stepped buttresses to keep it in place. Turner made great play of these in his sketch, and also recorded a now disappeared well in the foreground, busy with women.

His third sketch (*NOE* 44), of the castle seen from the north-west across the bridge (Pl. 97) was used in the late 1820s as the basis of one of the most beautiful and unusual of the watercolours in his series *Picturesque Views in England and Wales* (Pl. 98).[20] He set the scene at night, with a full moon rising. The effect is to give the scene the air of a poem by Sir Walter Scott. The most powerful effect, however is one of quiet. Still enough for us not to disturb the deer, and for us to imagine that we might almost hear the quiet plop of salmon surfacing in the river.

98. *Alnwick Castle, Northumberland*, exh. Egyptian Hall, London, 1829.
Watercolour, 283 x 483 mm, Art Gallery of South Australia, Adelaide (W.818).

Dunstanburgh
Northumberland

8m NE Alnwick. Bamburgh 10m NW. Access on foot only from Craster (1½m S) or Embleton (2m N). Castle, English Heritage, open daily April–October, Wednesday–Sunday November–March, admission charge. Turner's viewpoints freely accessible around castle perimeter and on foreshore.

Dunstanburgh is remote even today. Begun by Edmund, Earl of Lancaster in 1313, it sits on a wide sea-turfed headland, on basalt crags of Whin Sill, fronting the wind and sea.[21] The only means of visitor access is on foot, either across the two miles of Embleton sands, or along the slightly shorter shoreline from Craster. It had obvious appeal to the Romantic imagination,[22] but on none made such a deep impression as on Turner. The 1797 sketchbooks contain only three sketches from his visit,[23] one from the south (*NOE 45*), another of Egyncleugh tower from the foreshore (*NOE 46*)[24] and another in watercolour of the Lilburn tower, looking out to sea at sunrise (Pl. 100). In order to make the latter, he must have slept out overnight, or set out in the dark from Craster, and the experience seems to have engraved itself indelibly on his mind. Dunstanburgh inspired as much work as almost any other single subject of his career, and all of it is set at dawn.

After his return to London, his first idea seems to have been for a small oil painting now in New Zealand (Pl.

99. Dunstanburgh Castle, *c.*1797–8. Possibly Turner's first attempt at developing his north of England material in oils. Oil on canvas, 470 x 690 mm, Dunedin Art Gallery, New Zealand (B&J 32).

100. Dunstanburgh Castle, sunrise, 1797. Turner must have slept out overnight, or set off in the dark from Craster in order to witness this scene. Pencil and watercolour, 230 x 270 mm, 'North Of England' sketchbook, Tate Gallery, London, TB XXXIV 46A.

101. Dunstanburgh Castle from the south, *c.*1798. Watercolour, 349 x 483 mm, Laing Art Gallery, Newcastle, (W.284).

99). Turner at this stage had little or no experience in painting landscape in oils, and he rehearsed the composition first in a rough charcoal study (TB XXXVI T). The resulting canvas is an energetic and fluid composition but

the unsophisticated handling betrays the work of a novice. He nevertheless learned enough from it to utilise the experience in another series of compositions. This series probably originated in a lost sketch, for it is taken from further forward than the small oil, immediately to the left of the fisherman's cottage, with the Lilburn tower now on the right of the gateway. He began with a chiaroscuro study (Pl. 104)[25] and developed this through a colour study (Pl. 105) into an oil painting exhibited at the Royal Academy in 1798 (Pl. 106).

Not long afterwards, both compositions were repeated in watercolour. That of the small oil almost exactly (Pl. 101), but that of the exhibited oil with subtle changes to the lighting effect (Pl. 107),[26] now plunging the Lilburn tower into shade, to increase the sense of the fitfulness of the weather and the freshness of the conditions. In 1808 he returned to the subject for a composition for his series of prints, the *Liber Sudiorum* (Pl. 103), using the capacity of the dawn light to reveal form, to contrast the solid

geometry of the castle with the chaos of rocks and sea, and to create a sense of the inevitablility of the one returning to its natural state in the other.

About 1828 he returned to the subject for his series *Picturesque Views in England and Wales* (Pl.108). The background is closely observed from the sketch, and the dawn setting from experience, but the foreground has transposed the wide sands from Embleton Bay to the north, to the normally rocky foreshore of the south. As at Tynemouth, shipwreck and salvage is his theme, but here deployed not just for sublime effect, but to tell something of the human aspect of life in these parts. For the coastal villagers of Northumberland, salvage would have been a regular and vital source of income, a paradoxical source of sustenance out of tragedy. The profit to be made might therefore have been the source of some temptation, and required policing. The most prominent figure in the composition is a treasury officer,[27] equipped with horse to arrive as expeditiously as possible to ensure

102. Dunstanburgh Castle from the south.

Photograph, the author.

that the ship was not looted. One wonders how welcome his presence would have been.

Salvage was almost as hazardous an occupation as sailing, and the desperate efforts of one group trying to bring cables and timbers ashore in the teeth of moutainous waves is the subject of Turner's last and most sublime composition of Dunstanburgh exhibited at the Royal Academy in 1834. *Wreckers off the Coast of Northumberland, with a Steam-Boat assisting a Ship Off Shore* (Pl.107) shows the castle in the distance apparently now attacked on all sides by the elements. Offshore a two-masted coaster has been driven on to rocks by a fierce

easterly storm. In all this there has arrived an interesting note of modernity and progress; the sailing ship is at the mercy of the elements, and has been wrecked, but the brand-new steamship is independent and can sail against the wind to attempt the rescue. We have entered a new technological age when man will no longer be so much at the mercy of nature. But how much of a good thing will this be? The wreckers in the foreground will become redundant. Turner's world is always eponymously characterised by circles of change. Nothing is ever one thing without having a tendency to become another, often the very opposite of what it now seems.

103. Dunstanburgh Castle from the south, *c*.1808. The basis of the mezzotint published in the 'Liber Studiorum', 10 June 1808.
Watercolour, 188 x 269 mm, Tate Gallery, London, TB CXVI Q.

104. Dunstanburgh Castle from the south, 1797. Chiaroscuro study for his Royal Academy exhibit, Pl. 106.
Watercolour, 263 x 335 mm, Tate Gallery, London, TB XXXVI S.

105. Dunstanburgh Castle from the south, 1797. A rehearsal for his Royal Academy exhibit, Pl. 106.
Watercolour, 198 x 278 mm, Tate Gallery, London, TB XXXIII S.

106. *Dunstanburgh Castle, N.E. Coast of Northumberland. Sunrise after a Squally Night*, exh. R.A., 1798, no.322.
Oil on canvas, 920 x 1230 mm, National Gallery of Victoria, Melbourne, Australia (B&J.6).

107. Dunstanburgh Castle from the south, *c*.1802.
Watercolour, approx. 305 x 432 mm, National Trust, Wallington Hall, Northumberland (not in Wilton).

108. *Dunstanburgh Castle, Northumberland, c.1828.*
A customs officer arrives on horseback to supervise the salvaging of a wreck.
Watercolour, 291 x 419 mm, Manchester City Art Gallery (W.814).

109. *Wreckers – Coast of Northumberland, with a Steam-Boat assisting a Ship off Shore*,
exh. R.A., 1834, no.199.
Oil on canvas, 914 x 1219 mm, Yale Center for British Art, Paul Mellon Collection, New Haven, USA (B&J.357).

Bamburgh
Northumberland

Dunstanburgh 10m SE. Lindisfarne 6m NW. Castle, home of Lady Armstrong, open Maundy Thursday to last Sunday in October, guided tour, visitor facilities, admission charge. Turner's viewpoints readily accessible on beach and dunes.

Bamburgh from the seaward side is one of the most dramatic sites in Britain, perched on the crags of Whin Sill above the endless space of the beach. It is also a site rich in history. First occupied by Celtic tribes around the first century BC, and then used by the Romans as a beacon, it became a royal Saxon fortress in the mid sixth century. In 635 the court founded a monastery on nearby Lindisfarne, and in the couple of centuries that followed this northern outpost became one of the leading centres of scholarship and art in the world. The keep and massive walls were built by the Normans, and thereafter the castle remained impregnable until beginning a slow decline from the later sixteenth century. Restoration work was carried out in the 1750s, but the castle had to wait until its purchase by Lord Armstrong in the late nineteenth century to be fitted up in the full baronial splendour we see today.[28]

Turner made three sketches at Bamburgh, two from the dunes to the south *(NOE 47, 48)* and another from the beach to the north (Pls 110, 111), from where the castle appears at its most impressive. As at Tynemouth and Dunstanburgh, this is a perilous coast, busy with coastal trade beween Edinburgh, Berwick and the south, and fraught with shallow waters, hidden rocks, and frequent onshore storms. Bamburgh was the centre of a highly organised system of marine rescue. Thomas Pennant described 'apartments fitted for the reception of shipwrecked sailors. . . A constant patrol. . . along this tempestuous coast, for above eight miles, the length of the manor. . . By signals the country people are directed to the spot they are to fly to; and by this means frequently preserve not only the crew, but even the vessel, for machines of different kinds are always in readiness to heave ships out of their perillous situation.'[29] Turner saw the results of this for himself, and his sketch includes a two-master brought ashore having lost its upper masts, and being unloaded or possibly dismantled into a cart waiting alongside.

The subject had to wait for forty years to be developed

110. Bamburgh Castle from the north, 1797. The basis of the colour-beginnings (Pls 115–17). Pencil, 230 x 270 mm, 'North Of England' sketchbook, Tate Gallery, London, TB XXXIV 49.

111. Bamburgh Castle from the north. Photograph, the author.

into a finished watercolour, but when Turner took up the theme, he took it up with a vengeance. He made no fewer than three full-sized studies (Pls 115–17) in which he worked out the colour harmonies and contrasts, as well as the underlying lighting effect. The resulting finished watercolour is at present untraced, but when exhibited in 1837 was described as 'one of the finest water-colour drawings in the world.'[30] The storm is in full spate and a coaster is being driven ashore, one mast already lost, and its hull broadside to the full force of the sea. To the left a distress rocket rises against the black sky. Two figures in the foreground miserably cling to the rocks, and in the back-

Lindisfarne
Northumberland

Bamburgh 6m SE Berwick upon Tweed 12m NW.
Access to island only across tidal causeway. Priory,
English Heritage open all year, admission charge.
Castle National Trust, open April–October, admission
charge. Turner's viewpoints accessible in abbey and
near St Cuthbert's Island at low tide.

Lindisfarne is a site of epic appeal. In 1797 it must have seemed a good approximation to the edge of the world, cut-off, windswept, and bare except for the remains of the monastery, a small castle and a village of a few houses. Its population even now is less than it was in the twelfth century.

Its sense of remoteness, yet proximity to the royal fortress of Bamburgh brought some of the best-known figures of the seventh and eighth centuries. In 635 St Aidan came from Iona to establish the first monastery. He was succeeded by St Cuthbert, in whose lifetime the Lindisfarne gospels were written, and because of whose death the community found international fame. His body refused to decay, and the miracle attracted pilgrims and riches from all over Europe. The monastery was abandoned during the Danish settlements of the ninth century and St Cuthbert's remains endured a peripatetic existance thereafter, being shifted from place to place until they were permanently laid to rest in 1104 in the great new cathedral then being built at Durham. Soon after its completion about 1130, the monks of Durham decided to build a new church to St Cuthbert on Lindisfarne. It was modelled on, and was only slightly smaller than, their own. This became a new monastery, which in turn mouldered away after the Dissolution, but there can be few ruins in the world through which history blows with quite such romance.[31]

Turner's most direct route from Bamburgh was by boat, and one of his first sketches (*NOE 51*) is the view from the landing near St Cuthbert's Isle (Pl. 115). The small parish church of St Mary is to the left, then the priory ruins, and the castle to the right. If his recollection of the subject thirty years later in *Picturesque Views in England and Wales* (Pl. 116) can be taken as a guide, he might well have enjoyed an eventful crossing. A ferry-boat has just landed in the teeth of a fierce squall, and passengers paddle to the shore, no doubt relievedly. A gale has whipped up, and one of the boatmen has to hold on to the boat to prevent it drifting away. One cannot

115. Lindisfarne Priory and Castle from St Cuthbert's Isle.
Photograph, the author.

imagine much enthusiasm for the return crossing. More cautious boatmen have sheeted their boats on the beach.

His main subject of attention on the island was the priory, and he made a total of five sketches of the ruins. The first was a study of the chancel from the north aisle of the nave (Pl. 120), his second of the west end of the nave (*NOE 52*), the third of the nave from the chancel (*NOE 53*), the fourth of the nave arcades from the south (*NOE 54*) and the fifth of the west end from the north aisle (Pl. 119). Lindisfarne is a subject that Turner would certainly have discussed with his friend Thomas Girtin who visited in 1796 and exhibited two watercolours of the subject at the Royal Academy in 1797 just before Turner set off. It cannot be coincidence that some of

116. *Holy Island, Northumberland*, exh. Egyptian Hall, London, 1829.
These are perhaps not the best conditions for taking the Bamburgh ferry.
Watercolour, 292 x 432 mm, Victoria and Albert Museum, London (W.819).

Turner's sketches were of exactly the same subjects recorded by Girtin (Pl. 118).[32]

Turner made two watercolours himself, one large commissioned by a Mr Munden, and another small commissioned by Mr Lambert.[33] We do not known what has become of either of these compositions.[34] The larger was exhibited at the Royal Academy in 1798 and it seems possible that this might have been the same view of the nave arcades that Turner worked up in 1808 as a print for his series the *Liber Studiorum* (Pl. 117). The image is one of Turner's most direct confrontations with masses of crumbling stone, cropped to prevent any escape of the eye but through its mazes of columns and arcades. He had arrived just in time to record it, and before 1820 large parts of the building had collapsed. Small parts were rebuilt but modern visitors will find they have to search carefully for his viewpoints.

117. Holy Island Cathedral, *c*.1808. The basis of the mezzotint published in Turner's 'Liber Studiorum', 20 February 1808, showing the nave arcades from the south, now mostly disappeared.
Watercolour, 185 x 256 mm, Tate Gallery, London, TB CXVI N.

118. Thomas Girtin, St Cuthbert's, Holy Island, 1797. Girtin's visit to the north in 1796 must have been an important source of ideas for Turner. It is perhaps not surprising that the two friends should have taken similar views, *see* Pl. 119.
Watercolour, 255 x 302 mm, Yale Center for British Art, Paul Mellon Collection, New Haven, USA (B1975.4.1215).

119. Lindisfarne Priory, west end from the north aisle of nave, 1797
Pencil, 270 x 230 mm, 'North Of England' sketchbook, Tate Gallery, London, TB XXXIV 55.

120. Lindisfarne Priory: from the north aisle, looking east, 1797.
Pencil and watercolour, 270 x 230 mm, 'North Of England' sketchbook, Tate Gallery, London, TB XXXIV 50.

Berwick upon Tweed
Northumberland

Lindisfarne 12m SE. Norham 6m SW. Turner's viewpoint at the south end of the old bridge is freely accessible.

Berwick was the most northerly point of Turner's tour of 1797, and by the time he arrived there he must have been away for well over a month and covered 500 miles. He made two sketches. The first (Pl. 122) records the view north across the Tweed and old bridge to the town and town hall. (Pl.121) The bridge had been built between 1610 and 1624 and its barriers and gate-house remind us of the town's vulnerability at the most northerly tip of England.[865] His second sketch (Pl. 123) is taken from the same spot, continuing the panorama right to the river's mouth and the sea, and is a much more empty composition. He took advantage of the space to flood his sheet with pools of colour. The tide was low, boats lay beached in the harbour or at anchor in the bay, and the only movement was that of a rowboat pulling slowly across the slack water. He seems almost to have been resting.[36]

121. Berwick upon Tweed, bridge and town from the south. Photograph, the author.

122. Berwick upon Tweed, bridge and town from the south, 1797
Pencil, 230 x 270 mm, 'North Of England' sketchbook, Tate Gallery, London, TB XXXIV 56.

123. Berwick upon Tweed harbour, 1797.
Taken from the same viewpoint as Pl.122, continuing the panorama to the right.
Pencil and watercolour, 230 x 270 mm, 'North Of England' sketchbook, Tate Gallery, London, TB XXXIV 56a.

Norham Castle, Northumberland

Berwick 6m NW. Kelso 16m SW. Castle, English Heritage, open daily all year, visitor facilities, admission charge. Turner's viewpoint on river bank upstream, accessible by footpath.

In 1831 Turner revisited Norham on his way to Scotland to make illustrations for the work of Sir Walter Scott. He was travelling with Scott's publisher Robert Cadell. As their coach made its way up the hill past the castle, Turner took off his hat and made a bow. Cadell was puzzled and made enquiries as to the meaning of this odd gesture: 'Oh', was the reply, 'I made a drawing or painting of Norham several years since. It took, and from that day to this I have had as much to do as my hands could execute.'[37]

Turner had also made a series of quick sketches at Norham in 1801,[38] but it was those of 1797 which provided the basis of a series of work including two colour studies, four finished watercolours, a *Liber Studiorum* composition[39] and a late oil painting. Only one other sketch from the same tour, that of Dunstanburgh (q.v.),

124. Norham Castle and Mill, 1797. Probably a page detached from the 'North of England' sketchbook.
Pencil, 210 x 267 mm, Tate Gallery, London, TB XXVII U.

125. Norham Castle on the Tweed, 1797.
The unpromising basis of one of the most important subjects in Turner's career.
Pencil, 230 x 270 mm, 'North Of England' sketchbook, Tate Gallery, London, TB XXXIV 57.

126. Norham Castle, sunset.
Photograph, the author.

was to prove as inspirational to him. Here, at the furthest reaches of his tour into the northern wilds, he seems to have found himself.

There is little obvious evidence of this in the 1797 sketches themselves. One comparatively quick study of the view from upstream (Pl. 125) and another, more detailed study of the castle and mill (now disappeared) from a nearer viewpoint (Pl. 124). It is striking, however, that all the subsequent work, apart from two watercolours connected with Scott,[40] was set at dawn, and it seems likely that the reason for the brevity of his first sketch is that he was looking straight into the sun and blinded. From the intensity of its subsequent effect, he might well have been *en route* to Damascus.

His first project was to develop a major watercolour for exhibition at the Royal Academy in 1798 (Pl. 129). His poetic source at this time was James Thomson, and it would certainly have been significant for Turner that Thomson was intimately associated with the Tweed valley.

He was born at nearby Ednam, spent his childhood at Southdean and went to school in Jedburgh, and it is easy to imagine that the scenery described in his poetry is shot through with recollections of the Tweed. The finished watercolour was exhibited with some lines describing sunrise from *The Seasons*:

But yonder comes the powerful King of Day,
Rejoicing in the East: The lessening cloud,
The kindling azure, and the mountan's brow
Illumin'd – his near approach betoken glad.
(*Summer* 81–5)

The passage closes a paean to the dawn which includes some inspirational advice to early rising. Turner made a practice of the latter throughout his life, but the realisation of Thomson's effects in paint was more problematic. He started work with a large first colour study (Pl. 127) the purpose of which seems to have been to work out some means of achieving Thomson's effect of 'kindling azure'. For the first time we find Turner managing perfect control of a large pool of colour, imperceptibly shifting from the brilliant yellow of the sun to the deep azure of the sky above. A closer inspection of the edges reveals that this effect was built up from layers of bright carmine and yellow, overlaid with the blue. Turner was satisfied enough with the luminosity and the sense of peace created by the management of these washes to offer them up for comparison with Thomson at the exhibition.

127. Colour-beginning, Norham Castle, sunrise, 1797–8.
Watercolour, 660 x 813 mm, Tate Gallery, London, TB L B.

128. Colour-beginning, Norham Castle, sunrise, 1797–8.
Watercolour, 540 x 743 mm, Tate Gallery, London, TB L C.

129. *Norham Castle on the Tweed, Summer's Morn*, exh. R.A., 1798, no.353.
Watercolour, 509 x 735 mm, Private Collection (W.225).

There was one aspect of Thomson, however, which he had not resolved in the exhibited picture. The poet actually described his subject 'Illumed *with fluid gold*', and Turner suppressed the analogy in his quotation at the exhibition. Presumably he found 'kindling azure' difficult enough for one picture, but he did not let the matter rest, and a second colour study (Pl. 128) found a way of achieving 'fluid gold' by using a complex stopping-out procedure, which left the brilliant yellow underwash revealed, but created an illusion of a thick, golden impasto being laid across the surface. He developed this effect

130. *Norham Castle, Sunrise*, 1798.
A version of the exhibited subject painted for Edward Lascelles of Harewood.
Watercolour, 501 x 705 mm, Cecil Higgins Art Gallery, Bedford (W.226).

into a second finished watercolour (Pl. 130), which was bought by Edward Lascelles of Harewood,[41] and as if to draw attention to the relationship with Thomson's analogy, makes the light on the water seem as if it were a luminous material literally floating on the surface, clinging unctuously to the rocks which jut into its stream.

In the early 1820s he returned to the subject for his series of watercolours *Rivers of England* (Pl. 131). By then his colour effects were fully mature and the picture pulsates with prismatic strokes and irridescent effects. As is usual with his work of this time, however, the composition is full of anecdotal detail. To the right cattle water themselves, and sail-boat crews begin their day's work. To the left fishermen busy themselves around their bothy. He seems to intend that we remember this is the border for the most prominent figure at the left wears plaid. In this light we ought probably to consider the contrasts on each side of the river. On the English side is the imposing bulk of Norham, but on the left a mere bothy. The Scots

131. *Norham Castle, on the Tweed, c.*1824.
Watercolour, 156 x 216 mm, Tate Gallery, London, TB CCVIII O (W.736).

work with rowboats but the English with sail. The cattle are to the right. The contrast in wealth is obvious, and this contrast has been the source of conflict that had required the castle. It seems relevant that in 1822 not long before this watercolour was published, Turner had been to Edinburgh to witness the state visit of the newly crowned George IV. The uprising of 1745 was not yet that distant a memory. The picture seems to call for some still-required resolution of differences.

His final treatment of the subject (Pl. 132) dates from the last years of his life, and returned to the peace of his first treatments. Once again it was the pools of colour, the dissolving power of light, and a space of ineffable tranquility that came to the fore. In reviewing his origins, and the contact with the world which was so vital to him, the forms of his past emerge from the paint like *pentimenti* floating to the surface. It is perhaps one of his most moving tributes to the kind of experience that he had devoted his whole life to witnessing.

132. *Norham Castle, Sunrise, c.*1845.
Oil on canvas, 910 x 1220 mm, Tate Gallery, London (B&J 512).

Kelso Abbey
Roxburghshire

Norham 16m NE. Melrose 14m W. Abbey , Historic Scotland, near north end of Kelso bridge, free entry, no visitor facilities. Turner's viewpoints from streets to north and west.

One result of Turner's interest in medieval buildings is an inevitable contrast between past and present, usually to the disadvantage of the latter. In Turner's account there seems a scale and spirit about the past which had all but disappeared. The Tweed valley offered plenty of scope for such comparison, a rich land full of castles and abbeys, but all in decay, and the majority of its citizens in 1797 living in comparatively mean circumstances.

The situation was clearly in evidence at Kelso, where the remains of the twelfth century abbey served time in the town as cow-shed, storehouse and quarry and proved an appealing subject to late eighteenth century artists.[42]

133. Kelso Abbey, north front, 1797. Turner contrasts the scale of past endeavour with that of the present.
Pencil, 270 x 230 mm, 'North Of England' sketchbook, Tate Gallery, London, TB XXXIV 58.

134. Kelso Abbey, west front, 1797.
Pencil, 270 x 230 mm, 'North Of England' sketchbook, Tate Gallery, London, TB XXXIV 59.

135. Kelso Abbey, west front.
Photograph, the author.

His first sketch from the north (Pl.133) made much of the contrast, with the crumbling giant of the church tottering above a tumbledown cottage, while figures, carts and other paraphernalia stand about outside. His second sketch (Pl. 134) is a study of the architecture of the west side (Pl. 135). For some reason it remained only partly completed. This is not at all typical of this tour, but the result is nevertheless interesting, for it shows the way in which he roughed out the placement of his general elements, and then began to build up details over this framework. It was not until 1831 that he returned to make an illustration for the work of Sir Walter Scott.[43]

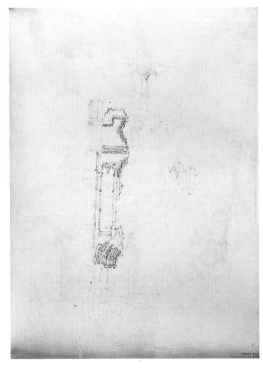

Melrose Abbey
Roxburghshire

Kelso, 14m E. Dryburgh 4m SE. Melrose Abbey, Historic Scotland, open daily all year, visitor facilities, admission charge. Turner's viewpoint from south accessible by footpath, but no right of way to that from east. Others in abbey precincts.

Melrose was one of the major sites of Turner's tour. He took out his large *Tweed and Lakes* sketchbook for the first time since Durham, and made three sketches, together with two more in his smaller *North of England* sketchbook. The abbey is one of the most exuberant examples of fifteenth-century architecture anywhere in Britain, being almost completely rebuilt after Richard II's devastation of southern Scotland in 1389. The masons probably came from Beverley in East Yorkshire (q.v.) where they were bringing the decorated style to perfection, and the project at Melrose continued for most of the next hundred years.[44] The result was one of the most complex subjects imaginable for the pencil.

The weather must have been good, for Turner obviously spent many hours outdoors making his drawings. He made two close-up studies, one of the north transept and nave from the cloister (*NOE* 60), and the other of

136. Melrose Abbey from the east, 1797.
Pencil, 274 x 370 mm, 'Tweed And Lakes' sketchbook, Tate Gallery, London, TB XXXV 18.

137. Melrose Abbey from mill to east, 1797.
Pencil, 230 x 270 mm, 'North Of England' sketchbook, Tate Gallery, London, TB XXXIV 61.

the interior of the north transept, looking across the east end *(T&L* 16).[45] It was the views of the exterior which occupied his attention most deeply, however, and he took views of the great east end from the north-east (Pl. 136),[46] a more distant view from the east (Pl.137),[47] and another of the south side (Pls 138, 139). These are some of the most complete and time-consuming drawings that he made on the tour, and with the sun reflecting from the red sandstone, a deep blue sky behind, and lush grass in the foreground, it is not hard to understand why. He would scarcely have needed any better reason than the pleasure of it, but although obviously enjoyed, nothing of this subject was developed until the 1820s and 1830s when he made two watercolours connected with the poetry of Sir Walter Scott.[48] For the moment, however, the being there seems to have been ample enough reward.

138. Melrose Abbey, south side, 1797.
Pencil, 274 x 370 mm, 'Tweed And Lakes' sketchbook, Tate Gallery, London, TB XXXV 17.

139. Melrose Abbey, south side.
Photograph, the author.

Dryburgh Abbey
Berwickshire

Melrose 4m NW. Jedburgh 10m SSE, near St Boswells. Abbey, Historic Scotland, open daily all year, visitor facilities, admission charge. Turner's viewpoint in the church is readily identifiable, that from St Boswells largely obscured by trees.

Dryburgh is one of the most idyllic monastery settings in Britain. It is hard today to imagine that it has been the scene of repeated destruction and butchery. Founded in 1150, it was destroyed in 1322, 1383, 1461, 1523 and 1545. After the last assault it has been allowed to sleep comparatively undisturbed.[49] Turner made two sketches in 1797. The first (Pl. 140) looks from the east end to the nave (Pl. 142). It is interesting to study Turner's method here, for the view is of too wide an angle to be taken in all at once. It will be discovered that he shifted position at least once, sketching the chapels of the north transept (to the right) from one viewpoint, and the walls of the south transept (to the left) from another. His second sketch was made from the opposite side of the river at St Boswells (Pl. 141). He returned to a similar viewpoint in 1831 to take a view to illustrate the work of Sir Walter Scott.[50] The following year Scott was buried in one of the chapels of the north transept.

140. Dryburgh Abbey, nave from choir, 1797.
Pencil, 230 x 270 mm, 'North Of England' sketchbook, Tate Gallery, London, TB XXXIV 62.

141. Dryburgh Abbey from the banks of the Tweed near St Boswell's, 1797.
Pencil, 230 x 270 mm, 'North Of England' sketchbook, Tate Gallery, London, TB XXXIV 23.

142. Dryburgh Abbey, nave from choir. Sir Walter Scott is buried in the chapel to the right.
Photograph, the author

Jedburgh
Roxburghshire

On the A68 between Newcastle and Edinburgh. Dyburgh 4m NW. Keswick 95m SW. Abbey, Historic Scotland, open daily all year, visitor facilities, admission charge. Turner's viewpoints readily identifiable outside west front, and SE from road by new parish church.

Jedburgh is the best preserved of the four border abbeys visited by Turner in 1797, and seems to have been designed to provide a spectacular welcome to travellers arriving in Scotland along the main road from the south. Despite being repeatedly damaged between 1305 and 1545 it was always repaired, and even after the dissolution survived in partly functional condition, serving as the parish church until a replacement was built in 1875.[51]

It was a subject which Turner would have discussed with Girtin, for his friend exhibited two watercolours of the subject at the Academy in 1797,[52] just before Turner set out. It seems likely that both Turner's views were modelled on Girtin's example. His view of the west front (Pls 144, 145) exactly follows a view by Girtin (Pl. 143) probably one of the Academy exhibits. Turner's sketch is firmer in drawing, hardly surprising given the amount of

143. Thomas Girtin, Jedburgh Abbey, West Front, exh. R.A. 1797, no.423 or 466. Turner would have seen this at the Academy shortly before he set out on his tour to the north.
Watercolour, British Museum, London, 1855–2–14–61.

144. Jedburgh Abbey, west front, 1797. A knife-grinder's stone stands to the left of the abbey portal.
Pencil, 270 x 230 mm, 'North Of England' sketchbook, Tate Gallery, London, TB XXXIV 64.

145. Jedburgh Abbey, west front.
Photograph, the author.

practice he had on this tour, but Girtin's is an entertainingly picturesque contrast of ruin and contemporary life. He includes Scotsmen in plaid, women carrying water from the well and a man mending a cart outside the west portal. It seems likely that all this detail was derived from observation on the spot.

Turner's second sketch (Pl. 147) shows the more distant view from the south-east (Pl. 146). We know that Girtin exhibited a drawing of a similar subject with women washing clothes in 1797,[53] but this cannot now be identified with certainty. Turner's drawing is one of the best of the tour , recording with great accuracy the startling impression created by the abbey as one comes to the town from the south. The foreground is likewise populated with washer-women, presumably a characteristic sight in the town at this time. He returned to a similar subject in 1831 for Sir Walter Scott.[54]

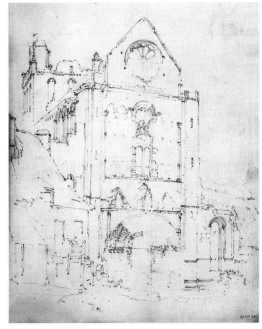

146. *left* Jedburgh Abbey from the south east.
Photograph the author.

147. *above* Jedburgh Abbey from the South East, 1797.
Washerwomen seem to have been a characteristic sight at Jedburgh.
Pencil, 230 x 270 mm, 'North Of England' sketchbook, Tate Gallery, London, TB XXXIV 63.

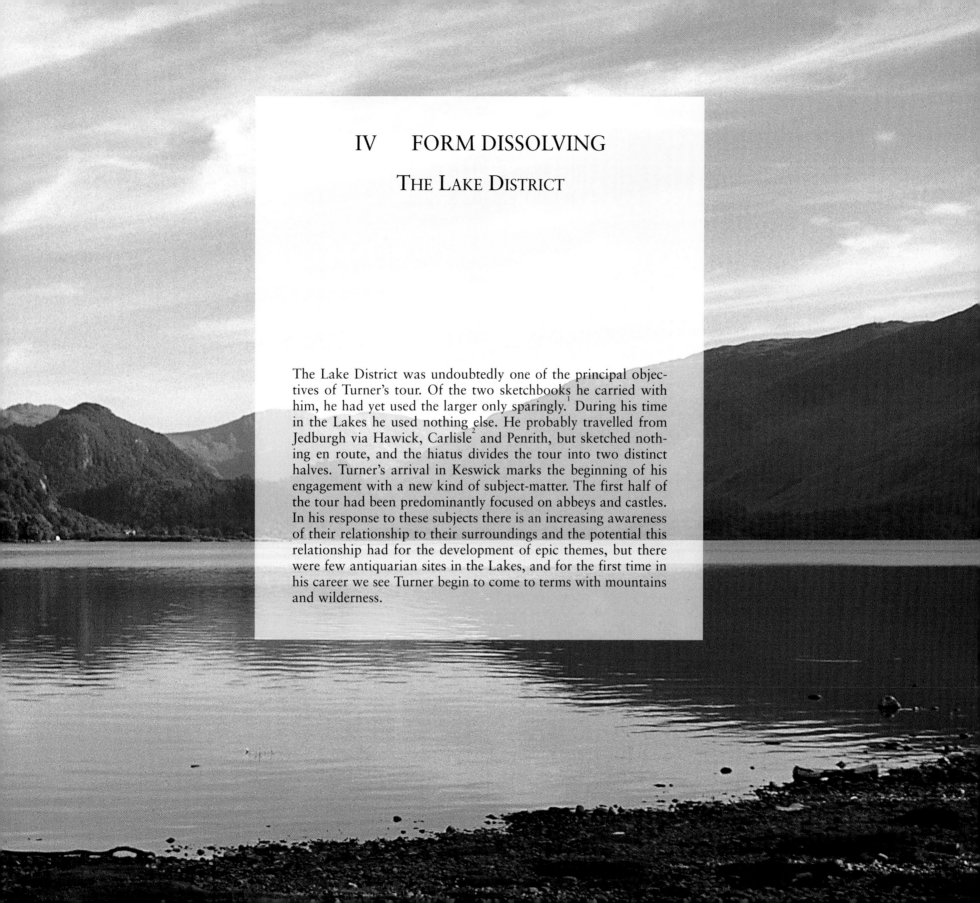

IV   FORM DISSOLVING

THE LAKE DISTRICT

The Lake District was undoubtedly one of the principal objectives of Turner's tour. Of the two sketchbooks he carried with him, he had yet used the larger only sparingly.[1] During his time in the Lakes he used nothing else. He probably travelled from Jedburgh via Hawick, Carlisle[2] and Penrith, but sketched nothing en route, and the hiatus divides the tour into two distinct halves. Turner's arrival in Keswick marks the beginning of his engagement with a new kind of subject-matter. The first half of the tour had been predominantly focused on abbeys and castles. In his response to these subjects there is an increasing awareness of their relationship to their surroundings and the potential this relationship had for the development of epic themes, but there were few antiquarian sites in the Lakes, and for the first time in his career we see Turner begin to come to terms with mountains and wilderness.

Derwentwater
Lake District

From Jedburgh 95m. Borrowdale 3m s. Buttermere 8m sw via Newlands. Turner's viewpoints around lake all freely accesible by road and footpath and all readily recognisable.

Turner made Keswick his base for the first few days of his stay,[3] and from there made excursions around Derwentwater, into Borrowdale and further afield to Cockermouth,[4] Buttermere and Crummock Water. Few visitors had much to say for Keswick itself: 'a neat town. . . at present renowned for nothing so much as the lake it stands near', as it was described in West's *Guide*,[5] but everyone was impressed by the setting. One of the first to describe it was Dr John Brown who in 1767 wrote: 'You have at Keswick a vast amphitheatre, in circumference above twenty miles. . . a noble, living lake, ten miles round, of an oblong form, adorned with a variety of wooded island. . . on one side of the lake, see a rich and beautiful landscape of cultivated fields, rising to the eye, in fine inequalities. . . on the opposite shore you will find rocks and cliffs of stupendous height, hanging broken over the lake in horrible grandeur. . . and beyond these at various distances, mountain rising over mountain, among which, new prospects present themselves in

148. *previous page* Derwent Water: Lodore Falls and Borrowdale from Calfclose Bay. Photograph the author.

149. Derwentwater: Castle Head and Derwent Fells from above Keswick, 1797. Pencil, 274 x 370 mm, 'Tweed And Lakes' sketchbook, Tate Gallery, London, TB XXXV 26.

150. Derwentwater, Lodore Falls and Borrowdale from Calfclose Bay, 1797. Pencil, 274 x 370 mm, 'Tweed And Lakes' sketchbook, Tate Gallery, London, TB XXXV 19.

mist, till the eye is lost in agreeable perplexity. . . *beauty, horror,* and *immensity* united.'[6] Two years later Thomas Gray approaching from Penrith described his first impression as of 'the vale of Elysium in all its verdure; the sun then playing on the lake; and lighting up all the mountains with its lustre.'[7]

Turner recorded his own first impression in a pencil sketch taken from Manor Brow (Pl. 149), where the road from Penrith begins its steep descent into the town. The exact view has now been obscured by the development of private houses, but the distinctive form of Castle Head, flanked by the lake is readily recognisable. It is perhaps symptomatic of Turner's interests that he carefully cropped the composition to exclude any sign of the town of Keswick, which is beyond the right hand edge. The Lake District is seen as a place in which the presence of man ought best to appear modest, a place in which nature can besport herself unadorned. This is not a condition in which it would have been wise for Turner to

151. Derwentwater, Lodore Falls and Borrowdale from the headland beyond Calfclose Bay, 1797. The basis of an unfinished studio watercolour, Pl. 153.

Pencil and watercolour, 274 x 370 mm, 'Tweed And Lakes' sketchbook, Tate Gallery, London, TB XXXV 82.

have conducted himself, for while he was there it seems to have rained most of the time. The Derwent fells in the background of this sketch are almost invisible for mist, and the same conditions seem to have prevailed throughout most of his stay. All too frequently the high mountain summits were invisible for cloud.

Tourists found many fine viewpoints in the immediate vicinity of Keswick,[8] but in 1797 Turner seems to have preferred to distance himself a little from the town. His first sketches were taken a mile or so south of Keswick at Calf Close Bay, one from the bay itself (Pl. 150, cf. Pl. 148) and another from the headland beyond (Pl.151). Both look south towards Lodore Falls, left of centre, with the entrance to Borrowdale towards the right guarded by the pyramidial bulk of Castle Crag. It would appear that the weather conspired to present the subject in sublime mood, for both sketches record low cloud scudding across the fell tops. Conditions were not so adverse to prevent him working the second sketch up in watercolour, albeit of a sombre hue, but if we might judge from the conspicuousness of Lodore Falls, normally dried to a trickle in the summer,[9] the recent weather must have been wet. For the moment at least the lake is still, and the heavy atmosphere is accentuated by the bright block of the old Lodore Hotel reflected in the dark water. We might almost imagine that we can hear the rumble of the falls beyond.

One of the artists whose work Turner might well have studied for ideas about the Lake District, was the senior Academician Joseph Farington who had been resident at Keswick from 1776 to 1781, and published a series of twenty *Views in the Lakes &c of Cumberland and Westmorland* in 1789. These would have been widely known since they were advertised in the third edition of West's *Guide*.[10] After the tour Turner frequently sought Farington's advice and support and even invited him to chose a subject from the north of England sketchbooks to be worked up as gift.[11] He eventually agreed to take a finished version of the watercolour sketch of Derwentwater and Lodore, and his name is inscribed on the back of the sketch.[12]

Turner seems to have begun the project soon after, and made a large watercolour (Pl.152), enthusiastically dramatising the mountain profiles and weather conditions, and carrying the work near to completion. It is hard to see quite why he should have left off, but in the event Farington had to wait until 1801 to receive his gift

152. *Head of Derwentwater with Lodore Falls*, 1801. Probably painted from nature while at Keswick in August 1801.
Watercolour, 355 x 524 mm, Private Collection (W.282).

153. Derwentwater, Lodore Falls and Borrowdale from the headland beyond Calfclose Bay, 1797.
Watercolour, 493 x 629 mm, Tate Gallery, London, TB XXXVI H.

(Pl. 153). The watercolour with which he was presented is inscribed 'To Joseph Farington Esqre with W Turner's Respects' and signed 'JMW Turner Keswick Augt 1801'. This seems to want some explanation. In 1801 Turner made a tour of Scotland and arrived at Gretna Green on his way south on 5 August.[13] He must presumably have revisited Keswick then. By this time Turner had evolved a

154. Derwentwater from Friar's Crag, near Keswick, 1801. Probably painted from nature while at
Keswick in August 1801.
Watercolour, 383 x 549 mm, Tate Gallery, London, TB XXXVI I.

practice of making large colour studies directly from nature. Most are now identified as scenes in north Wales dating from 1799,[14] and one as of Scotland dating from 1801.[15] The topographical detail of Farington's watercolour, particularly the clarification of Grange Fell – the low hill to the right of Lodore – suggests fresh observation independent of the 1797 sketches, and the broad treatment is untypical of Turner's usual work in the studio. It is significant in this respect that another large unfinished watercolour in the Turner Bequest (Pl. 154), shows the same bright colour and ambitious handling of the north Wales and Scotland studies, but depicts a view of Derwentwater taken from the shore of Friar's Crag[16] at Keswick. Given the lack of any pencil sketches from this viewpoint, it seems highly probable that this was painted directly from the motif. This being the case it would seem equally possible that Farington's watercolour was painted from nature, and worked up to completion while Turner was still in Keswick.[17]

In the years following Turner's visit, Keswick became famous as the haunt of poets. Coleridge stayed at Greta Hall for a couple of years from 1801, and was succeeded there by Robert Southey, who stayed until his death in 1843. Many more came to visit: Keats, Shelley, Rogers, Hazlitt, Lamb, Scott, Ruskin, De Quincey and of course Wordsworth. Of these, Turner was particularly associated with Samuel Rogers and moved freely in his circle.[18] In the 1820s he made illustrations for an edition of his poems, and included two Derwentwater scenes, the view of Lodore (Pl. 155) and another of St Herbert's Isle.[19] In 1831 he returned to Keswick when collecting material for his illustrations to Sir Walter Scott,[20] and developed a view of Skiddaw from the south end of the lake.[21] His last treatment of the subject, however, was a watercolour published in 1837 in his series *Picturesque Views in England and Wales* (Pl. 156) in which he returned to the viewpoint of his first visit. At the height of his power he transmuted the scene into dazzling colour, but as is frequently the case in this series, the sublimity is offset by a sense of human comedy. In the foreground a group of figures staggers away from a boat. They have obviously been caught in the shower on the lake, and are no doubt relieved to be back on dry land. A cover for the boat stands propped against a rock in the foreground, apparently unused.

The boating party is worth closer inspection. It consists of an elderly gentleman with distinctive black hair,

155. *Keswick Lake. c.* 1824. Derwentwater and Lodore Falls. Painted as an illustration to the poems of Samuel Rogers. Watercolour, 112 x 140 mm., Tate Gallery, London, TB CCLXXX 181. W.1182.

supported by two young women, one of whom tries to protect him from the elements with a tiny umbrella. One is forced to wonder who this might be. In 1831 Turner seems to have been quite close to Robert Southey. Only two years earlier the poet laureate had written a poem entitled 'Stanzas Addressed to JMW Turner Esq RA on his view of the Lago Maggiore from the Town of Arona' which was published in the *Keepsake* of 1829, along with the engraving of Turner's watercolour.[22] The admiration seems to have been mutual, and in 1816 Turner used some lines of Southey's poetry as an epigraph to one of his Royal Academy exhibits.[23] They must certainly have met through Samuel Rogers, and it seems highly likely that when Turner was in Keswick in August 1831 he would have called on the celebrated poet to pay his respects.[24] For a 'Lake Poet' Southey was somewhat handicapped by much preferring life indoors, and he was less than enthusiastic about exposing himself to the elements.[25] Wordsworth on the other hand obviously relished it, and for Turner it constituted nothing less than the central purpose of his life It would also have been quite typical of him to repay Southey's poetic compliment in his own wry way.

From Keswick Turner made an excursion to Borrowdale. His first stop was to make a watercolour study of Lodore Falls (Pl. 157). The stream tumbles prettily down

156. *Keswick Lake, Cumberland, c.1835.*
Watercolour, 276 x 438 mm, British Museum, London, 1958–7–12–442 (W.871).

a rocky cleft among trees and is occasionally dramatic in winter or in spate. It had even been compared to Niagra in height if not in volume, but if Turner was in expectation of spectacle he was to be disappointed. The flow of water seems to have subsided considerably since he made his views from Calf Close Bay.

Lodore was a popular spot nevertheless and he would have been lucky not to have been disturbed during the hour or two that he spent there, but the viewpoint of his second stop was rather more sequestered. The summit of Grange Fell is somewhat off the beaten track even now, but offers a sensational view north to Skiddaw with the river Derwent serpentining to the lake at its foot. It is hard to imagine that Turner would have found out this spot unaided, and it seems likely that he was using the

157. Lodore Falls, 1797.
Pencil and watercolour, 370 x 274 mm, 'Tweed And Lakes' sketchbook, Tate Gallery, London, TB XXXV 85.

158. Derwentwater and Skiddaw from Grange Crag, 1797.
Pencil and watercolour, 274 x 370 mm, 'Tweed And Lakes' sketchbook, Tate Gallery, London, TB XXXV 77.

services of a guide.[26] It is a spot that in good conditions visitors will find hard to leave quickly, and Turner enjoyed the view leisurely, working up one of the most complete colour studies of his trip (Pl. 158).

Borrowdale
Lake District

3m s from Keswick, via Lodore, Grange and Rosthwaite, returning through Grange and on w shore of Derwentwater. Turner's viewpoints freely accessible by road and footpath.

He continued from Grange Fell down Borrowdale, making a sketch of Castle Crag (*T&L* 21) on his descent. His viewpoint was not far from the Bowder Stone. The giant boulder lies close by the road and was one of the most conspicuous and frequently visited curiosities of the area, and it is significant of Turner's interest that he did not take the opportunity to sketch it. He pressed on up the valley to make a sketch from above Longthwaite looking towards Seathwaite and Taylorgill Force (Pls 159, 160). At first sight there seems to be no obvious reason why he should have sketched this of the many views in Borrowdale, or why he should have chosen this spot, not far upstream from the present Longthwaite Youth Hostel, in particular. Again he seems to have had advice,

159. Borrowdale, Seathwaite valley from above Longthwaite, 1797. Looking towards the Scafell range. Borrowdale graphite mine on the slopes to the right.
Pencil, 274 x 370 mm, 'Tweed And Lakes' sketchbook, Tate Gallery, London, TB XXXV 22.

160. Seathwaite valley from above Longthwaite.
Photograph, the author.

161. Borrowdale, Longthwaite Bridge and Castle Crag, *c*.1809?
With a glimpse of Skiddaw in the jaws of the valley, right.
Watercolour, 346 x 533 mm, Private Collection (not in Wilton).

for this is the one viewpoint in the valley bottom from which it is possible to have sight of Lingmell End, part of Scafell, the highest range in England. Unfortunately the weather was against him, and he could see nothing beyond Seathwaite Fell, less than half the distance to Scafell. Another attraction of this view might have been that it included, on the slopes of Grey Knotts to the right, the site of Borrowdale graphite mine, which would have interested Turner since its ore was well known for its use in the manufacture of pencils.[27]

His next sketch (*T&L* 88) was from Longthwaite Bridge looking down the valley. Again he must have had advice, for this particular viewpoint, unfortunately now obscured by trees, afforded a glimpse of Skiddaw framed in the jaws of the valley to the right of Castle Crag. A finished version of the composition (Pl. 161) was commissioned by a Mr Knowles and his name was inscribed on the back of the sketch.[28] The closest comparison in terms of style is with watercolours of Alpine subjects made about 1808 for his Yorkshire patron Walter Fawkes,[29] and his experience of the Alps seems to have influenced his memory of Borrowdale. One might be forgiven for mistaking it for the first sight of Mont Blanc from the bridge at St Martin.

Returning towards Grange, he completed his survey of Borrowdale with two sketches looking to Rosthwaite Fell and Glaramara from the road into the valley under Castle Crag (Pls 162, 163). Late in the day, conditions seem to have lifted sufficiently for him to again take out his watercolours. Although Glaramara is still wreathed in mist, Rosthwaite Fell is bathed in soft evening sunlight, and the trees on the valley floor cast long shadows across the meadows. He returned to Keswick along the west shore of Derwentwater making sketches of Skiddaw from Brandlehow Woods (*T&L* 24)[30] and of Falcon Crag and St Herbert's Isle from the shore at Hause End (*T&L* 25). The sketches are too slight to be worth reproducing, and no doubt the light was beginning to fade. Nevertheless evening light on Falcon Crag can be impressive, and it seems that Turner's day ended in peaceful mood. An economical note scribbled on the sketch manages to say a very great deal: 'Perfct Refln'.

162. Borrowdale, Rosthwaite Fell and Glaramara from the road under Castle Crag, 1797. Evening light on the fellsides. Pencil and watercolour, 274 x 370 mm, 'Tweed And Lakes' sketchbook, Tate Gallery, London, TB XXXV 83.

163. Borrowdale, Rosthwaite Fell and Glaramara from the road under Castle Crag. Photograph, the author.

Buttermere and Crummock Water
Lake District

Buttermere village 9m SW from Keswick via Newlands. Crummock Water 1m NW of Buttermere. To return to Keswick via Whinlatter pass, 14m. Turner's viewpoints all accessible by road or footpath, and all readily recognisable except view from above village (*T&L* 28).

Turner's next excursion was over the Derwent Fells to Buttermere.[31] It was a place of dramatic impact: In 1802 Coleridge found 'an enormous Basin mountain-high of solid stone, cracked in half and half gone; exactly in the remaining half of this enormous Basin, does Buttermere lie, in this beautiful and stern Embracement of Rock.'[32] The village of Buttermere was no more than sixteen houses but one of these was the Fish Inn where Turner would no doubt have sought refreshment. He might well have beeen served by Mary Robinson, daughter of the landlord.[33] As a fresh-faced girl of about fifteen in 1792 she had become an early victim of media coverage when rather over-enthusiastically described by Joseph Budworth in his *Fortnight's Ramble to the Lakes*. As if this exposure were not enough, she became a national *cause celebre* as the Maid of Buttermere when the story later broke of her having fallen prey to a professional bigamist called John Hatfield who, masquerading as the flashy Hon. Alexander Augustus Hope, seduced her into marriage and was hanged for his sins at Carlisle in 1803.[34]

Not entirely distracted from sublimity by beauty, Turner made sketches of the lake and valley head from above the village (*T&L* 28)[35] and from the lake shore (Pl. 164). The viewpoint of the first is now difficult to distinguish for later building and tree growth, but that of the second is perfectly recognisable (Pl. 165), taken from near the river exit with Fleetwith Pike dominating the composition to the right of centre, and the entrance to Honister Pass to its left.

He returned to Keswick via Crummock Water where he made two further sketches, one of Crummock Water from near its northern end (T&L 29),[36] and another from Buttermere Hause (Pl. 167), looking over the southern end of the lake back towards Buttermere. The old road over the Hause which Turner would have used has been replaced by a modern road on the lake side and has become a pleasant route to walk. His viewpoint from above the lake is readily recognisable (Pl.166), looking back from where the road turns the point, to Fleetwith

164. Buttermere, Fleetwith Pike and Honister Pass, 1797. Looking south from the stream at the foot of the lake. Pencil, 274 x 370 mm, 'Tweed And Lakes' sketchbook, Tate Gallery, London, TB XXXV 27.

165. Buttermere, Fleetwith Pike and Honister Pass. Photograph, the author.

Pike in the distance left, Haystacks right of centre and High Stile to the right. Though conditions seem to have been poor, he worked up the sketch in watercolour to a degree unequalled thus far. Heavy clouds drift across the mountains, the colours are cold grey and peat moss, and the lake is 'black' according to a note pencilled on the water. In the midst of all this gloom, however, a whitewashed cottage gleams, and light breaks through the clouds to sparkle on Buttermere in the distance, and to hang shimmering in a curtain of rain at the centre.[37]

During the following winter Turner developed this subject into one of his first major landscapes in oil exhibited at the Royal Academy in 1798 as *Buttermere Lake, with part of Cromackwater, Cumberland, a Shower* (Pl.

168).[38] None can ever have depicted a shower, even one in Cumberland, quite so enthusiatically. As the conditions had been relieved by light on his visit, however, he developed the theme of optimism by turning the shimmering effect of light in the sketch into a rainbow in the finished composition. Even though this would be strictly impossible from this viewpoint – the sun would have to be in the north – rainbows would nevertheless have been a frequent sight during his exploration of the Lakes. The idea of the rainbow might also have been part of the experience in another way. One of the most popular books on the Lakes was William Gilpin's *Observations Relative to Picturesque Beauty made in the year 1772, in several parts of England, particularly the Mountains and Lakes of Cumberland and Westmorland*, which had been first published in 1786. Gilpin's description of the scenery around Keswick quoted some lines from James Thomson's *Seasons*.[39] The same lines were quoted by

166. Crummock Water from Buttermere Hause, Buttermere in the distance.
Photograph, the author.

167. Crummock Water from Buttermere Hause, Buttermere in the distance, 1797. The basis of one of Turner's most impressive early paintings Pl.168.
Pencil and watercolour, 274 x 370 mm, 'Tweed And Lakes' sketchbook, Tate Gallery, London, TB XXXV 84.

Turner as an epigraph to *Buttermere Lake* when it was exhibited at the Academy:

Till in the western sky the downward sun
Looks out effulgent – the rapid radiance instantaneous strikes
Th' illumin'd mountains – in a yellow mist
Bestriding earth – the grand ethereal bow
Shoots up immense, and every hue unfolds

(*Spring*, ll 189–205)

Turner edited down his source to form virtually a new poem appropriate to the picture. But if we look out the source, another reason for its selection becomes apparent. Both published poem and Gilpin's quotation in the *Observations*, begin 'Thus all day long the full distended clouds/ Indulge their genial stores. . .' We can see from these and many other sketches how appropriate this passage would have been to Turner's experience of the Lakes in 1797.[40]

168. *Buttermere Lake, with part of Cromackwater, Cumberland, a Shower*, exh. R.A., 1798, no. 527.
Seldom can anyone have painted a shower so enthusiastically.
Oil on canvas, 915 x 1220 mm, Tate Gallery, London (B&J 7).

Ullswater, Lake District

Grasmere 8m SW. To Ambleside from Patterdale 10m S via Brothers Water (3m) and Kirkstone Pass. All Turner's viewpoints except that of the church readily accessible and recognisable; on W lakeshore from road, Aira Force by footpath (National Trust), Side Farm and campsite by footpath, Goldrill Bridge and Brothers Water by road.

From Grasmere Turner went next to Patterdale at the southern end of Ullswater. His most likely road was the most direct route over Grisedale Hause. At just over 2000 feet the hause would have been the highest point on the tour, and given the conditions recorded at Grasmere, almost certainly in cloud. It is disappointing, but perhaps inevitable, that he made no sketches on the journey.

He would have put up at Patterdale possibly at the King's Arms where as William Gell found a few weeks earlier, 'the people are very civil and gave us a very good dinner'.[47] He began his exploration of the lake by making eight sketches on an expedition up the western shore towards Gowbarrow Bay.[48] His first (Pl. 176) suggests some confusion as to what he thought he was looking at. Taken from the craggy shore near Stybarrow Crag, it records the view past Glenridding to Patterdale with Hartsop Dodd prominent in the centre, flanked by Arnison Crag to the right and the slopes of Place Fell to the left. On the evidence of the inscription below, he

176. Ullswater from near Glenridding, looking south, 1797
Pencil, 274 x 370 mm, 'Tweed And Lakes' sketchbook, Tate Gallery, London, TB XXXV 37.

177. Ullswater, looking south from Aira Park, 1797. St Sunday Crag in centre largely obscured by cloud. The basis of two finished watercolours, Pls 180, 181.
Pencil, 274 x 370 mm, 'Tweed And Lakes' sketchbook, Tate Gallery, London, TB XXXV 42.

178. Ullswater from Aira Park. Photograph, the author.

appears to have been under the misapprehension that Hartsop Dodd was Helvellyn. He would have known from any description of Ullswater that Helvellyn stood near the head of the lake, but the mountain is in fact barely visible from any part of the west lake shore except at the northern end.

He nevertheless managed to find out Aira Force,[49] which lies in a wooded valley half a mile back from the lakeside, about three miles from Patterdale, where he made a careful sketch which he partially worked up in watercolour (Pl. 179). The view which proved most useful to him he found on the shore near where Aira Beck issues into the lake(Pl. 177). Strangely this is one of the least detailed of any of the sketches made on this tour. The weather seems to have got the better of him entirely. To the left we can see Place Fell and Silver Crag and to the right Glenridding Dodd, but the principal feature of the centre of the view (Pl. 178), the great whale-backed ridge of St Sunday Crag, was invisible to him.

Perhaps the very paucity of information gave him scope for artistic invention, for he returned to the subject twice in later years to make major watercolour compositions.

The first (Pl. 180) was painted about 1815 for his Yorkshire patron Walter Fawkes. Only the left side is at all recognisable in the sketch. Beyond that he has created a great shimmering amphitheatre of mountains piling to the clouds like the Himalayas. Nearly twenty years on from his visit, the experience has now been transmuted into pure imaginary form, the silence of which is broken only by the single exclamatory gesture of the cowherd.

His second version of the subject was published in 1835 in the series *Picturesque Views in England and Wales* (Pl. 181). Imagined mountains now gleam transubstantially in the setting sunlight, which casts long purple shadows over the lake. On this extraordinary evening a

179. Aira Force, 1797.
Pencil and watercolour, 370 x 274 mm, 'Tweed And Lakes' sketchbook, Tate Gallery, London, TB XXXV 78.

180. *Ullswater Lake, from Gowbarrow Park, Cumberland, c.*1815. Based loosely on the sketch of the view from Aira Park, Pl. 177.
Watercolour, 280 x 413 mm, Whitworth Art Gallery, Manchester (W.551).

party of bathers has come down to the lake. At this point the picture begins to make more subtle implications. We cannot help noticing that the cow on the right is particularly thin, almost as skeletal in fact as the sticks in the water nearby. The billy-cans are empty. The bathers' nakedness seems somewhat waifish. The composition gives an impression of emptiness as much as of spaciousness. In the midst of all this scenery there is only a bare threshold of means. Turner clearly intended us to give this some consideration. To contrast perhaps this aboriginal beauty with the world from which it was being viewed. That is the world of ourselves as the privileged consumers of this as art, in a situation in which our comforts are so numerous as to include this on top of all else. Basic as the luxuries of the bathers might seem, it is they who enjoy immersion in nature in fact, for us it is merely vicarious.

After exploring the west shore of the lake, Turner next took a stroll around Patterdale. His first sketch (*T&L* 44) was taken near the hotel looking north over the church to the lake. Sometime after the tour[50] Joseph Mawman commissioned a finished watercolour (Pl. 182) of the subject to be engraved as one of the illustrations

184. Ullswater, Cumberland, *c*.1835.
Despite the evident beauty of the scene, the details seem to suggest impoverishment.
Watercolour, 330 x 426 mm, Private Collection (W.860).

conditions were now clear, and all his sketches give uninterrupted views of the mountains. It was on this same bridge that five years later Wordsworth composed his poem 'The Cock is Crowing'. For him too the weather had just cleared up:[52]

There's joy in the mountains;
There's life in the fountains;
Small clouds are sailing,
Blue sky prevailing;
The rain is over and gone!

Brothers Water was a favourite spot for Wordsworth and he described the scene with enthusiasm in his *Guide*: 'having gone along the western side of Brothers-water and passed Hartsop Hall, a stream soon after issues from a cove richly decorated with native wood. This spot is, I believe, never explored by Travellers; but from these sylvan and rocky recesses, whoever looks back on the gleaming surface of Brothers-water, or forward to the

185. Brothers Water from the east shore.
Photograph, the author.

186. Brothers Water, from the east shore, looking to Dove Crag, 1797. Hartsop Hall in the centre middle distance.
Pencil, 274 x 370 mm, 'Tweed And Lakes' sketchbook, Tate Gallery, London, TB XXXV 48.

187. Brothers Water, from above the inn looking north, 1797. The inn flourishes to this day, though much redeveloped.
Pencil, 274 x 370 mm, 'Tweed And Lakes' sketchbook, Tate Gallery, London, TB XXXV 49

precipitous sides and lofty ridges of Dove Crag, &c., will be equally pleased with the beauty, the grandeur, and the wildness of the scenery.'[53] This was the subject of Turner's second sketch (Pl. 186), taken from the eastern shore, just below the road, with Hartsop Hall in the centre middle distance backed by the impressive crest of Black Brow and Dove Crag. The view is virtually unchanged today, and with the lake still as in Turner's sketch, amply worth the scramble down from the road to reach it (Pl. 185).

His final sketch (Pl. 187) was taken from just above the Brothers Water Inn, looking back over the lake towards Place Fell. We can see the inn sign hanging over the road to the right. Apart from the buildings being redeveloped, the site is little changed today, and we might well imagine Turner taking full advantage of its facilities to refresh himself before beginning the haul over Kirkstone to Ambleside.

ing boat in these sketches, to travel the five miles or so down the lake to Bowness. Modern visitors can travel in grander style on one of the many steamers which ply the route today.

Bowness is a hubbub of tourist activity. There are busy piers and marinas, barkers filling up pleasure steamers and hire boats, private yachts and cruisers, hotels, gift shops, pubs, cafés, and ice cream stalls . It can seem as if all human life throngs along its promenades. When Turner made his sketch of the Bay (Pl. 190) from a viewpoint now overlooking the modern piers (Pl.191), with the northern end of the lake dominated by the summit of Fairfield, there were already signs of its growing popularity. The shore in the foreground is filled with boats, and a rowing party pushes off on to the lake.[63]

He returned to the subject forty years later in a watercolour published in *Picturesque Views in England and Wales* in 1837 (Pl. 192). His final sketch at Windermere in 1797 was a quick note looking north over Belle Isle[64] from Hawkshead ferry landing (*T&L* 56). The *England and Wales* watercolour combined the information from

190. Windermere, from Waterhead looking west towards Langdale.
Photograph, the author.

191. Windermere, from Waterhead looking west towards Langdale, 1797. The Langdale fells obscured by mist, slate barge being loaded in the foreground. Used as the basis of a finished watercolour, Pl.000.
Pencil, 274 x 370 mm, 'Tweed And Lakes' sketchbook, Tate Gallery, London, TB XXXV 52.

this with that of Bowness Bay to construct a composite view as if taken from the ferry looking north.[65] The result is a consummate celebration of the pleasures of the lake. In the background the sun sets over the fells, dissolving them in mist. Although the position of the sun is too far north to be possible, Bowness is nevertheless on the sunset side of the lake and evening light is one of its most memorable delights. Not long before he painted the watercolour, Turner might have revisited Bowness when he was in the area in 1831 and travelled from Kendal to Keswick. Visitors were by then flocking to the Lake District in their thousands, and Bowness would have been bustling as Turner shows it. The lake is thronged with pleasure seekers in craft of all descriptions, getting into one another's way and dipping their hands in the water.[66] On the shore the less affluent also gather to enjoy the spectacle. The whole cross-section of society is gathered here, bound in one common purpose, to enjoy the moment in whatever way they can, communicants in a celebration of being. No picture ever treated tourism so positively.

192. *Windermere*, 1821.
A fanciful adaptation of the 1797 sketch, Pl. 191.
Watercolour, 292 x 407 mm, Private Collection (W.555).

193. Windermere, from Bowness looking north, 1797. Fairfield at the head of the lake in the distance, and a boating party pushing off onto the lake. Used as the basis, with adaptations, of a later watercolour, Pl.195.
Pencil, 274 x 370 mm, 'Tweed And Lakes' sketchbook, Tate Gallery, London, TB XXXV 55.

194. Bowness.
Photograph, the author.

195. *Winander-Mere, Westmoreland, c.*1835. Winandermere is the old name of Windermere.
The view from the Hawkshead ferry looking north, with Belle Isle in the middle distance.
Watercolour, 290 x 460 mm, Manchester City Art Gallery (W.874).

Coniston
Lake District

Bowness 8m E via Hawkshead and Ferry. Furness Abbey 20m SSW via Ulverston. Turner's viewpoints accessible by footpath, except that of Coniston Old Hall (not open to public) from SE, on private land.

Turner began his work at Coniston by making two sketches of the ruins of the sixteenth century old hall on the lake shore;[67] one of the entrance front with a glimpse of the lake and fells to the east (*T&L* 59), and another (Pl. 196) from immediately to the south east. The weather seems for once to have been fine, and he enjoyed uninterrupted views to the fell tops, with Coniston Old Man visible to the left, and in the centre Coppermines valley, with the sun in the south west picking out the ridge of Black Sail rising to the summit of Wetherlam. The dereliction of the hall contrasts with a busy scene of boating activity in the foreground, as slate and ore is loaded for shipping to the southern end of the lake.

Coppermines valley offers one of the quickest routes to the sublime in the Lake District. Half an hour's walk up from the village by the south side of Church Beck leads to an amphitheatre of hills lent an increased sense of desolation by the ruins of the old copper mine workings.[68] Turner went up just so far as he needed and stopped by the main waterfall, just below the threshold of the amphitheatre, to record the view from the left bank where the high fells first reveal themselves (Pl. 197).[69] Again, as at Ullswater, he was mistaken about what he was looking at, the summit of Coniston 'Old Man' as he inscribed his sketch, being well outside the

196. Coniston, Old Hall from the Lake, Old Man beyond, 1797. The exact viewpoint is on private land, but a similar view may be had from the lake.
Pencil, 274 x 370 mm, 'Tweed And Lakes' sketchbook, Tate Gallery, London, TB XXXV 58.

197. Coniston, church beck falls and Coppermines Valley, 1797. Looking to Wetherlam, Old Man well out of the field of view to the left. The basis of the oil painting, Pl.197.
Pencil, 370 x 274 mm, 'Tweed And Lakes' sketchbook, Tate Gallery, London, TB XXXV 57.

198. Coniston, Church beck and Coppermines valley.
Photograph, the author.

199. *Morning amongst the Coniston Fells, Cumberland,* exh. R.A., 1798, no. 196.
Oil on canvas, 1230 x 897 mm, Tate Gallery, London (B&J.5).

composition to the left. He was in fact looking towards Wetherlam, but seems to have been able to snatch only glimpses of the hills for mist, and those in his sketch bear only patchy resemblance to reality (Pl. 198).

No-one ever had less sense of adversity than Turner. The worse the conditions, the more vividly they seem to have stuck in the memory, and during the following winter Turner transformed his sketch into one of his finest early oil paintings, *Morning amongst the Coniston Fells, Cumberland* (Pl. 199) which he exhibited at the Academy in 1798. His unfailingly positive attitude is reflected in the quotation he selected to accompany the painting in the catalogue: Ye mists and exhalations that now rise

> From hill or streaming lake, dusky or gray,
> Till the sun paints your fleecy skirts with gold,
> In honour to the world's great Author, rise.

The passage was taken from Milton's *Paradise Lost*[70] in which Adam and Eve, still enjoying life in Eden, make their regular morning praises of the beauty of creation. It has been observed that the shepherd and shepherdess leading their flock to the hills might well be an allusion to the First Couple.[71] There are other details in the painting, however, which locate the scene in the here and now. Although there is no sign of the mine in the sketch, Turner introduces some buildings into the painting at the very crest of the road, which tell us that he knew it was there.[72] On the road towards the bottom right, is a horse having great difficulty holding back a cart, heavily loaded no doubt with ore[73] being carried down to the lake. Some of the mists and exhalations rising here must be smoke from the mining operations. This is emphatically not the landscape of Eden, but Turner is not intending to be ironic, or nostalgic. He was forging a relationship with the world as he found it. Fallen from innocence it might have been, but it was nevertheless dramatic, and he was constantly aware that his ability to tour the world and enjoy its sights as he did was a privilege. He could do no less than share that privilege through his work.[74]

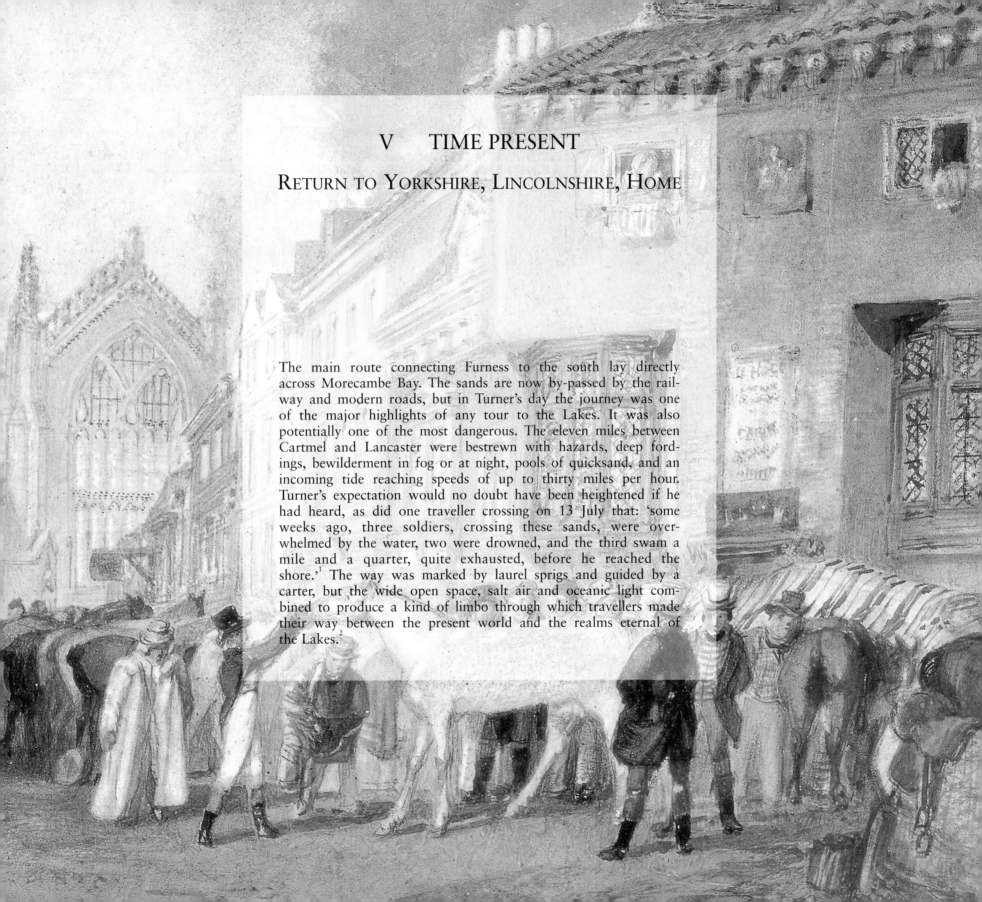

V TIME PRESENT

RETURN TO YORKSHIRE, LINCOLNSHIRE, HOME

The main route connecting Furness to the south lay directly across Morecambe Bay. The sands are now by-passed by the railway and modern roads, but in Turner's day the journey was one of the major highlights of any tour to the Lakes. It was also potentially one of the most dangerous. The eleven miles between Cartmel and Lancaster were bestrewn with hazards, deep fordings, bewilderment in fog or at night, pools of quicksand, and an incoming tide reaching speeds of up to thirty miles per hour. Turner's expectation would no doubt have been heightened if he had heard, as did one traveller crossing on 13 July that: 'some weeks ago, three soldiers, crossing these sands, were overwhelmed by the water, two were drowned, and the third swam a mile and a quarter, quite exhausted, before he reached the shore.'[1] The way was marked by laurel sprigs and guided by a carter, but the wide open space, salt air and oceanic light combined to produce a kind of limbo through which travellers made their way between the present world and the realms eternal of the Lakes.[2]

Furness Abbey
Lake District

Coniston 20m NNE via Ulverston. Barrow 1½m SW. To Lancaster over Sands via Ulverston, 20m ESE. Furness Abbey, English Heritage, open daily April–October, Wednesday– Sunday November–March, visitor facilities, admission charge. Turner's viewpoints (except for gateway) readily recognisable in abbey precincts.

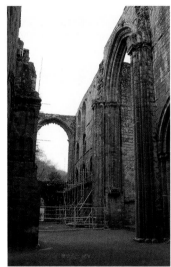

Previous page Louth, detail of Pl. 248.

200. Furness Abbey, north transept and crossing from south transept, 1797. Taken from the night stairs into the transept from the dormitory. Pencil, 370 x 274 mm, 'Tweed And Lakes' sketchbook, Tate Gallery, London, TB XXXV 60.

201. Furness Abbey, north transept and crossing from south transept. Photograph, the author.

Furness Abbey was founded in 1127 and by the time of its dissolution had become one of the wealthiest monasteries in Britain.[3] The extensive ruins set in a quiet valley near the tip of the Furness peninsular made it a site of considerable imaginative appeal to early tourists. As Johnson Grant described it, just a few weeks before Turner's visit:

The approach is lined by venerable old trees, which envelop the ruin in their awful listening gloom. The way is strewed with fragments of desolation. Reached, through these, the silent contemplative remains of the tall pile; and a train of ideas of the most serious nature rush upon the mind; melancholy from remembrance, calm with stillness, breathing 'love of peace and lonely musing.' We are struck with an extensive ruin exactly in a proper state of decay, to shew the depredations of time, without effacing the grandeur of what it once was.[4]

Turner made three sketches, one of an ivy-covered gateway (*T&L* 61),[5] another of the infirmary chapel from the east (*T&L* 62), and another looking across the crossing to the great window of the north transept (Pl. 200). The view is perfectly recognisable today (Pl. 201) except for a number of minor losses and restorations, but the exact viewpoint poses something of a problem. Turner was sitting on the night stairs leading down into the south transept from the dormitory. Close inspection of the sketch, however, will reveal that the ground level was then several feet higher than today, covered with debris from collapsed walls and vaulting. With all that now removed the night stairs are inaccessible, ending some five feet above current floor level.[6]

Lancaster
Lancashire

Barrow in Furness 20m WNW over sands via Ulverston. Bolton Abbey 50m ESE via Settle and Skipton. Turner's viewpoints accessible, but views somewhat altered. Aqueduct still fully functional, and accessible along towpath.

Lancaster is crowned by John O'Gaunt's castle and twelfth-century church, it is steeped in history stretching back to the conquest and beyond. Turner's interest could hardly fail to be engaged, and he made three sketches, one (*T&L* 64) showing the view from the north across the now-disappeared medieval bridge and another (Pl. 202) recording the panorama of the town from the east with the recently-constructed steeple (1784) of St John's at the left and the old bridge and busy port at the right. The third sketch (Pl. 203), although not the most complete of the three, is possibly the most remarkable. It shows the aqueduct which stands on the edge of the town to the north east. This was a radical departure of subject, for the aqueduct was new. Designed by John Rennie to carry the north Lancashire canal, it had in fact only just been completed, opening in the very year of this visit, 1797. Its five huge arches, 221 yards in length, carrying the canal fifty-one feet over the river Lune below made it one of the greatest civil engineering feats in

202. Lancaster from the east, near St John's church, 1797. Pencil, 274 x 370 mm, 'Tweed And Lakes' sketchbook, Tate Gallery, London, TB XXXV 67.

203. Lancaster from the aqueduct, 1797. The aqueduct was brand-new, being opened in the year of the sketch. Pencil, 274 x 370 mm, 'Tweed And Lakes' sketchbook, Tate Gallery, London, TB XXXV 65.

Britain. As one recent commentator has put it, the modern equivalent of this as a subject would be the carriageway of the M6 motorway which flies across the Lune just a few hundred yards further upstream.[7]

Here for the first time on the tour was Turner engaging with the modern world, and there seems little doubt that he was impressed to have found a modern structure with the nobility and ambition to rival those of the medieval world. He makes the equation by framing the old castle and church in the left hand arch of the new bridge, and he gave the aqueduct all the careful attention that he had hitherto invested in abbeys and castles. He even counted up the individual courses of stonework, and noted the results of his arithmetic at various points on the drawing. It was a subject to which he returned in 1816 and worked up in about 1825 into a finished watercolour,[8] but although he resketched the aqueduct, he used it in the watercolour only as a viewpoint for the old town. Perhaps by then his interest in the modern had faded.[9]

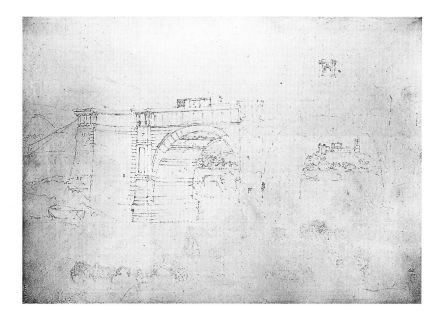

Bolton Abbey
Yorkshire

Lancaster 50m WNW via Settle and Skipton. York 40m E via Harrogate and Knaresborough. Access to priory and surroundings free (fee for parking), visitor facilities in village. Priory church of St Mary & St Cuthbert open daily all year.

From Lancaster, Turner returned to Yorkshire, travelling to York. His journey must have been time-consuming and complex, coaching via Settle to Skipton, and completing the journey via Harrogate and Knaresborough.[10] The only sketch made *en route* was a hurried and inaccurate view of Bolton Abbey (*T&L* 68). The sketch is so faint and scrappy as to be unreproducible, and so inaccurate, misrecording for example the window to the right of the transept as the same size as those of the rest of the choir (Pl. 204), as to make it doubtful that it was made from observation at all. He was to take a much greater interest in the twelfth-century priory, one of the most beautifully situated in Yorkshire,[11] in later years,[12] but for now we must wonder what occasioned the brevity of his first visit. Travelling by coach from Skipton, he would have had a short break at Bolton Bridge to take on fresh horses for the long haul up over the moors to Harrogate. Unfortunately the priory is the best part of a mile above the bridge, and the coachmen would hardly have been sympathetic to being delayed by any artistic diversion. It is an entertaining thought to imagine him rushing up the riverside to catch a quick glimpse, worried that the coach might leave without him. It would have been most prudent to set down what he could remember once safely back on board.

Under these circumstances it seems a little odd perhaps that he later[13] used this sketch as the basis of a watercolour, or at least the beginnings of one (Pl. 205). The sheet is a pair to an equally fanciful adaptation of a sketch of Kirkstall (Pl. 26), although in the latter case he had much more information to work with. It seems likely that in both cases he was using the sketches as a starting point for poetic meditation and composition, in a space free of all but imaginative concerns. Even though his art was normally rooted in sound and detailed knowledge, he needed to stretch his creative legs free of such matters from time to time.

204. Bolton Abbey from the south.
Photograph, the author.

205. Bolton Abbey from the south, *c.*1800? A poetic adaptation of an unusually inaccurate sketch. A pair to a composition of Kirkstall Abbey, Pl. 26.
Watercolour, 239 x 355 mm, Tate Gallery, London, TB CXXI I.

York
Yorkshire

Bolton Abbey 40m w via Harrogate and Knaresborough. Harewood, 22m wsw via Wetherby. Turner's viewpoints, or close approximations mostly readily accessible and recognisable, even where redeveloped. Minster open daily all year.

Turner's main purpose in returning to Yorkshire was to visit Harewood House (q.v., following), and given that his route from Lancaster passed by Bolton Abbey, and therefore through Harrogate, it might seem a little eccentric for Turner to have visited York before Harewood.[14] It would, however, have been proper for Turner to establish a base and wait on the family's convenience. In the meantime he made full use of his few days in York.

We have some evidence of where he might have stayed. His first sketch (Pl. 206) records the view down Pavement, looking past St Croix church (demolished 1883) to the old market cross (demolished 1813) and All Saints Church (survives). To the left is a three storey building with gables, and at first floor level a sign on which Turner has written 'Black H'. The Black Horse, Pavement reappears in sketchbooks used on a later visit to York in 1816,[15] and it seems possible that he used the inn on both occasions. It cannot have been the most modern hotel in the city, for the building is an old timber-framed structure, that had clearly seen better days.[16] Present-day visitors will find it has now disappeared, but despite the widespread modernisation of buildings in the area, the general scene is recognisable and one of the busiest thoroughfares in the city. It seems possible that Turner had been recommended the site by his friend Thomas Girtin, for his young contemporary made a watercolour of exactly the same view (Pl. 207) following his tour of 1796.[17] Although the architectural detail is less assured than Turner's, he was still careful enough to include the sign of the Black Horse. By the time Turner arrived at York, he would have been on the road for at least six weeks, through mud and rain, travelling light enough to carry everything with him, and must have been in serious need of an overhaul. York had every amenity the modern world could boast, baths, laundery, scent, barbers, cobblers and paved streets. He would not have wanted to visit Harewood without making full use of these facilities.

Another sketch (Pl. 208)[18] shows the Minster with

206. York, Pavement, looking to All Saints, 1797. Now-disappeared church of St Croix to the right, sign of the Black Horse Inn to the left. Pencil, 274 x 370 mm, 'Tweed And Lakes' sketchbook, Tate Gallery, London, TB XXXV 66.

207. Thomas Girtin, York, Pavement, c.1796. Exactly the same view as Turner's sketch. Perhaps both artists stayed at the Black Horse. Watercolour, 273 x 375 mm, Private Collection.

211. York Minster from Lendal Wall.
Photograph, the author.

212. York Minster and Lendal Tower from the south west, 1797. Possibly a leaf from the 'Tweed and Lakes' sketchbook.
Pencil, 238 x 375 mm, Tate Gallery, London, TB XXXVI B.

213. Pupil of J.M.W. Turner? York Minster and Lendal Tower from the south west, *c*.1797.
Watercolour, 64 x 94 mm, Tate Gallery, London, TB XXXVI C.

passenger, perhaps not unlike his own, together with figures on the opposite quay, and a smart carriage and four, complete with driver and postillion, crossing the bridge. In order to make the view as complete as possible, he even added a view of the Minster in the background. He could not have seen this from river level, and must have added it afterwards from the bridge. Unfortunately very little of this can be seen today. The bridge was at the very end of its life. In 1809 St William's Chapel was demolished, and the bridge followed soon after. Its successor, a plain but efficient three-arched structure was opened in 1820. The only building which is readily identifiable today is the Kings Arms pub, the squat timber-framed building on the far shore directly under the tower of St Michael's, Spurriergate.

His next group of sketches was taken a little further upstream at Lendal and St Mary's gardens. The first of these (Pl. 212) records the view of the Minster from just outside the walls with Lendal tower in the centre then in use as the city's main water tank. The view is obscured today by later developments but a close approximation can be had from the walls nearby (Pl. 211). It seems possible that Turner was planning a finished watercolour of his subject, for the sketch was made to a specific size.[22] No such composition is known, but a small blue and grey wash drawing does survive in the Turner Bequest which was certainly derived from this sketch (Pl. 213). Although the handling is weak, very specific details of the

scene of the *fracas* in 1132 that led to a breakaway faction leaving to found Fountains, and had been a major centre in its heyday. Its city site had made it a convenient source of building materials, and relatively little was left standing, but it was nevertheless a popular subject with visitors to York.[25] Turner invested his customary intelligent observation in the difficult angles and detail of the portal, however, and was struck by the pathos of such a once-grand building now reduced to service as a cart shed.

The subject to which he devoted the greatest attention in York was inevitably the Minster.[26] York is one of the major sites in the Christian world. Constantine was hailed emperor in York in 323 and on his journey back to Rome had a vision, which confirmed him in the new

sketch are carried over, such as the exact angles of the boat masts. The most likely explanation is that it was made by someone to whom Turner himself was giving instruction at this time.

Another sketch from the south bank of the river (Pl. 214) shows the view looking to the Minster from further upstream, with St Mary's tower in the foreground and St Mary's Abbey to the left. The real interest of the sketch, however is in the shoreline detail at the centre. Beyond St Mary's tower is the fourteenth century Hospitium, which was then in use as a boatyard run by one Cornelius Hill.[23] It enjoyed a profitable life servicing and building coal barges until 1845 but after the coming of the railway it went into decline. The view is now obscured but the main buildings are preserved in St Mary's gardens. Again there is a connection with Girtin, for a watercolour by him at Harewood House[24] shows exactly the same scene. The comparison is so close as to make one wonder whether Girtin in this case might not have worked from Turner's sketch.

Turner also made a detailed study of the west portal of St Mary's Abbey (Pls 215, 216). St Mary's had been the

214. York, St Mary's and the Minster from opposite St Mary's tower, 1797. The fourteenth-century hospitium then in use as a boatyard.
Pencil, 274 x 370 mm, 'Tweed And Lakes' sketchbook, Tate Gallery, London, TB XXXV 70.

215. York, St Mary's Portal, 1797.
Pencil, 274 x 370 mm, 'Tweed And Lakes' sketchbook, Tate Gallery, London, TB XXXV 71.

216. York, St Mary's Portal. Photograph, the author.

217. York Minster, south side, 1797.
Pencil, 274 x 370 mm, 'Tweed And Lakes' sketchbook, Tate Gallery, London, TB XXXV 86.

218. York Minster, south side.
Photograph, the author.

faith. One of the first Saxon churches in the kingdom of Northumbria was built here in the seventh century, and a succession of buildings followed on the site to culminate in one of the largest and most magnificent cathedrals in Europe. Close to, however, it reveals itself only at the last minute, as if it has filled all the available space around it to bursting-point. Turner's sketch of the south side from Deangate (Pls 217, 218) seems designed to make that very point. From this close viewpoint the building cannot be contained in a single perspective. The south transept is seen frontally, while the west end is seen obliquely. The result both in Turner's sketch and comparative photograph seems oddly distorted, like a giant ocean liner sliding by a quayside through a fish-eye lens. Another artist might have tried to resolve this difficulty by translating the information into a single perspective,[27] but this would sacrifice the sense of actually grappling with the scale on the spot.[28]

Inside the Minster he made five sketches, one from the north transept looking to the south (*T&L* 73), two from the south transept looking across the crossing (*T&L* 74, 76) and another of the south transept aisle from the nave (*NOE* 66). The fifth, looking from the nave to the crossing and choir (Pls 219, 220)[29] must suffice to give an idea of the astonishing level of sustained interest and concentration that the series contains. It might seem odd given the huge investment of effort that Turner made in his sketches of York that he made no further use of them. The overriding impression that they leave, however, is of the vitality and delight with which he engaged with these subjects. They are maps as much of his spirit as of the subjects they record. Perhaps it would seemed inappropriate to translate that sense of being into studio work. They were already complete as works of art in themselves.

219. York Minster, crossing and choir from the nave, 1797.
Pencil, 370 x 274 mm, 'Tweed And Lakes' sketchbook, Tate Gallery, London, TB XXXV 75.

220. York Minster, crossing and choir from the nave.
Photograph, the author.

Harewood
Yorkshire

Turner's route around the north of England perhaps requires some explanation. There seems to be some significance, however, in the fact that the huge figure of eight that he traced is centred on Harewood House and he must have passed the gates on his way north between Kirkstall Abbey and Knaresborough,[30] and on his way south must have passed nearby on his way to York.

221. Harewood House, north front.
Photograph, Harewood House Trust

York 22m ENE via Wetherby. Howden 36m ESE via Selby. Turner's viewpoints to the south freely accessible on public footpath from Lofthouse gates, and all apart from distant view SW readily recognisible. Others in grounds of house. Harewood House, the home of the Earl and Countess of Harewood, midway betwen Leeds and Harrogate, open daily mid March–November, full facilities, admission charge. No public access to castle, though viewpoints on N side of river accessible by public footpath.

222. Harewood House from the north east, 1797.
Watercolour, 495 x 645 mm, Harewood House (W.218).

Turner was invited to Harewood by Edward Lascelles, eldest son of the first Earl of Harewood (Pl. 2, *see* Part I p. 3). One of the most flamboyant *beaux* of the Regency age, Lascelles fully indulged himself in all the latest fashions and luxuries, and had a particular taste for the art of young up-and-coming artists.[31] He naturally chose the most exciting young architectural draughtsman of the day to make views of his family's new seat in Yorkshire and Turner made a series of six large watercolours, comprising four views of the house and two of the castle nearby. Lascelles's personal account books record that he paid ten guineas for each of the watercolours, and that they were delivered in two batches, the first two in November 1797,[32] and the remaining four in March 1798.[33]

His immediate difficulty was what to draw on. His enthusiasm at York had left him with only the smaller of his two sketchbooks unfilled, and he required some larger sheets to make the serious survey of Harewood that he was intending. Perhaps Lascelles supplied him with paper, or perhaps he bought some in York, but he managed to obtain a few sheets of his favourite stout Whatman paper and scissored them down to a useable size.[34]

His starting point was the view of the house from the north-east (Pl. 221), for this was the subject of one (Pl. 222) of the first two finished watercolours to be delivered in November 1797. This was derived from two sketches, one concentrating on the architectural detail,[35] and the other on the surroundings.[36] The care invested in the latter, noting every particularity of the trees and of the view beyond the house, but ignoring the house almost entirely,[37] suggests that his interests were developing, almost as he worked, beyond those of the mere architectural draughtsman, into those of a painter of landscape.

He was also interested in the occupants of that landscape, and the finished picture includes a lively foreground of estate workers enjoying a picnic at the end of their day's work. A wheelbarrow, pickaxe and shovel lie by, and the results of their endeavours, a large felled tree, can be seen being carted away in front of the house. The second watercolour to be completed was a view of the opposite side of the house from the south-west (Pl. 223). The time of day is again evening, and it has clearly been warm for the cattle are gathered under the shade of the trees. Conditions seem to have overpowered one of the figures in the foreground who has fallen into slumber on

223. Harewood House from the south west, 1797.
Watercolour, 510 x 654 mm, Harewood House (W.219).

the ground, but have not prevented the woman looking down on him from working, for she has been gathering reeds, to judge from the bundle under her arm. One might imagine that she had good cause to upbraid her companion for his indolence. Out on the lake others take to the water in the last rays of the sun. In their various ways all these figures express something of what it means to be outdoors and in contact with the landscape, precisely the brief that Turner had discovered for himself on this tour.

By the time his second pair of watercolours of the house (Pls 224, 229) was delivered in March 1798 he was very firmly a painter of landscape. From his viewpoints on the lane running from Lofthouse gates across the southern edge of the estate (now a public footpath), the house is now pushed into the distance, and seen against the wide sweep of Wharfedale crowned by Almscliffe Crag (Pls 226,[38] 228). In the process Turner had developed a depth of colour and solidity of handling

which carried watercolour painting into new territory, demonstrating that the medium could rival the aesthetic strength and substance of oils. The results were even presented like oils, close-framed in weighty gold mounts. It is appropriate in view of the role of Edward Lascelles in encouraging this development, that watercolours surviving from his collection at Harewood today, have recently been reframed and rehung in the kind of setting for which they were intended, and in the house in which they were conceived (Pl. 225).[39]

He continued his work at Harewood by making a series of sketches of Harewood Castle.[40] In 1797 this fourteenth century fortified house (Pl. 230) was a major landmark in an open position overlooking Wharfedale from Harewood Bank, and Turner made a series of eight sketches in the *North of England* sketchbook (*NOE* 67-74) in which he recorded the ivy-clad ruins from inside and out, and distant views from vantage points on the north bank of the river opposite the mill and below the bridge. The ruins themselves are today inaccessible in private woodland, but still form a prominent landmark when seen over the tree tops from the riverside or from

224. Harewood House from the south, 1798.

Watercolour, 470 x 661 mm, Harewood House (W.220).

225. The Watercolour room at Harewood.

Photograph, Harewood House Trust.

the Leeds to Harrogate road north of Harewood Bridge. The subject elicited from Turner some of his best work (Pls 227, 231), in which he took his customary care over the architecture, but also bestowed the same care on every hedgerow and shrub in the landscape. In succeeding years Edward Lascelles came to admire Girtin's work even more than that of Turner, saying that Girtin had the greater genius while Turner tended to effect his purposes more by industry.[41] That industry, however, was in fact one of Turner's greatest strengths. His sketches teach us the possibility of levels of intelligent, enquiring engagement with experience that few artists have ever rivalled.

The sketches provided the basis of a pair of finished watercolours. The view from the east (Pl. 233)[42] sets the time of day early in the morning. It promises to be a fine day. A milkmaid carrying a jug on her head makes her way up the hill accompanied by a young girl. Both seem to have been observed on site (Pl. 227). Beyond them a labourer makes his way to work in the fields, and beyond all this Wharfedale stretches out in the morning sun, and we can trace the course of the river all the way from the bridge at the right, past the mill and weir until it loses

itself at the foot of the moors above Farnley in the distance. The view from the north bank of the river (Pl. 232) sets the time of day as evening. A strong wind has blown up from the west and the sky threatens rain. Work still goes below the castle and the results of the day's hay-cutting lies in rows in the field. In the foreground a wagon hurries away to get at least one load under cover before the rain comes on. Between them the pictures describe a day's work. In the normally suspended world of images, there is a sense of real time elapsing. His own sketches also measure out a day's work, and he referred to the time he had spent in his observations by introducing himself into the landscape. In the left foreground of the view from the east (Pl. 233) is an artist sketching in a large sketchbook of exactly the form used by Turner on this tour (frontispiece). It is extremely tempting to see these as representing Girtin besides Turner. It is not impossible that they were together at Harewood in 1797, for the date of the first payment to Girtin in the account books, 17 February 1798,[43] is contemporary with the payments to Turner for work resulting from his visit, and might suggest at least the possibility of a visit the previous summer.[44] Turner works, assiduously engaged in effecting his purposes by industry, while his companion languishes idly by, effecting his, no doubt, by genius.

226. Harewood House, distant view from south east, farm in foreground, 1797.
Pencil, approx. 279 x 400 mm, Tate Gallery, London, TB LI L.

227. Harewood Castle from the west, 1797. The figures used in the finished watercolour, Pl.233.
Pencil, 230 x 270 mm, 'North Of England' sketchbook, Tate Gallery, London, TB XXXIV 68.

228. Harewood House from the south east.
Photograph, the author.

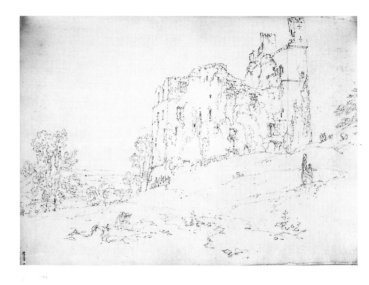

229. Harewood House from the south east, 1798.
Watercolour, 474 x 645 mm, Harewood House (W.217).

230. *left* Harewood Castle from the east. There is no public access to the castle.
Photograph, the author.
231. *above* Harewood Castle from the east, 1797.
Turner's sketches are a model of intelligent engagement with visual experience.
Pencil, 230 x 270 mm, 'North Of England' sketchbook, Tate Gallery, London, TB XXXIV 67.

232. Harewood Castle from the north, 1798.
Watercolour, 457 x 652 mm, Harewood House (W.221).

233. Harewood Castle from the east, 1798.
Watercolour, 470 x 661 mm, Private Collection (not in Wilton).

Spofforth Castle
Yorkshire

Harewood 6m SW. Plompton 2m NW. Castle, English Heritage, open all year, free admission, no facilities. Turner's viewpoint accessible by disused railway track (now cycle way).

Spofforth is a quiet village between Wetherby and Harrogate. It seems to have enjoyed rather greater prominence in the fourteenth century when Henry Percy built his fortified manor house to oversee his Yorkshire property. Turner had already visited two Percy castles at Alnwick and Warkworth,[45] and riding from Harewood to Plompton took the opportunity of sketching Spofforth (Pl. 234).[46] The house survives almost exactly as he recorded it (Pl. 235), and might well strike the visitor as somewhat at odds in grandure with its otherwise sleepy village. This aspect seems also to have interested Turner, for he contrasts the castle with the more modest farm buildings to the left.

234. Spofforth Castle, 1797.
Pencil, 230 x 270 mm, 'North Of England' sketchbook, Tate Gallery, London, TB XXXIV 75.

235. Spofforth Castle.
Photograph, the author.

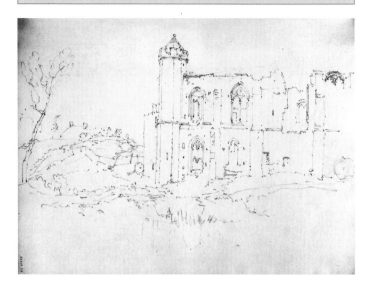

162

Plompton Rocks
Yorkshire

Between Harrogate and Wetherby. Spofforth 2m SE. Harewood 7m SW. Private grounds, open all year, admission charge. Turner's views readily recognisable.

Not long after inheriting, Lord Harewood decided that the house needed some improvements. One of his first decisions was to block up two doors in the saloon, four being quite sufficient, and to fill up the space with paintings.[47] Although Turner had yet little experience of painting landscape in oils he seems to have been in the right place at the right time and was commissioned by Lord Harewood to make two paintings of Plompton Rocks, a Lascelles family property not far away from Harewood, near Knaresborough.

Plompton has one of the greatest concentrations of weathered gritstone outcrops in the area, second only to Brimham Rocks, and with the making of a lake in the 1760s, was transformed into a pleasure garden of exceptional interest.[48] Although now much more assisted by nature than by art, it is an attractive site to explore today, and most of the features recorded by Turner can be readily recognised.

From his sketches at the site, one of which he worked up in watercolour,[49] perhaps to give Lord Harewood some indication of what he might do with the subject, Turner developed two views of the lake and rocks, one from the north end (Pl. 236) and another from the top of the dam to the south (Pls 237, 238).[50] In both the time of day is evening and in the view from the north some fishermen are at work on the lake. In the view from the south they have finished and are tipping the boat to empty it of water. In the background a pleasure party sets out from the inlet. Perhaps this is a little unwise given the shower clouds that are gathering overhead. As early essays in oil, it is perhaps not surprising that Turner's style closely follows that of the eighteenth-century painters he admired, particularly Richard Wilson. He seems to have succeeded in following their lead too well, for when his friend Joseph Farington visited Harewood in 1801 he mentioned only 'Landscapes, views of Knaresborough, Plimpton Rocks, Harwood Castle etc',[51] thus failing to distinguish Turner's work from the overdoors by Nicholas Thomas Dall, which were part of the

236. Plompton Rocks, 1798. From the lake head looking south, fishermen at work on the lake.
Oil on canvas, 1220 x 1375 mm, Harewood House Trust (B&J 27).

237. *over* Plompton Rocks, 1798. From the dam looking north, fishermen packing up for the night.
Oil on canvas, 1220 x 1375 mm, Harewood House Trust (B&J 26).

238. *over* Plompton Rocks.
Photograph, the author.

original scheme dating from the 1770s. He should perhaps have looked a little more closely, for he would have noticed that the paintings contain exquisite touches of colour chosen to harmonise with the salmon pink colour scheme of the room,[52] and that the angle of light in each painting exactly reflected that of the sunlight falling into the room. It was perhaps a gamble for Lord Harewood to have given Turner his first commission for landscapes in oil, but it turned out to be both a success and a bargain. He paid Turner £32.9.0 for the paintings in June 1798.[53] Just a few years later Turner was charging more than ten times that sum for paintings of a similar size.

Howden
Yorkshire

20 miles SE of York. Harewood 36m WNW via Selby.[54] Beverley 20m ENE. Ruined chancel and chapter house, English Heritage, outside viewing only, all year, free. Turner's viewpoints readily accessible and recognisable.

From Harewood, Turner next headed east across Yorkshire to Howden, about halfway between York and Hull. The minster church of St Peter is obvious testimony to the prosperity of the town in the middle ages. Howden was the site of a Saxon church, and after the Norman conquest developed into a sub-house of Durham Cathedral and grew wealthy enough to attain collegiate status in 1267, and for the nave, chancel and chapter house to be rebuilt in the fourteenth century.[55] After the dissolution, funds for maintenance gradually dwindled away and use of the church retreated to the nave, allowing the east end to fall into disrepair until the roof of the chapter house finally collapsed in 1750. By then, however, this kind of subject had begun to attract the attention of antiquarians and artists.[56] Turner's conscientious sketches of the chapter house (Pl. 239) and east end (Pl. 240),[57] were part of a growing body of work which raised consciousness of such remains, and by taking them out of time in pictures, contributed to the development of a desire to preserve. In 1842 the Yorkshire Archaeological Society contributed to the establishment of a restoration fund and the old walls were clamped and strengthened, and in 1972 the ruins were taken into the care of the state.

239. Howden Minster, east end, chapter house, 1797. Continued to right in Pl. 240.
Pencil, 270 x 230 mm, 'North Of England' sketchbook, Tate Gallery, London, TB XXXIV 78.

240. Howden Minster, east end, old choir, 1797. Continued to left in Pl. 239.
Pencil, 270 x 230 mm, 'North Of England' sketchbook, Tate Gallery, London, TB XXXIV 77.

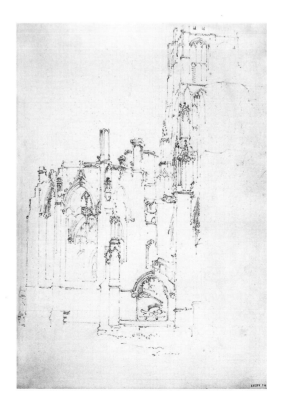

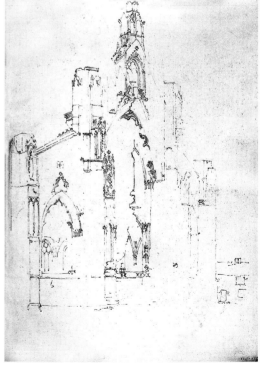

Beverley
Yorkshire

Approx 7 miles N of Hull. Howden 20m WSW. Brocklesby 25 SSE via Humber crossing to Barton. Minster open all year, Turner's viewpoints readily recognisable.

From Howden Turner travelled east to Beverley. It seems hard to imagine today that this quiet market town was in 1377 ranked the eleventh largest town in England. As at Howden a great church grew from agricultural prosperity, but in contrast Beverley Minster survived intact. The church, as the word *minster* suggests, has a history going back to Saxon times when John of Beverley, late Bishop of York, retired in 718 to a small monastery on the site. John was canonised in 1037 and his veneration in the

241. Beverley Minster, north side, 1797
Pencil, 270 x 230 mm, 'North Of England' sketchbook, Tate Gallery, London, TB XXXIV 91.

242. Beverley Minster, interior, Percy Tomb, 1797.
Pencil, 206 x 257 mm, Tate Gallery, London, TB XXXVI N.

north was second only to that of St Cuthbert of Lindisfarne and Durham. This building as it survives encompasses a history from about 1220 at the east end, to about 1500 at the west.[58]

Turner made three sketches of the building. The first (Pl. 241) records the Early English north transept to the left and the exhuberantly Perpendicular west end to the right. The second is a much quicker sketch (*NOE 79*) recording the same material from a slightly more distant viewpoint, looking down the street to the north porch. The third (Pl. 242)[59] records a view in the interior, looking from the north east corner of the north east lesser transept across the Percy tomb to the choir. The tomb of Eleanor, wife of Henry, first Lord Percy of Alnwick, is one of the most exquisite examples of Gothic carving in the country and ranked among the finest achievements of medieval European art.

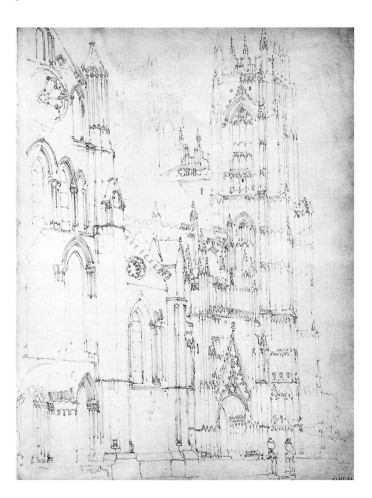

Brocklesby Park
Lincolnshire

8 miles WNW Grimsby. Beverley 25m NNW via Humber crossing at Barton. Louth 22m SSE. Private house and park of Earl of Yarborough. No public access to house, mausoleum may be visited by special arrangement with Brocklesby estate office.

After Beverley, the next subject in Turner's sketchbooks was Louth, nearly fifty miles south east, not far from the Lincolnshire coast. Turner must have crossed the Humber estuary by ferry from Hessle to Barton and then followed the main road through Great Limber past Grimsby and so across the east Lincolnshire wolds to Louth. As a route back to London from Harewood, this was somewhat less than direct. Interesting as the sites that Turner visited undoubtedly are, some particular purpose seems suggested by the distance involved.

One aspect of the explanation is supplied by Brocklesby Park, the seat of Lord Yarborough, which lies directly between Beverley and Louth. The following year Turner told Farington that he had 'been in Lincolnshire at Lord Yarborough's and made 3 drawings of his Mausoleum.'[60] The Mausoleum was designed by James Wyatt as a memorial to Lord Yarborough's wife Sophia

243. Brocklesby Mausoleum.
Photograph, the author.

244. Brocklesby Mausoleum, 1797.
Pencil and watercolour, 430 x 636 mm.
Tate Gallery, London, TB CXXI U.

who had died in 1787. The building was completed by 1792, and Turner no doubt on the basis of his reputation as an architectural draughtsman was commissioned to record it.

Six loose pages detached from a large, landscape format sketchbook[61] record Turner's visit to Brocklesby, comprising four detailed pencil sketches of the mausoleum from viewpoints near and far in the park,[62] one study of an urn decorated with figures,[63] another of a cow grazing.[64] A seventh sketch records the view from Richmond Hill.[65] The house had been built about 1710 to replace an older structure, and during the eighteenth century the park had been developed by Capability Brown and others into an arcadian landscape punctuated by grottos, temples, bridges, urns and grassy rides. One of these rides can be seen in the foreground of Turner's sketch, leading away towards the house, and beyond to

the north Lincolnshire flats, and a glimpse of the Humber in the distance to the right.

Pevsner considered the mausoleum (Pl. 243) to be 'undoubtedly Wyatt's masterpiece',[66] but not every visitor has been quite so enthusiastic. Viscount Torrington was positively vituperative when he visited in 1791 and saw the work still in progress. His capacity for appreciation, it has to be said, had been jaundiced by the catering at the local pub:

At early noon, we came to Gt Limbe[r], near to which Mr P[elha]m in his grounds is erecting a mausoleum, (a little Ratcliffe library) of which Mr W[yat]t, the famous architect gives the plan, and directs the execution. – Below it, for the sake of contrast, and miserable comparison stands (for the reception of the living) an alehouse so bad, as not even to afford cheese. . . We did get a slice of baked beef, not to be eaten, beer and bread as bad, and a glass of brandy and water, – We then walk'd up to this, not yet finish'd mausoluem, a fine effort of Mr W.'s genius! And a fine sum it will cost! A lumbring Grecian building, whose lower story is to be the deposit for the dead; and the upper circular hall will be fill'd with monuments. . .this is adorn'd with festoons of flowers, and there are stone baskets at the top: I never saw a heavier clump! – and the expense will be as heavy as the clump.[67]

In addition to the pencil sketches Turner also made a study in watercolour (Pl. 244),[68] possibly as a try-out for the finished work he intended to develop. Unfortunately the finished drawings were destroyed in a fire, but one survives in the form of a coloured aquatint by F.C.Lewis which was made about 1800.[69] Turner also made a large watercolour of the interior of the mausoleum (Pl. 245), which he used as an illustration to his lectures as Professor of Perspective at the Royal Academy.[70] Given the lack of any separate studies, it remains something of a mystery as to where Turner could have obtained his information unless it was painted directly from the subject.[71] Above, light pours through the glass lantern painted by Francis Eginton, dimly illuminating the marbles in the background, whilst softly bathing the central cause of the mausoleum, the tender statue of Sophia carved by Joseph Nollekens in about 1791.

245. Interior of Brocklesby Mausoleum, 1797?
Watercolour, 640 x 490 mm, Tate Gallery, London, TB CXCV 130.

Louth
Lincolnshire

Brocklesby 22m NNW. Boston 34m S. St James's church open daily, all year. Turner's principal viewpoint readily accessible and identifiable.

Turner continued south from Brocklesby to the old market town of Louth. Nestled between the grazing of the wolds to the west and the rich soil of the marshes to the east, it became wealthy in the middle ages supporting a large abbey (now disappeared) and lively market. At the peak of this prosperity the townsfolk built themselves St James's church, completed in 1441, and between 1501 and 1515 capped it with a spire 294 feet high, now widely regarded as one of the finest in Britain.

Turner made two sketches. One (*NOE* 81) is too faint to be easily seen in reproduction but shows the town from its northern approaches, but the other (Pl. 247) is much more detailed, recording the view looking to St James's from the junction of Mercer Row and Upgate, the main north-south street of the town. The view is readily recognisable today (Pl. 246), and it is remarkable how many of the buildings can be identified, including

246. Louth, Upgate and St James's church from Mercer Row.
Photograph, the author.

247. Louth, Upgate and St James's church from Mercer Row, 1797.
Pencil, 270 x 230 mm, 'North Of England' sketchbook, Tate Gallery, London, TB XXXIV 80.

the old Assembly rooms[72] half way down the street on the left, and the medieval building to the right, now in use as a Tandoori restaurant. It will be found, however, that Upgate is rather narrower than Turner's sketch implies and he must have shifted viewpoints at least twice in order to include all his detail, especially that of the east end of the church, which only becomes visible some way further down the street on the left hand pavement.

The street in the sketch has a strangely deserted air for such a central thoroughfare, as if it was very early in the morning, but Turner's landscape was a human landscape, and when, thirty years later he came to develop the subject into a finished watercolour for his series *Picturesque Views in England and Wales* (Pl. 248), he dramatically widened the street so that it could include one of the most extraordinary throngs of humanity that he ever

painted. It is market-day,[73] and the whole cross-section of society is gathered in the street. To the right country farmers and squires look on while a gentleman examines a fine white stallion, no doubt being bought to match the outfit of his lady who is dressed in a white full-length coat. At the opposite side of the street various members of the lower classes including a peasant farmer with cheeks as red as apples and dressed in a traditional smock, stand and watch in wonder. Behind them people crowd around the stalls. Rich and poor, old and new, sun and cloud, warm and cold, all come together in a vibrant chiaroscuro of opposites and complementaries. To the right, a woman leans out of an upstairs window to watch the spectacle. The most telling detail however is probably in the woman immediately above the black and white dog, who holds up a pair of scales as she weighs out goods from the stall. In a picture full of contrasts it is the sense of a balanced range of interests and sympathies which is one of its strongest features. One recent commentator[74] has related Turner's depiction of a cross-section of society in this watercolour to increasing agricultural unrest in the 1820s. This seems highly plausible, and although it would be difficult to say that he unequivocally took sides, it seems clear that he intended the picture to raise questions of social relations and difference, and of the balance between the two.

Louth might also offer another explanation for Turner's excursion into Lincolnshire. Inside the front cover of the *North of England* sketchbook (*see* Part VII The Sketchbooks) is a list of commissions which records that a Mr Howlett ordered two small watercolours of *Louth Church* and *Boston Church*. Bartholomew Howlett[75] published a series of *Select Views in the County of Lincoln* which included ten plates by Girtin published between 1797 and 1800. Two of these plates featured Louth and Boston,[76] and it seems possible that Girtin's work was preferred to Turner's, for there is no record of Turner's watercolours ever having been completed. Turner did however make watercolours of Grantham (q.v.) and Sleaford (q.v.) for Howlett, and it does seem possible that one of Turner's motives for his tour of Lincolnshire was to gather material for Howlett, however relatively unsuccessfully this transpired.

248. *Louth, Lincolnshire*, exh. Egyptian Hall, 1829.
Upgate is too narrow for such a market ever to have taken place.
Watercolour, 285 x 420 mm, British Museum, London, 1910–2–12–278 (W.809).

Boston
Lincolnshire

Louth 33m N. Sleaford 17m W. St Botolph's church open every day, all year. Turner's viewpoints S of church porch and from quay E of town bridge.

Approaching from the north, Turner would have seen Boston Stump, the tower of St Botolph's church from more than ten miles away rising like a pencil from the fens.[77] Hardly anywhere in England is it possible to have a greater sense of making some real contact with the great age of medieval prosperity. Boston today is five times larger than in 1797,[78] and full of modern industry and housing, but the journey there gives the impression of a town cut off in both space and time from the rest of teeming Britain.

In the middle ages Boston was Britain's second busiest port, and in 1289 raised more in customs duty than even London.[79] From Norman times until after the Renaissance it thronged with ships, traders and goods from all over Europe, and for many years had more communication with Antwerp, Bruges, Rotterdam, Hamburg or the ports of Scandanavia than with most other towns in England. St Botolph's fair was one of the major markets not only in the country but also in Europe, as great quantities of fleeces, hides and grain were traded for wines, timber and finished goods from the continent.

It is said that St Botolph's was built to rival the great cathedral of Antwerp,[80] and it has been described as the largest and most impressive parish church in Britain,[81] and might with credit be compared to the churches of Bruges or Ghent. The foundation stone was laid in 1309 and the gigantic tower, reaching nearly 300 feet high, and carrying a lantern whose light could be seen by sailors steering into the Wash, was finished in 1460. The town's influence spread even to the New World when seventeenth-century puritans emigrated to America to found new colonies in Massachusetts.

Turner made two sketches, the first (NOE 81A) a detailed study of the church from near the south porch, and the second (NOE 82) a view of the church from the quay to the east of the town bridge,[82] less detailed with regard to the church but careful in its study of the riverside buildings, old wooden bridge and boats tied up at the quay. As with Louth, Bartholomew Howlett commissioned a small watercolour of the church,[83] but this does not seem to have been completed and the subject had to wait thirty years for Turner to work up a finished composition for his series *Picturesque Views in England and Wales*. He developed the composition in a colour study (Pl. 249),[84] in which he began to think himself back into the subject. The finished composition (Pl. 250) is full of characteristic detail: women raising eel pots from the river to the left, barge-families settling down for the evening to the right while the sun lifts from the river. By now Turner had studied such things so much for him to have a greater knowledge of them than almost anyone, and he demonstrated this knowledge in one striking detail. The lower half of the tower and the body of the church is dissolved in light as the warm air shimmers in the last rays of the sun. Above, however, the air is colder and more clear, and the detail can be seen much more crisply. Few artists have ever developed the representation of phenomena with such imagination. Few have ever had such a wealth of experience with which to work.

249. Colour-beginning, Boston church from the south, *c*.1833. Watercolour, 298 x 493 mm, Tate Gallery, London, TB CCLXIII 21.

250. Boston, Lincolnshire, c.1835.
Watercolour, 280 x 419 mm, McMaster University, Canada (W.859).

Sleaford
Lincolnshire

Boston 17m E. Grantham 17m ENE. St Denys church open every day, all year. Turner's viewpoint in market square.

Sleaford has good claim to be Lincolnshire's oldest town. It has been successively the site of Iron Age, Roman and Anglo Saxon settlements, and in Norman times developed into a market centre of some importance.[85] The church of St Denys was built in the late twelfth and early thirteenth centuries, and with its solid Early English broach spire was a substantial enough building in itself, but as population and prosperity increased so it became necessary about 1350 to expand the church with wide aisles down the full length of both sides. The traceried windows with which these aisles were punctuated have made the church famous.

Turner sketched the view of the west end from the market-place (*NOE* 83), which he translated into a finished watercolour (Pl. 251) engraved for Bartholomew Howlett's *Select Views in the County of Lincoln* published in 1801.[86] He followed the details of the sketch very closely,[87] and obviously took great care over the architectural details of the church. Once again, though, this is a living environment, and the foreground is dotted with people and activity. A few straggling market-folk sit chatting before packing up their stalls and unsold produce for the night. To the right a water-carrier makes his way down the street. In the distance a heavy timber-wagon pauses in the square to give its three horses a rest. The watercolour repeatedly makes allusion to the weight of things; the bulk of the tree-bole, the water-butts carried on a yoke over the shoulders, the baskets and barrows of produce, the mass of the church and its tower contrasted with the lighter structures of the stalls. This is a site of endeavour, and also, at this moment in time, of rest. The setting sun casts long shadows across the square and plunges the space of the day's activity into shade, drawing the work to a close. Turner's placement of the sun is worth noting. The church faces west, so the sun must be in the north-west, or even slightly further north. This could only be at midsummer when the days are at their longest, and it would now be close to 9.30 in the evening.[88] Given the presence of the church, viewers might reasonably have been expected to notice this, and

251. Sleaford Church, Lincolnshire, *c.*1797-8. Commissioned by B. Howlett for *Select Views in the County of Lincoln*, published 1801. Watercolour, 237 x 347 mm, Museum of Rhode Island School of Design, USA (W.240).

therefore to give consideration to how long a day this has been, and how deserved the rest that the workers now enjoy.

Grantham
Lincolnshire

Sleaford 17m w. Stamford 21m s. St Wulfram's Church open every day. Angel and Royalty Hotel in High Street. Turner's view in marketplace readily recognisable.

Grantham, like other Lincolnshire towns enjoyed sufficient prosperity in the middle ages to fund the building of a great church. St Wulfram's was completed in the early fourteenth century and boasts a spire of nearly 300 feet which in its day was the tallest in Britain. Turner already knew the church through having previously made a watercolour of it, working from another artist's sketch, which had been engraved by Bartholomew Howlett for his *Select Views in the County of Lincoln*, and published on 1 March 1797 not long before he set off.[89] Strangely, however, on this occasion Turner did not make the church the focus of his study. He preferred instead to sketch the market place (Pl. 252), looking to the gateway of the Angel Hotel in the High Street, with the spire of St Wulfram's appearing almost incidentally over the rooftops to the left. This marks something of a shift in interest for this tour.[90] He had visited many towns, Pontefract, Wakefield, Leeds, Knaresborough, Ripon, Richmond, Durham, Warkworth, Alnwick, Berwick, Kelso, Melrose, Jedburgh, Keswick, Lancaster, all of which offer considerable interest in their streets and market squares, but this aspect only appears in his sketches, if at all, in order to place the major landmarks of castles, abbeys, bridges or churches in context. Only in the latter part of the tour, and particularly at York, did he begin to take much interest in the towns themselves. Grantham stands on the Great North Road, and much of the life of the town revolved around its great coaching inns and the trade and traffic flowing along its great arterial road. Turner's main reason for being there was to join that Great North Road, and begin his journey south back to London. He probably put up at the Angel Hotel, which is the principal subject of the sketch, and his subject seems to suggest more of his time was spent waiting for the coach than recording the major features of Grantham.

The Angel Hotel was nevertheless a subject of considerable architectural antiquity. The gateway frontage, with its oriel window supported by an angel with outstretched wings, dates back to the fifteenth century, and

252. Grantham market Square, 1797. Oriel window of Angel Hotel visible in high street. Note Turner's interest in the names of the shops.
Pencil, 230 x 270 mm, 'North Of England' sketchbook, Tate Gallery, London, TB XXXIV 84.

would have been seen by Richard III when he stayed there to sign the death warrant of the Duke of Buckingham in 1483.[91] Besides this, however it was the more day-to-day features of the subject, the interesting variety of buildings and shop frontages, crowded shoulder to shoulder around the square which engaged at least as much of his attention. He even took care to note the names on the various signs.[92]

Stamford
Lincolnshire

Stamford has been described as 'one of the two or three most beautiful towns in England',[93] and few can boast such a variety of historic buildings in such a concentrated space, and so unaffected, at least in the southern part of the town, by modern development. It is also one of the most ancient towns that Turner had yet visited on this tour. Its name derives fron the prehistoric paved (stone-) ford and one report has it that there was a University founded here in 863 BC.[94] The Romans had a ford here, and a camp nearby, and the Danes made it one of the five great cities of their kingdom. After the conquest it became rich on the wool trade and its cloth market was internationally known. In the town's medieval heyday there were fifteen churches, six priories, hospitals, charities, schools and nearly a University when a breakaway college of Brasenose was established in 1334.

Trade flowed through Stamford along the Great North Road and Turner made this his subject, taking the view from the London Road at St Martin's looking north across the river valley to the town (Pl. 253). Virtually every building can be recognised at the site today (Pl. 254), but not all, it has to be said, at the same time. The street, as at Louth (q.v.), is actually much narrower than the sketch suggests and in order to be able to see the spire of All Saints to the left, one has to stand on the pavement outside the Bull and Swan to the right. Likewise in order to be able to see the spire of St Mary's to the right, one has to stand on the pavement opposite. Thirty years later Turner developed the sketch into a finished watercolour for his series *Picturesque View in England and Wales* (Pl. 255). It is a consummate celebration of his life on the road. To the left the northbound coach disgorges its passengers, superintended by the coachman and guard. One lady seems to be complaining about her luggage being piled on the ground. In the centre of the street a cleric with umbrella makes his way to the inn for refreshments, attended by a porter in peasant dress. In the background nature puts on its most vivid display. By all accounts Turner came to exhibit all too

253. Stamford, Lincolnshire, 1797. From oustide the Bull and Swan inn, looking north along the London road to St Martin's church.
Pencil, 230 x 270 mm, 'North Of England' sketchbook, Tate Gallery, London, TB XXXIV 86.

254. Stamford, Lincolnshire. In his sketch Turner conflated two viewpoints on opposite sides of the street.
Photograph: the author.

clearly the signs of having travelled on coaches in conditions such as these. One chronicler tells us that as a result of habitually riding as an outside passenger his skin was as red as that of a boiled lobster and as tough as that of a rhinoceros.[95]

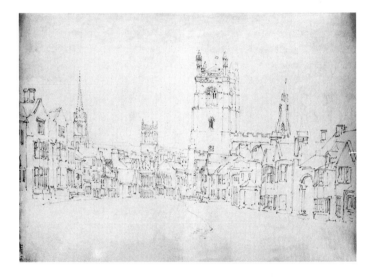

255. *Stamford, Lincolnshire, c.*1828.
Watercolour, 293 x 420 mm, Usher Art Gallery, Lincoln (W.817).

Burghley House
Cambridgeshire

Stamford 1½m N.[96] Peterborough 11 m SE. London 88 m S. Home of Marquess of Exeter, open daily early April–early October, full facilities, admission charge. Turner's viewpoint in park to NW freely accessible all year, except during horse trials, early September.

From Stamford Turner did not rush off straight away home, but while he still had the energy and some spare pages in his sketchbook, he took in Burghley House and Peterborough before finally heading for London. Burghley is undoubtedly one of the finest Elizabethan houses in the country. Built 1565–87 by William Cecil, Lord Burghley, the Queen's Lord High Treasurer, it rises out of the parkland bristling with spires, chimneys and cupolas, and when its limestone walls gleam in the sun has as one writer put it, more the 'consequence of a town',[97] than of a country house. Turner recorded the view of the house from the north west (Pls 256, 257), taking in the two most important facades. To the right in the centre of the west range is the great square tower which was the first part of the house to be built, and to the left is the north range which was the last and most elaborate, with its extraordinary entrance bay surmounted by festoons of grotesque ornament.

256. Burghley House from the north west, 1797.
Pencil, 230 x 270 mm, 'North Of England' sketchbook, Tate Gallery, London, TB XXXIV 85.

257. Burghley House from the north west.
Photograph, the author.

Burghley is as spectacular inside as it is out, and boasts one of the greatest decorated suites of seventeenth-century England, painted by Antonio Verrio in the 1680s. It also houses one of the finest collections of seventeenth-century Italian paintings in private hands. Although none of this is recorded in Turner's sketchbooks, it would seem highly likely that he would have taken the opportunity of extending his education by studying the collection. We might surmise that he did so by the very fact that he sketched the house at all. Beautiful as Burghley is, Turner had passed many fine country houses on this tour, without sketching any other than those at Harewood and Brocklesby at which he had business.

178

Peterborough
Cambridgeshire

Stamford 11 m NW. London 85 m S. Cathedral church of St Peter open all year. Turner's viewpoints outside west front and from west end of nave freely accessible.

Turner's final site of the tour was Peterborough. The cathedral of St Peter was built between 1118 and 1238 and thereafter was extended and remodelled at various times up to the sixteenth century. It was a site with which Turner was already familiar through a visit in 1794 at the end of a tour of the midlands, when he made several sketches of the cathedral[98] resulting in a number of finished watercolours, one, a view from the north being published in the *Copper-Plate Magazine* on 1 May 1796,[99] and another, a view of the west front being exhibited at the Royal Academy in 1795.[100] At that exhibition Turner found his view of Peterborough somewhat upstaged by a rather more dramatic treatment of the same subject by his young friend Thomas Girtin,[101] and it may be that Turner revisited the cathedral in 1797, to find a riposte.

He made two sketches. The first (Pl. 258) is a view of the west front with it unique giant arcade and porch,

258. Peterborough Cathedral, west front looking through west gateway, 1797.
Pencil, 230 x 270 mm, 'North Of England' sketchbook, Tate Gallery, London, TB XXXIV 87.

259. Peterborough Cathedral, nave and choir from porch, 1797.
Pencil, 230 x 270 mm, 'North Of England' sketchbook, Tate Gallery, London, TB XXXIV 88.

taken from underneath the western gateway to the old monastic precincts.[102] His second (Pl. 259) is a view from the porch down the nave to the choir closed by the screen with the organ above.[103] With these last two sketches his books were full. He had collected over two hundred sketches in an itinerary of over a thousand miles, and filled his mind and memory with the colours, light, weather, tribulations, textures and sensations of at least two months on the road. A simple day's journey now by coach down the Great North Road brought him back to London, to begin the task of translating as much as he could manage of this experience into paint.

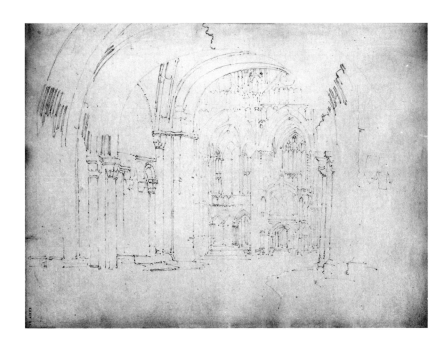

VI LOOKING BACK

STUDIO WORK AND REVISITS

Finished work for exhibition and commissions 1797–8

Back in London during the autumn and winter Turner immersed himself in his memories of the north. The first works that we know him to have completed are two watercolours for which Edward Lascelles paid twenty guineas on 21 November 1797[1] and five more for which he paid fifty guineas on 15 March 1798.[2] These can be identified as four watercolours of Harewood House (Pls 222, 223, 224, 229), two of Harewood Castle (Pls 232, 233) and one of Kirkstall Abbey (Pl. 39).[3] Lascelles's commission of the views of Harewood Castle and of Kirkstall is recorded in a list inside the front cover of Turner's *North of England* sketchbook:[4]

Mr Lacelles	Harwood[5] Castle L[arge]
Mr Lacelles	Harwood Castle L[6]
Mr Munden	Holy Island L[7]
Mr Lambert	Holy Island S[mall][8]
Mr Kirshaw	Harwood Castle S[9]
Mr Lambert	Ambleside Mill[10]
Hon Mr Lacelles	Kirkstall L[11]
Mr Howlett	Boston Church V[ery] S[12]
Mr Howlett	Louth Church VS[13]

Facing page Fishermen and their boat, detail of Pl. 237.

Turner seems to have shown his sketchbooks to prospective patrons and supporters over a considerable period of time, for Farington records being shown the *Tweed and Lakes* sketchbook on 24 October 1798:

> I . . . called upon him, at his Father's a Hair Dresser, in Hand-Court, Maiden Lane. – The apartments to be sure, small and ill calculated for a painter. He shewed me two Books filled with studies from nature – several of them tinted on the spot, which He found, He said, were much the most valuable to him. One of the books contained studies [from his tour to Wales that year]. . . The other Book, studies at Doncaster,[14] York, Durham, Melross, the English Lakes, Lancaster, Richmond in Yorkshire, Fountains Abbey. He requested me to fix upon any subject which I preferred in his books, and begged to make a drawing or picture of it for me, I told him I had not the least claim to such a present from Him, but on his pressing it I said I would take another opportunity of looking over his books and avail myself of his offer. Hoppner, He said, had chosen a subject at Durham.[15]

The *Tweed and Lakes* sketchbook has a washline mount inside the cover, and it seems likely that Turner worked up some small example of his work to give prospective customers an idea of what a finished example might look like.[16] It cannot have served this function for long, however, for in the space within the frame Turner noted the commissions of Mr Lambert for Ambleside Mill (as also listed in the *North of England* sketchbook) and the commission by Hoppner for Durham, which Farington recorded above.[17] In addition to these records individual pages of the sketchbooks record commissions, and the *Tweed and Lakes* sketchbook includes the name of a Mr Knowles on the back of a sketch of

Longthwaite Bridge in Borrowdale (cf. Pl. 161),[18] a Mr Taylor on the back of a sketch of the interior of Durham Cathedral (cf. Pl. 74),[19] Mr Farington, having finally made a selection, on the back of a sketch of Derwentwater (cf. Pl. 152),[20] and the *North of England* sketchbook records the name of one William Blake on the back of a sketch of Harewood Castle.[21] Clearly the sketchbooks impressed many of those who looked at them.

Apart from the commissions, Turner's immediate preoccupation was with what he might develop for exhibition at the Royal Academy the following year. Having attracted favourable notice at previous exhibitions, it would have been clear to him that there was a great deal at stake for his developing reputation. In 1796 he had exhibited his first oil painting, a seapiece of *Fishermen at Sea*[22] which had been praised by the reviewers, and in 1797 he had exhibited two more oils, another seapiece, *Fishermen coming ashore at Sun Set, previous to a Gale*,[23] and a *Moonlight, a Study at Millbank*.[24] The critic of the *Morning Post* for 5 May commented on the former that it showed 'an undeniable proof of the possession of genius and judgement',[25] and the critic of the *St James's Chronicle* for May 20–3, declared one of the watercolours in the same exhibition, *The Transept of Ewenny Priory*,[26] to be 'one of the grandest drawings he had ever seen, and equal to the best pictures of Rembrandt... there is mind and taste in everything the man does – and yet he is not of the Royal Academy.'[27] He had already raised expectations and been given enough encouragement to nurture ambitions of becoming a member of the Royal Academy. His north of England subjects were in these circumstances vital to him in furthering that reputation and in securing him admittance to the Academy.

Of the ten works that he exhibited in 1798, nine were north of England subjects:[28]

Winesdale, Yorkshire, an Autumnal Morning [untraced, *see* below]
Morning amongst the Coniston Fells, Cumberland [Pl.199]
Dunstanburgh Castle, NE coat of Northumberland. *Sun-rise after a squally night* [Pl. 106]
Refectory of Kirkstall Abbey, Yorkshire [Pl. 24]
Norham Castle on the Tweed, Summer's morn [Pl. 129]
Holy Island cathedral, Northumberland [untraced, *see* p. 82]
Ambleside mill, Westmoreland [Pl. 188]
The dormitory and transept of Fountain's Abbey – Evening [Pl. 54]
Buttermere Lake with part of Cromackwater, Cumberland, a shower [Pl. 168]

Of the first, *Winesdale*, there is no subsequent record, and except for the fact that the critic of the *St James's Chronicle* for 1–3 May 1798 said that it consisted of 'a beautiful variety of tints, all in perfect harmony',[29] we have no idea at all of its appearance. Its subject is made even more mysterious by the fact that there is no such place in Yorkshire, or indeed anywhere on his north of England itinerary of 1797. It has been pointed out that there were numerous typographical errors in the catalogue of the

exhibition that year, and suggested that the printer might have mistaken the intended identification of Wensleydale,[30] but on the evidence of the sketchbooks, Turner did not visit Wensleydale in 1797[31] and only sketched the Ure[32] at Ripon (q.v.). Another suggestion that has been made is of Wyresdale near the Trough of Bowland, which Turner might have passed through on his way from Lancaster to Bolton Abbey,[33] but there is again no evidence of this in the sketchbooks, nor would the route have been by any means the most direct or convenient, and in any case Wyresdale is in Lancashire not Yorkshire. The most likely possibility is Wharfedale. Given that the printer would have been working from a handwritten list, it would have been easy to mistake the *h* of Wharfedale for an *i*, and the *f* for an *s*, and the letters between for *ne* to produce Winesdale. In any case it would seem most likely that the subject is contained somewhere in the pages of the sketchbooks, and Wharfedale is certainly a subject that Turner visited and sketched in 1797 while he was at Harewood.[34]

The missing *Winesdale* seems to have been an oil,[35] as were certainly three other exhibits which survive, *Morning among the Coniston Fells* (Pl. 199), *Dunstanburgh Castle* (Pl. 106) and *Buttermere Lake* (Pl. 168). In the autumn of 1797, however, his experience in oil painting was somewhat limited. Other than the seapieces and the small Millbank study he had painted nothing that prepared him to tackle such major subjects in landscape, and he must have been extremely anxious about the exhibits he was preparing for the exhibition. He seems to have begun his work in oils with a half-sized canvas of *Dunstanburgh Castle* (Pl. 101, which was in large measure a seascape, and thus at least started out with material with which he could feel confident. By the standards which he attained over the next few years, the paintwork is perhaps somewhat naïve, but the nervous flicks and touches of colour nevertheless manage to charge the whole composition with a sense of energy, and the painting was judged enough of a success to find a buyer, even if he did not feel confident enough to exhibit it at the Academy. He learned enough from the exercise to develop a full-sized version of the subject (Pl. 106) and although he needed to rehearse the composition with a chiaroscuro study (Pl. 104) and a colour study (Pl. 105), before committing himself to canvas, he developed through these a dynamic distribution of mass, light and colour, and a convincing sense of the dawn sun slanting in over the cold sea, which possessed sufficient authority and weight of design to stand association with the work of one of the most admired poets of nature, James Thomson.

A recent rule change regarding the Academy catalogues allowed artists for the first time in 1798 to give a few lines of explanation in addition to the titles of their works.[36] Turner took advantage of the opportunity to quote passages of Thomson in relation to four of his exhibits, *Dunstanburgh Castle* (p.74), *Buttermere Lake* (p.116), *Norham Castle* (p.90) and *Fountains Abbey* (p.38), and a passage from Milton's *Paradise Lost* in relation to *Morning amongst the Coniston Fells* (p.136). He was the only landscape painter to do so, and in so doing made a remarkably ambitious claim for his work to be seen to have the same weight of literary and poetic content as the more prestigious genres of historical or literary painting. To make this claim at the same time as exhibiting his first major series of oil paintings was a bold and risky step, on the success of which his ambitions critically depended and he must have been extremely concerned about the outcome. On 5 January 1798, when he would have been most fully immersed in finishing his work for the exhibition, the portrait painter John Hoppner told Farington that he had called at the studio in Maiden Lane: 'Hoppner mentioned two pictures by Turner – Rainbow and Waterfall – a timid man afraid to venture'. He had seen *Buttermere Lake* (the rainbow) and *Morning amongst the Coniston Fells* (the waterfall) which were probably the two most dramatic and sublime compositions that Turner exhibited that year, and indeed of his whole early career, and it is difficult to conceive quite how Hoppner can have thought that the pictures were either timid or unadventurous. It is not hard, however, to imagine that Turner must have been in a state of high anxiety about how his new work would be received, and that he might easily have seemed to Hoppner apprehensive and in fact deeply afraid of how his venture would succeed.

He must have been gratified by the response. The critic of the *Oracle* for 23 April said 'W Turner has a variety of Picture worthy the attention of the *Cognoscenti*. He takes a distinguished lead in the present Exhibition, and rises far superior to our expectation on forming an opinion of his previous works.'[37] The reviewer of the *London Packet* for 9 May commenting on *Dunstanburgh* noted the pretensions of equating his work with Thomson's poetry, but allowed that the comparison stood up to scrutiny: 'This is a really good picture – the phenomenon of Nature which the painter has given charmingly is that of the sun rising on the coast after a squally night. The idea is sublime and we here excuse his giving a quotation of eight lines from his favourite Thompson.'[38] The *Monthly Magazine* for July said 'This artist's works discover a strength of mind which is not often [even] the concomitant of much longer experience: and their effect in oil or on paper is equally sublime. He seems thoroughly to understand the mode of adjusting and applying his various materials; and, while colours and varnish are deluding one half of the profession from the path of truth and propriety, he despises these ridiculous superficial expedients, and adheres to nature and the original and uneering principles of the art.'[39] The critic of the *London Packet* noted the ambition of the paintings but preferred the less dramatic beauties of the watercolours: 'This is a very aspiring artist, but he appears rather too much inclined to shackle Nature in the magic bonds of Poetry, than give her chaste beauties their full and unaffected display. Mr T's drawings in general much surpass his pictures.'[40] The *Whitehall Evening Post* for 2 June described *Norham Castle* as ' a work upon which we could rivet our eyes for hours and not experience satiety. . . Every repeated view of it discovers new perfections. The light and shade are so skilfully managed and

the perspective so inimitably just, that every division of the picture at once strikes the eyes and seems rather nature in miniature than a transcript.'[41] The *St James's Chronicle* for 1–3 May said of the same watercolour that it had ' the force and harmony of oil painting. It is charmingly finished and the effect is bold and natural. In short we think it the best Landscape in the present Exhibition'.[42]

One of the purposes of the poetic quotations was to imply that the paintings constituted a response to nature of the same merit and profundity as the greatest poetry. But the quotations also served to highlight the richness and particularity of sensation which informed the paintings. This is also suggested by the precisely identified locations spread across a wide area of the country, from sequestered inland abbeys of Yorkshire to airy coastal promontories in Northumberland, to a castle overlooking the borders of Scotland to mountainscapes and ancient mills in the Lake District. It is further reinforced by the specific times of day and effects of weather alluded to in the titles. An additional effect of the poetic quotations is to suggest a process of experience succeeding experience through time and space; mists. . . exhalations. . . hill. . . streaming lake. . . dusky. . . gray. . . precipice. . . blacken'd flood. . . ruins glitter. . . briny deep. . . pointed promontory's top. . . blue horizon. . . floating gleam. . . kindling azure. . . mountain's brow Illumin'd. . . sober evening. . . thousand shadows. . . downward sun. . . rapid radiance. . . yellow mist. . . ethereal bow shoots up immense. We are given the idea of someone who has moved through the world and employed his full range of senses in the process. The quotations enabled Turner to educate his viewers' eyes to enter into his compositions and explore them as if exploring the site in actuality, and he seems to have been successful at least with the reviewer of the *Whitehall Evening Post* quoted above who entered into 'every division' of *Norham Castle*, and writing on 10 May described *Morning amongst the Coniston Fells* as 'A beautiful and well-executed landscape. The distance is so admirably preserved, as to induce a momentary deception, and appears as if the Spectator might actually walk into the picture.'[43] At this level of engagement Turner could direct his audience beyond the ostensible subjects of his pictures to a sense of engagement with the physical stuff of which they were composed, rock, water, light, trees, fields, clouds, mists, showers of rain, buffeting winds, the warmth of the sun, colours, textures, and forms, and the sense of the artist having moved over and through such things as to know them so thoroughly as to be able to recreate them in paint.

The principal subject of Turner's 1798 exhibits is the experience that lay behind them. Any dialogue with art is less in evidence. Piranesi and Cuyp might come to mind with regard to *Kirkstall*, Ruisdael in relation to *Ambleside*, Rembrandt in the case of *Buttermere*, Wilson with regard to *Dunstanburgh*, but it is hard to think of any obvious precedent for *Morning amongst the Coniston Fells*, or *Norham Castle*, and in no case except perhaps *Kirkstall* does the analogy seem intended to be obvious. Most commentators have focused rather more on their comparative stylelessness. Lawrence Gowing, for example, observed: 'In Turner's first pictures imagination and reality seem like opposite alternatives. *Buttermere Lake*, which he exhibited when he was twenty-three, is real. We are hardly aware of the picturesque arrangement of the scene. The banks of shadow have the gentle breadth of tone that Turner had learned copying watercolours by J.R.Cozens, in the company of Girtin, but the picture seems almost styleless.'[44] Andrew Wilton has remarked of *Buttermere* that Turner describes the subject as a shower in order to locate it in common reality: 'Turner has carefully elaborated the detail of his subject rather than supressing it in favour of generalised grandeur: We feel that his intention was to persuade by the accuracy of his statement rather than by aiming at a stark grandeur. Why indeed did he so carefully inform the viewer that he was painting a 'shower' – which in itself is far from being a sublime phenomenon?' He goes on to describe it as 'an honest attempt to copy these incidents direct from nature; a young man's homage, as it were, to the self-sufficiency of his raw material. The coloured sketch that he made of the subject in one of his notebooks (Pl. 167) is evidence that he painted what he saw, and embellished only just sufficiently to round out his design.'[45] One of the most striking features of his treatment of the material gathered in his sketches, is how little Turner seems to have felt the need to exaggerate. There is a naturalism of scale and perspective in the sketches which is adopted without demur in the finished work. In later life this was by no means his practice, but for now it is as if the world was sufficiently impressive in its own right to require no more of him than to convey the way he found it. This is particularly striking at Buttermere, where the forms of the hills are recorded in the sketch as if needing nothing but transcription, and when transposed to the painting are if anything diminished by the boating party introduced into the foreground (Pls 166, 167, 168). Nothing could be more at odds with Gilpin's conception that reality required remoulding to make it conform to the precepts of taste and judgement, that the 'rough-hewn matter' of the north of England was by itself incorrect, deformed, irregular, stubborn, inglorious, and, he clearly implies, uncouth. Such things might have been transformed by a practised eye, a judicious hand, creative power, and a refined sensibility into something worthy of the title art, but Turner was apt to take it as it came. Nature was something to be taken for real, and not to be dressed up into the image of the decorations of some eighteenth-century curate's drawing-room.

If Turner used his poetic quotations and titles to indicate a sense of actually moving through the landscape, he also began to develop devices recording the same sense in his sketchbooks. To some extent, of course, the sequence of pages already did this for him, but in 1797 there is evidence of his linking sketches together in such a way that it is possible to build up a knowledge of the three-dimensional geography of his subjects, and of the very ground over which he moved. The opposed views of the bridge and castle at Barnard Castle are one example, and others might be found in his circuit of Durham, or of Dunstanburgh, or the series of sketches along the shore at Ullswater, and the pairs of sketches of the quayside at Waterhead, or Coniston Hall. The most extended exercise of mapping space and recording his movement through it occured at Harewood where he took views of the house from all angles, including a series of sketches moving across the southern edge of the park making sketches from viewpoints only a few hundred yards apart, with the common elements of house, lake, farm, Wharfedale and Almscliffe Crag coming together in different relations to measure the geography of the valley and the ground across which he moved. In the three watercolours commissioned by Edward Lascelles of views of the house from the south (Pls 223, 224, 229), he was able to translate this into paint. At Harewood, however, he made an even more complete circuit of the castle, making a total of eight sketches of views from all sides, and then moving down into the valley and along the riverbank, recording the scene at intervals as he went, and including figures who moved through the space as he did. The sketches measure time as well as space, and if we allow thirty minutes to one hour for each one, then we can see that there must be a full day's work accounted for by the series. In making a pair of watercolours of the subject (Pls 232, 233), he based one on the first sketch in the series, and the other on that made at the furthest remove from the castle. The first he set at early morning with the day promising to be still and warm, and the second at evening with the weather now changed, and showers blowing up from the west. In the first a labourer goes off to work, in the second the results of the day's work lies cut in rows in the field. Apart from the customary attention to detail, to the stuff of which the world is composed, he has also introduced the processes of time and change by which reality is characterised.

Harewood offered him the opportunity to develop this further in a pair of oil paintings of *Plompton Rocks*. He must have been working on these alongside his Academy exhibits, or even while the exhibition was open for they were paid for on 14 June 1798 (*see* p.163). The paintings take views from opposite ends of the lake, one from the north (Pl. 236) and the other from the south (Pl. 237). The same range of rocks is depicted in each, and in order to make this more obvious he has placed a boat near the centre of each composition which is at exactly the same spot on the lake, that is at the head of the boat-house inlet. These pleasure-boaters are contrasted with working boatmen in each foreground, in one netting fish, and in the other tipping water out of their craft. Again he uses the element of time. In the view from the north the sun is in the west, but in the view from the south it has moved further north, so that we might judge that an hour or two has passed betwen one and the other. In each cloud builds up from the south-east, but in the later view this is somewhat more pronounced and the sky is beginning to look distinctly threatening beyond the rocks and to the right.[46] It would seem to be a good time for the fishermen to be packing up, and a somewhat less opportune moment for the pleasure-boaters to be embarking upon the water. Turner obviously invested considerable care in the relationship between the two compositions, and intended us to give it some thought. The working lives of the fishermen routinely exposes them to the elements, and gives them an understanding of nature's processes. For the pleasure-boaters this is less likely to be the case. For them the experience of nature is a leisure activity. Turner might seem even to have been a little mischievous in sending them out in conditions which seem set to give them a soaking.

In contrasting those whose lives give them contact with nature with those for whom it was exceptional, Turner introduces a theme which stands at the heart of his own situation and mission as an artist. Born in the heart of London, his was essentially a metropolitan sensibility. Throughout the eighteenth century an increasing proportion of the population came to live in towns and cities. For ever larger numbers the greater part of life was spent indoors, either by necessity of work in trade, offices or factories, or by desire to be enured from any unpleasant contact with reality. For these nature became an entertainment, tourism or a trot or stroll in the park, or taken in the form of paintings, or travel journals or the poems of James Thomson. Turner's audience was one for whom nature was something they had become distant enough from to desire, even if more in vicarious forms than in reality. Turner on the other hand was one for whom such contact was his *raison d'être*. As an artist concerned with this situation, his background was something of an asset. His origin as the son of a hairdresser placed him rather closer in class to that of the fishermen at Plompton than to that of the pleasure-boaters. By and large it was always such people, given a natural sensibility by birth and situation, with whom he sympathised and by whom his pictures were populated.[47]

Very few of Turner's finished compositions lack a human element, and the sketches, although primarily concerned with buildings and landscape, so frequently include figures as to suggest that he regarded the human dimension as an integral part of his subject-matter. There are cowherds shepherds, gardeners, grave tenders, timber-cutters, millers, carters, market traders, travellers on foot, on horseback and in smart coaches and carriages, bargemen, oarsmen, fishermen, milkmaids, washerwomen, children, knife-grinders, lime burners, fieldworkers and slate handlers. He was constantly interested in those whose working lives bound them to a place in a way that his mobility did not, and the way that their lives gave them a relationship to and understanding of nature from which the metropolitan sensibility was becoming increasingly alienated.

In the finished work resulting from the tour there are several examples in which he seems to have set out to demonstrate that he had acquired a knowledge of nature comparable to that of the countryman. In 1799 he exhibited a watercolour of *Warkworth Castle, Northumberland – Thunder storm approaching at sunset* (Pl. 91). Prominent in the foreground is a group of fishermen at work on the river. Beyond them on the bank below the castle another figure tends a small fire and the smoke drifts away up the hillside. The sun is setting low in the west but the last rays still shine brightly on the castle. This is a scene of tranquility and

security except for the title 'Thunder storm approaching at sun-set'. Of this thunderstorm there seems little sign. The smoke indicates that the wind blows from the left, but the sky to the left is clear and the sun, although low, shines brightly from that direction. The dark cloud is to the right, where it must evidently be blowing away. The sense of peace and security seems well founded, and Turner obviously intended that the incongruity between the picture and its title be considered. In fact the ground winds before a thunderstorm are sucked into the advancing cloud, so the cloud beyond the castle is not blowing away but approaching. The apparent contradiction can be resolved by the kind of knowledge that the fishermen would have possessed, but Academy visitors would be more likely to have remained confused.[48]

There are other subtle but striking demonstrations of Turner's knowledge. In both 1798 watercolours of *Norham Castle* (Pls 129, 130) he introduces a plume of smoke rising from a small fire on the riverbank below the castle. 'Rises' is perhaps the wrong word for it is driven almost horizontally away from the fire. This would suggest a considerable gale from the right except for the fact that the rest of the composition seems calm. The water reflects the cows and castle clearly, and the sail of the boat hangs limply in one version, and in the other suggests that what little breeze there is in the sail blows in the opposite direction to the smoke. Again Turner poses an apparent contradiction, which requires resolution through understanding. It is dawn and in settled summer conditions a morning breeze generally blows from the cold land to the warmer sea. The effect here is being exaggerated under the castle bluff by the 'Venturi effect', that is the property of a fluid to travel faster the more confined the space, and thus the smoke is whisked along briskly to the point at which the valley widens, the wind slackens, and then begins to rise. It is probably a coincidence that the Italian physicist Louis Battista Venturi (1746–1822), who gave his name to the effect, was a contemporary of Turner's, for Turner might well have derived his understanding from observation, but there seems little doubt that the artist was intentionally drawing attention to the fact that his work contained an understanding of such matters, and that this was derived from his study in places like Norham.

One of the most subtle details of this kind occurs in the *Refectory of Kirkstall Abbey* (Pl. 24). Just to the right and slightly below the central doorway is a shadow silhouette of a cow's head. It might well seem odd, if not wilfully obtuse, to focus on such an apparently incidental feature, but the detail is not part of the original sketch, and for Turner to have been able to construct it at all implies some knowledge of the properties of shadows and sunlight. Since the sun is a source at a near infinite distance, any shadow in the same plane as the object which creates it will be the same size as that object. As with the Venturi effect, Turner need not have had a theoretical knowledge of the effect, but it seems clear that he intended to show that he had an understanding of the properties of sunlight in these circumstances. In the subtlety of the placement of this detail, we might also detect that he was making something of a test of the capacity of his audience to find and recognise such things.[49]

Turner's north of England material provided a springboard from which he launched his bid for recognition and success. Although still only in his early twenties he had been exhibiting regularly at the Academy since 1790 and he hoped now to cultivate support for election as a member. As we have already seen he showed his sketchbooks around widely, and offered gifts of finished watercolours or paintings to Academicians who might support his cause. The first beneficiary of this strategy was John Hoppner who by 24 October 1798 had chosen a view of Durham (Pl. 70). Turner might have had a double reason for making a gift to Hoppner for he was a close friend of the Lascelles family,[50] and could have had some influence in Turner being commissioned to visit Harewood in 1797. Turner's main concern in October 1798, however was the forthcoming ballot of Academicians for new Associate members. On the same day that Turner told Farington that Hoppner had chosen the view of Durham, he had been to see Farington in the morning to discuss his prospects in the election. 'Turner has called and had promises of votes from Bacon, Nollekens, Bourgeois, Gilpin, Stothard, &c to be an Associate. I told him I saw no necessity for further application. I thought his chance so certain that I would wait the event which He said He would do.' Later the same day (see p.181) Farington called at Turner's studio where he looked over the *Tweed and Lakes* sketchbook and was offered the gift of a painting or drawing. The election took place the following week and in the event Turner, although gaining the support of twelve members, including Farington, failed to be elected to either of the two places available, Martin Shee and Charles Rossi being preferred instead.

It was a strong showing, however, for one appearing in the lists for the first time, and he renewed his effort the following year. On 6 July 1799 Farington recorded, 'Turner called. I told him he might be assured of being elected, to remove his anxiety. . . Smirke and I, on our way to the Academy, drank Tea with him and looked over his sketchbooks. He said he had 60 drawings now bespoke by different persons.' It seems that Turner was still pressing his case on the basis of his north of England sketchbooks for when two days later Smirke and Farington again called, he pressed gifts of finished compositions from the *Tweed and Lakes* sketchbook. Smirke chose a view of Richmond, and Farington allowed Smirke to chose for him a view of Lodore and Derwentwater. It is not clear whether Smirke actually received his gift, for no finished composition is known (but cf. Pl. 57), and Farington had to wait until August 1801 for his to be completed (Pl. 152).[51] In any case on 4 November 1799 Turner was formally elected an Associate Member of the Royal Academy. He immediately joined the Academy Club and moved from the cramped quarters of his parents' house in Maiden Lane to a more respectable situation in Harley Street. At only twenty-four years of age, this constituted a meteoric rise to success, and one in which his tour to the north of 1797 had played a vital role.

Later work and revisits

Turner's travels took him far and wide after 1797, and he visited every corner of mainland Britain and most of Europe besides. Even though he was ever dedicated to visiting new places, he did occasionally have reason to return to some of the sites that he had visited in 1797 and from time to time to develop new work from the early sketchbooks. In 1801 he made an extensive tour of Scotland, and on his way north sketched on the Yorkshire coast and revisited Durham, where he made a number of new sketches (see p. 56), then travelled on through Northumberland where he resketched Norham Castle (see p. 88) before continuing to Edinburgh. On his way south he called at Keswick where he painted Farington's watercolour of Derwentwater (Pl. 152) and probably made a large colour study of the view down the lake from Friar's Crag (Pl. 154). Sometime after this he made a pair of watercolours of *Brinkburn Priory* and *Dunstanburgh Castle* (Pl. 107).[52] Strangely, although these have been hanging in full public view at Wallington Hall in Northumberland (National Trust), they seem to have escaped notice by modern scholarship.

From 1807 he began to produce designs for a series of mezzotint prints called the *Liber Studiorum* which he published in parts up to 1819. Four of the subjects were based on 1797 material, *Holy Island* (Pl .117) published 20 February 1808, *Dunstanburgh Castle* (Pl. 103) published 10 June 1808, *Kirkstall Abbey* (based on Pl. 24), published 14 February 1812, and *Norham Castle* (derived from Pls 129, 130) published 1 January 1816. It is possible that compositions based on a sketches of Kirkstall (Pl. 23) and Bolton Abbey (Pl 205) date from about the time of his first thoughts for the *Liber Studiorum*. In 1808 he revisited Yorkshire to make the first of what became annual stays with Walter Fawkes at Farnley Hall near Otley, and on this occasion revisited Bolton Abbey (see p.142) making a rather more leisurely inspection of the site than had been possible in 1797, and also revisited Harewood Castle and Bridge (see p.203 n.40). In 1809 he revisited the Lake District, and returned to Cockermouth where he made a series of detailed sketches which formed the basis of a painting for the Earl of Egremont exhibited at the Academy in 1810 (see p.200 n.4). His other sketches explored the west coast recording Whitehaven, St Bees and Calder Abbey, and also Lowther Castle near Penrith of which he made a pair of paintings for the Earl of Lonsdale.[53]

In 1816 he was commissioned by Longmans to illustrate Thomas Dunham Whitaker's *General History of the County of York* and he spent most of the summer touring Yorkshire and north Lancashire which took him back to sites visited in 1797 including Bolton Abbey, Knaresborough, Ripon, Fountains Abbey, Richmond, St Agatha's Abbey, Egglestone Abbey and Barnard Castle, as well as to Morecambe Bay and Lancaster. Some of the 1797 sketches, such as those of Richmond and St Agatha's formed the direct basis of watercolours for the project (Pls 56, 61), and other sites such as Ripon, Bolton, Egglestone and Barnard Castle were resketched from the same or similar viewpoints and in the case of Egglestone his new material was worked up as a finished watercolour (Pl. 000). The 1816 tour also provided Turner with the opportunity to visit a number of sites such as Jervaulx, Middleham, Bowes and Hornby Castle on the Lune, which were close to sites visited in 1797 but which were omitted from the earlier itinerary presumably for the sake of time. The comparison between the tours indicates something of the ways in which his sensibilities to landscape had developed in the interval. In 1816 for example he made a thorough exploration of Wensleydale, which he bypassed in 1797. He visited most of the waterfalls including Hardrow, West Burton, Aysgarth and Askrigg, but he also took in more general prospects of the valley which would not have been considered sufficiently noteworthy to have warranted depiction in 1797. In general we can detect a widening of the scope of his subject matter to include many more natural features, but also scenes which characterise the country *between* whatever landmarks it might contain. It is worth remarking also that through his long association with Farnley Hall he began to treat more local scenery such as that of Otley Chevin or the Washburn valley, or the sweeps of Beamsley Beacon between Farnley and Bolton Abbey.[54] Amongst these subjects are some of the first pictorialisations of the moorland scenery[55] for which the north became increasingly recognised as the nineteenth century progressed.

His association with Fawkes gave him the opportunity to develop two 1797 Lake District subjects into finished watercolours, the first of *Ullswater* (Pl. 180) c.1815 and the second of *Windermere* (Pl. 192) in 1821. During the 1820s Turner reworked a number of 1797 subjects in the context of poetry. For Fawkes at Farnley he made watercolours of Norham and Melrose as illustrations to Sir Walter Scott,[56] and late in the 1820s he utilised his memories of Derwentwater in two watercolours for the poems of Samuel Rogers, one reworking the view of Lodore that he had painted for Farington,[57] and the other concocting a Gothic fantasy of St Herbert's Isle.[58] In 1831 he returned through the north on his way to Scotland to make illustrations for an edition of Scott's poetry and revisited Derwentwater, Barnard Castle and Egglestone Abbey, together with the abbeys of the Scottish Borders at Jedburgh, Melrose, Dryburgh and Kelso. As we heard at the outset, in passing Norham on the way to Berwick, he was moved to pay homage to his debt to the tour of 1797.

During the 1820s and 1830s he was engaged in a number of projects which gave him occasion to revisit 1797 sites, or to make use of the earlier sketches. In 1824 he returned to Kirkstall to make sketches for a pair of watercolours for the series *Rivers of England* (*see* p.28), and in the same series reutilised the watercolour of *Warkworth Castle* (Pl. 91) which he had exhibited at the Academy in 1799.[59] In about 1822 he made a watercolour of *Tynemouth Priory* (Pl. 84) in connection with another series, the *Ports of England*[60] and shortly after this he embarked upon the most ambitious series of watercolours for engravings that he had yet attempted, *Picturesque Views in England and Wales*. The series was begun in 1825[61] and shortly before this Turner had gone through all his sketchbooks, sorted them into order and labelled them.[62] Leafing through the thousands of pages in 125 sketchbooks must have been a moving and reflective exercise and, in effect, *England and Wales* became a retrospective survey of his life and travels.

It is striking that of the ninety-six subjects completed from such a wide variety of material, seventeen were of subjects visited in 1797. Eleven were derived directly from 1797 sketches, and three more were of similar views based on sketches made in 1816. The number itself suggests the strength of impression that these subjects left in his memory, but the fact that many of these compositions such as Alnwick, Holy Island, Barnard Castle, Lancaster, Knaresborough and the Lincolnshire towns of Louth, Stamford and Boston, were worked up for the first time, suggests that their subject matter had somehow remained a priority waiting only for the opportunity to use it. The most obvious feature of most of the work in the series, moreover, is its human interest shot through with a profound sense of sympathy for the lives being so vividly wrought out of the various circumstances. This is most obviously typified by his watercolour of *Louth* (Pl. 248) in which he depicted with equal care and humour a complete cross-section of society milling about at the market. The north of England certainly did, as Ruskin imagined, introduce him to the peace and spectacle of nature, but it was always a world shared by all humanity. *England and Wales* positively celebrated, as did Turner throughout his life, the manifold conditions that constituted that life.

Turner's association with the north of England culminated in three Northumberland subjects from the 1830s and 1840s. The first of these was a final version of Dunstanburgh Castle entitled *Wreckers – Coast of Northumberland, with a Steam Boat assisting a Ship off Shore*, and exhibited at the Royal Academy in 1834 (Pl. 109). Once again we witness the effects of a storm, and the efforts of the local villagers to rescue what they can from the situation. In the foreground a ferocious tug-of-war takes place with the waves, as a group of figures attempts to drag cables and timbers ashore. It seems a hopeless task, and they are dragged down the shore, sucked almost into the sand under their feet, while a wall of angry water rises to smash them down.. In the background the castle has been cut off from the land and begins to seem as insubstantial as one made of sand. At the foot of the castle a coaster has been driven on to the rocks, its masts leaning askew from the pounding, while offshore a steamer is making an effort to tug the striken ship to safety. Once again Turner sets up an apparent contradiction. The plume of smoke demonstrates a fierce gale from the sea, but the storm is moving off to the right. Turner was using a similar device to that employed before at Warkworth (*see* p.68), for in a thunderstorm the tail winds, as well as the advance winds, blow contrary to the direction of the storm. The most striking feature of the painting, however, is the energy with which it has been painted, so that the very material of which the scene is composed whirls around in clumps and swathes. From beginning to end critics found Turner's depiction of the sea too substantial: 'like veins in marble slab', 'like a turnpike road', 'soapsuds and whitewash', but in its very materiality, and here more than anywhere, it becomes the image of the primordial forces of creation. Turner seems to have remembered Northumberland as a place so untamed that such forces were still at work in the present, and one into which human beings ventured at their peril. There is, however, some sign of the taming process advancing. The steamship can function even in these conditions.

Three years later he followed this with a watercolour of *Bamburgh Castle* exhibited at the Graphic Society in 1837. It seems likely that it was intended for engraving to represent the culmination of the powers and interests developed in the series *Picturesque Views in England and Wales*. In the event it was not engraved, but the exhibition catalogue described it as 'one of the finest watercolours in the world.' Turner seems to have been unusually concerned with its composition, and made no fewer than three full-scale colour-beginnings (Pls 112, 113, 114)[63] in which he rehearsed the colour structure and effects. It became the summation of all his storm and rescue themes on this coast. In the distance a rocket rises to attract attention, but there is already quite sufficient distress to occupy us on the foreground shore. Yet another coaster is on the rocks, crowds gather on the shore to assist, and in the foreground are two bedraggled figures amongst the flotsam and jetsam. Bamburgh was well-known to be a major centre for the rescue and relief of distress, and the painting portrays it as a site of hope and care as much as of tragedy and despair. As the composition formally demonstrates, it is a place where the most violent opposites compete equally, cold against warmth, dark against light, night against day, sea against land, chaos against form, a place where life was lost and lived in the most vivid and heroic circumstances.

His final north of England subject was an oil of *Norham Castle, Sunrise* (Pl. 130), painted in the last few years of his life. If *Wreckers* and *Bamburgh* presented nature at its most destructive, *Norham* presents it at its most creative. It is as if the very materials are in the process of moulding themselves and almost as we watch the paint begins to resolve itself into form. Jack Lindsay has described the effect brilliantly:

In his later work, if he is not directly depicting the forms and tensions of elemental violence, he is driven to depict a paradisaic earth in which the tensions of light-energy compose the forms. What we see [in *Norham*] is a field of force, but one which is assembling and constructing life out of its minute gradations, its overall movement from com-

plex asymmetries into a new controlling symmetry. Or, rather, the forms tremble on the edge of this new system; and that is what gives the definite but indefinable effect of irreversible time – something which so far Turner alone of artists has been able to master.[64]

It was perhaps fifty years since Turner first visited Norham, but the sights witnessed then were still etched in his memory, and valued here near the end of his life perhaps even more highly than at the beginning. The whole of the interval in between had been devoted to witnessing and depicting as much of that world as he could visit, and to observing the processes at work in that world. In the last few years of his life he painted a number of such canvases, many of which go back to subjects from the *Liber Studiorum* which were recorded in his youth.[65] All of these late paintings depict the process of the image emerging from the paint before the customary veneers of finish were applied. It seems that by this stage the process had become the subject in itself, as if the paintings were models of his memory at work. They give the sense of what stands behind them, that is of what is emerging, as much as what is actually present. It is not sufficient to see the painting as an abstraction distancing itself from the original engagement with Norham Castle, but rather we must recognise that it is all the more powerfully an act of memory made in direct relationship to an experience of that place. Kenneth Clark recognised the relationship: 'The logical connection between what we should have seen if we had been there and the faint touches of pink, blue and yellow with which Turner has stained his canvas exists – it is the essence of their beauty – but it is extremely complex, and could only be discovered by re-living Turner's experience.'[66] As we have seen in relation to Turner's north of England material, and doubtless this process could be traced through most of his work, right from the first Turner developed strategies to alert us to a sense of a living sensibility behind the work. He constantly directs us to a sense of his having travelled widely for the sake of engaging with the world, and in his sketches and drawings he left us a model of how intense that engagement could be made to be. In truth his purpose was never simply to make pictures, but rather to use his profession as a vehicle for attaining and then teaching a state of being as fully and as consciously alive as anyone could possibly be. Kenneth Clark seems to have doubted that re-living Turner's experience was either possible or even desirable. But that would be to ignore Turner's most fundamental message, that if he could attain such intensity of experience, so might we all.

VII   THE SKETCHBOOKS

258. The North Of England Sketchbook, 1797.
Tate Gallery, London. TB XXXIV.

The two sketchbooks on which this account is principally based are both in the Turner Collection at the Tate Gallery, London. Because of their vulnerability and fragile condition, handling of the originals is not normally allowed. Most of the sketches, however, are reproduced here, and for more critical work the Tate Gallery has a set of high-quality photographs. There are many single, mounted sheets in the Turner Bequest and these may be examined in the Tate Gallery study room by arrangement with the study room registrar.

TB XXXIV North of England *sketchbook, 1797*

Fully leatherbound sketchbook, fitted with four brass clasps. Containing ninety-three leaves, 270 x 230 mm, watermarked 'J Whatman 1794'. Inscribed on cover 'Derbyshire, Yorkshire, Durham, Northumberland, Tweedale Scotld, Lincolnshire, Northamptonshire'.

Turner's executors noted that this book was found with eighty-eight leaves, comprising '83 very careful sketches in pencil and 5 washed with colour (Yorkshire Northumberland)'. When A. J. Finberg compiled the *Inventory of the Turner Bequest* in 1909 he found a sequence of eighty-eight leaves including two virtually blank (21, 70), and four partly worked up in watercolour (1, 33, 35, 50). In addition he found seven sheets, four of which were inserted, more-or-less appropriately, into the main sequence as 10a, 46a, 56a and 81a and the remaining three at the end as 89–91. Of these, three (46a, 56a, 89) have been fully worked up in watercolour, one (10a) has details in watercolour, and three are pencil drawings. It seems impossible to determine which permutation of this material consititued the sequence noted by the executors. The composition of the sketchbook is further complicated by five separate sheets, all pencil drawings, which seem to have been detached from the book, mention of which is incorporated into the main sequence below (indicated by an #) after 10, 20 (two leaves), 57 and 79. Additionally Finberg noted leaves torn out after 33 and 78. No candidate has yet presented itself as the former, although a Tynemouth or Shields subject is suggested, but there are two candidates for the latter, as discussed in the listing. It seems possible that there are other loose sheets in the Turner Bequest, and perhaps some in other collections, which might yet be identified as belonging to this book.

Inside Cover

A list of commissions (for identifications see p. 181):

Mr Lacelles Harewood Castle L
Mr Lacelles Harewood Castle L
Mr Munden Holy Island L
Mr Lambert Holy Island L
Mr Kirshaw Harewood Castle S
Hon Mr Lacelles Kirstall L
Mr Howlett Boston Church VS
Mr Howlett Louth Church VS

\# An unnumbered leaf, on to which has been pasted a note by John Ruskin.

'Inventory No 178
Very valuable early pencil containing original sketches of Kirkstall and Egglestone of Yorkshire series. Dunstanborough of Liber, Alnwick and Boston of England and Bamborough large. A beautiful Jedburgh. Whitby, Tynemouth, Melrose &c 3 taken out namely York, Boston and Kirkstall Crypt.'

1 Wingfield Manor, Derbyshire, inner courtyard, with great hall to right. Part worked up in watercolour (Pl. 3).

2 Wingfield Manor, Derbyshire, from north west (Pl. 6).

3 Dronfield, Derbyshire, St John the Baptist from south east (Pl. 7).

4 Conisbrough Castle from the north, Walker's Mill and river Don to right (Pl. 12).

5 Doncaster Church from south west (Pl. 14).

6 Doncaster Church, from chancel looking north west to nave and crossing (Pl. 15).

7 Pontefract, All Saints church, south side (Pl. 16).

8 Pontefract, All Saints church, west end (Pl. 17).

9 Pontefract, All Saints church, crossing and nave from north east corner of chancel

10 Wakefield Bridge and chapel from south. The basis of a pencil composition study TB XXXVI A and watercolour, W.241 (Pl. 21).
Verso inscribed "G D"

\# TB XXXVI Q, Heath Hall from the river Calder not far downstream from Wakefield Bridge. A leaf detached from the *North of England* sketchbook.

10a Kirkstall Abbey, dormitory undercroft. Part worked up in watercolour. The basis of a watercolour, W.234 (Pl. 24), and *Liber Studiorum* drawing TB CXVII O and print published 14 February 1812.

11 Kirkstall Abbey, chapterhouse (Pl. 22). A watercolour in a private collection W.235, possibly derived from this.

12 Kirkstall Abbey, crossing and north transept (left), choir to right. Debris of collapsed tower in foreground (Pl. 25). The basis of a watercolour study, TB CXXI H (Pl. 26).

13 Kirkstall Abbey from west.

14 Kirkstall Abbey, east end (Pl. 30).

15 Kirkstall Abbey from Kirkstall Hill, Kirkstall forge in the distance (Pl. 34).

16 Kirkstall Abbey from south east, river Aire in foreground. The basis of a watercolour W.224 (Pl. 39).

17 Unidentified manor house between Kirkstall and Knaresborough.

18 Knaresborough Castle and castle mills from south (Pl. 42).

19 Ripon Cathedral from the south east. Canal to left, river Skell to right (Pl. 44).

20 Ripon Cathedral, west front (Pl. 45).

\# Ripon Cathedral from the north, Ure Bridge in the foreground. A leaf detached from the *North of England* sketchbook (Pl. 47). The view resketched in 1816, cf. TB CXLVI 8.

\# TB XXXVI E, Ripon Cathedral from the north east above the river Ure, from a viewpoint further north of XXXVI D, above. The view resketched in 1816 cf. TB CXLVI 9.

21 A few preliminary lines of an architectural drawing. ?Ripon or Fountains.
[f.89 originally taken from here?]

22 Unidentified estuary, with medieval ruin on far side of river. Out of seqence as f.23 following. Probably Durham or Northumberland coast given colliers loading in foreground.

23 Dryburgh Abbey from the river near St Boswells (Pl. 141). Out of sequence, see f. 62.

24 St Agatha's Abbey, Easby from downstream. The basis of watercolours W.273 (Pl. 58) and W.561 (Pl. 61) and of a colour beginning TB CCLXIII 360 (Pl. 60).

25 St Agatha's Abbey, Easby, north side.

26 Richmond from downstream, with St Martin's mill in foreground, and remains of St Martin's priory, left.

27 Egglestone Abbey on the Tees. Henry Cooke's paper mill in foreground (Pl. 62). Resketched in 1816, cf. TB CXLVII 31 verso, and made the basis of a watercolour, W.565 (Pl. 63).

28 Egglestone Abbey, presbytery and canon's dorter, Thorsgill bridge in foreground. Cf. f.90 verso, below – removed from here?

29 Barnard Castle and bridge from upstream (Pl. 66). Resketched in 1816, TB CXLVII 32 and 1831, TB CCLXVI 32–4, and developed into watercolour W. 793 (Pl. 68).

30 Barnard Castle and bridge from downstream (Pl. 65).

31 Durham, Elvet Bridge from downstream (Pl. 75).

32 Finchale priory from downstream.

33 Tynemouth Priory, east end from south aisle of nave, lighthouse to left. Part worked up in watercolour (Pl.80).

[Finberg notes a leaf torn out here]

34 ?North Shields.

35 Tynemouth Priory from south, across Prior's Haven. Part worked up in watercolour (Pl. 81). The basis of a study TB XXXIII T (Pl. 83), and finished watercolours W.545 (Pl. 84) and 827 (Pl. 85)

36 Bothal, two figures on a footbridge by the river 'Wernesbeck' i.e. Wansbeck, with Bothal church in the background (Pl. 86).

37 Bothal Castle from the north, with Bothal church to left (Pl. 88).

38 Warkworth Castle from east (Pl. 89).

39 Two sketches (Pl. 92);
i. Warkworth Castle from north west (faint).
ii. Interior of entrance hall to keep, looking out to gateway, right.

40 Warkworth Castle from west. The basis of a watercolour W.256 (Pl. 91).

41 Warkworth Castle and bridge from the north. St Lawrence's church through arch to right (Pl. 94).

42 Alnwick Abbey gatehouse (Pl. 95).

43 Alnwick, St Michael's church from the south (Pl. 96).

44 Alnwick Castle and bridge from the north west. The basis of a watercolour W.818 (Pl. 98).

45 Dunstanburgh Castle from the south. The basis of studies, TB XXXVI T, TB XXXIII S (Pl. 105), XXXVI S (Pl. 104), oil paintings B&J 32 (Pl. 100), 6 (Pl. 106), and 357 (Pl. 109) watercolours W.284 (Pl. 101), 814 (Pl. 108) and another not in Wilton at Wallington Hall, Northumberland (Pl. 107), together with a *Liber Studiorum* drawing, TB CXVI Q (Pl. 103) and plate published 10 June 1808.

46 Dunstanburgh Castle, Egyncleugh tower and Gateway from foreshore to east. A study from a similar viewpoint, TB XXXVI R.

46a Dunstanburgh Castle, Lilburn tower, looking east, sunrise. Worked up in watercolour, (Pl. 100).

47 Bamburgh Castle from the south.

48 Bamburgh Castle from the south, from further to the right than f.47.

49 Bamburgh Castle from beach to the north (Pl. 110). The basis of colour beginnings TB CCXLV 30, TB CCLXIII 334, 382 (Pls 112–14) and finished watercolour W.895.

50 Lindisfarne. St Cuthbert's Priory, crossing and chancel from north aisle of nave. Part worked up in watercolour (Pl. 120).

51 Lindisfarne. St Cuthbert's Priory and castle from St Cuthbert's Isle. The basis of a watercolour, W.819 (Pl. 116).

52 Lindisfarne. St Cuthbert's Priory, west end from nave.

53 Lindisfarne. St Cuthbert's Priory, crossing and nave from choir, north transept to the right.

54 Lindisfarne. St Cuthbert's Priory, looking across nave from south. The basis of a *Liber Studiorum* drawing, TB CXVI N (Pl. 117) and print published 20 February 1808, and possibly of an untraced watercolour exhibited RA 1798 (W.236).

55 Lindisfarne. St Cuthbert's Priory, west end from north aisle of the nave (Pl. 119).

56 Berwick bridge and town from the south (Pl. 122).

56a Berwick Harbour, looking east from the same viewpoint as f.56. Worked up in watercolour (Pl. 123).

57 Norham Castle from upstream (Pl. 125). The basis of colour beginnings TB L B, C (Pls 127–8), watercolours W. 225 (Pl. 129), 226 (Pl. 130), 736 (Pl. 131), *Liber Studiorum* drawing TB CXVIII D and print published 1 January 1816, and oil painting B&J 512 (Pl. 132).

TB XXVII U, Norham Castle and mill from a closer viewpoint than f.57. Probably a leaf detached from the *North of England* sketchbook (Pl. 124).

58 Kelso Abbey, north front (Pl. 133).

59 Kelso Abbey, west front (Pl. 134).

Reflc' and 'Do' i.e. Keswick.

26 Castle Head (middle distance, left of centre) from Manor Brow above Keswick, Swinside to right, with Derwent Fells in distance barely recognisable for mist. Inscr. 'Do' i.e. Keswick (Pl. 149).

27 'Buttermere', from north west corner, looking to Honister Pass (centre) with Fleetwith Pike to right (Pl. 164).

84 Crummock Water from Buttermere Hause, with Buttermere and Fleetwith Pike in the distance, Hay Stacks right of centre and High Stile to right (Pl. 167). The basis of the oil painting B&J 7 (Pl. 168). Worked up in watercolour. Inscr. on water 'Black'. Would be better placed after f.28

28 Buttermere, 'Do', from above village, Fleetwith Pike in distance left of centre.

29 'Cromeck Water', from road above north end of lake, looking south to Rannderdale Knotts (left) with Red Pike in mist to right.

30 'Bassenwath'. Overshot mill, possibly at Braithwaite, with Skiddaw in the distance left?

31 'Keswick', i.e. Derwentwater, from near boat landing, looking to Swinside?

32 'St John's Vale', looking to Helvellyn (in mist, centre) from Grasmere road near Castlerigg (Pl. 169).

33 'Grasmere', from west shore, looking north to Helm Crag right of centre, Dunmail Raise centre, and slopes of Helvellyn right, obscured by mist (Pl. 170).

87 Grasmere, looking to Rydal Water from near Dale End. Worked up in watercolour (Pl. 171).

34 'Rydal' Water, from Grasmere end, looking towards Rydal, Loughrigg to right (Pl. 173).

35 'Lead Mine', ?Grasmere Mine (Pl. 174).

36 'Langdale', Elterwater from the Grasmere road, looking south to Coniston Fells obscured in mist (Pl. 175).

37 'Ullswater', looking south from near Glenridding, Arnison Crag to right, Hartsop Dodd centre, erroneously inscr. 'Helvellyn' (Pl. 176).

38 'Do' i.e. Ullswater from near Stybarrow Crag, looking south.

39 'Do' i.e. Ullswater from near Stybarrow Crag (slightly further north of f.38), looking south.

40 'Do Gowbarrow' i.e. Ullswater and Aira Point from below Gowbarrow Park, looking south to St Sunday Crag left and Sheffield Pike right.

41 'Do' i.e. Ullswater from near Gowbarrow Bay, looking south to Sheffield Pike right of centre.

[f.78, bound after f.19, but fits better into sequence here. Aira Force. Part worked up in watercolour.]

42 'Do' i.e. Ullswater from Aira Point, below Aira Force, looking south

to St Sunday Crag centre obscured in mist (Pl. 177). The basis of watercolours W.551 (Pl. 180) and 860 (Pl. 181)

43 'Do' i.e. Ullswater, looking north from near Stybarrow Crag.

44 'Patterdale' old church, looking north to the lake. The basis of a watercolour W.229 (Pl. 182) engraved in Mawman's *Excursion to the Highlands and English Lakes*, 1805.

45 'Do' i.e. Patterdale from above Side Cottages, looking north to Side Farm. Sheffield Pike to left apparently obscured by cloud.

Patterdale Old Hall across south end of Ullswater from below Side Farm. Partly worked up in watercolour (Pl. 183). Evening light on Helvellyn in distance. Probably a leaf detached from the *Tweed and Lakes* sketchbook, now in the Fitzwilliam Museum, Cambridge, W.229.

46 'Goldrill Br[idge]', Patterdale, looking south to Hartsop Dodd.

79 Goldrill bridge, Patterdale, looking north to Ullswater. Partly worked up in watercolour. Morning light on Sheffield Pike to left (Pl. 184).

47 'Broad Water' i.e. Brothers Water from the north end with old bridge to right and Hartsop Dodd in background left.

48 'Do' i.e. Brothers Water from the east shore below road, looking to Hartsop Hall with Black Brow left and Dove Crag right, in background (Pl.186).

49 Brothers Water Inn, looking north over lake to Place Fell (Pl. 187).

50 'Rydal' Water from Rydal end, looking towards Grasmere, Loughrigg to left.

51 'Ambleside Mill' from lower bridge. The basis of a watercolour, W.237 (Pl. 188).

52 'Windermere', Waterhead near Ambleside, looking west towards Langdale fells obscured by mist (Pl. 191). Slate barge in foreground, the same boats in f.53 following. The basis of a watercolour W.555 (Pl. 192).

53 Windermere, Waterhead looking north to Fairfield (Pl. 189). Slate barge in foreground cf. f.52.

54 Windermere, looking south between Waterhead and Bowness.

55 'W[indermere]', Bowness, looking north to Fairfield from boat landing (Pl. 193). The basis with f.56 of a watercolour W.874 (Pl. 195).

56 Windermere and Belle Isle, looking north from the Hawkshead Ferry.

57 Church Beck Falls, Coniston, looking west to Wetherlam. Inscr. erroneously 'Old Man' (Pl. 197). The basis of a painting B&J 5 (Pl. 199).

58 'Coniston' Old Hall, looking west with Old Man left and Wetherlam centre (Pl. 196).

59 'Do' i.e. Coniston Old Hall, north front, looking east to lake.

60 'Furness' Abbey, north transept and crossing from night stairs in south transept (Pl. 200).

61 'Ditto' i.e. Furness Abbey, Infirmary chapel from the east.

62 'Ditto' i.e. Furness Abbey. Gateway and old manor house.

63 Lime kiln in Morecambe Bay.

64 Lancaster, old bridge, church and castle from the north.

65 Lancaster Aqueduct, with the church and castle seen through the right-hand arch (Pl. 203).

66 'York', Pavement looking to High Ousegate, with All Saints centre, and St Croix, Pavement to the right. 'Black H[orse]' inn to the left (Pl. 206).

67 Lancaster church, castle and town from the north east near St John's church (Pl. 202).

68 'Bolton Abbey' from the south. The basis of a watercolour study TB CXXI I (Pl. 205).

69 'York', Ouse Bridge and Minster from downstream (Pl. 210).

\# TB XXXVI B. York Minster and Lendal tower from outside the walls (Pl. 212). A leaf possibly detached from the *Tweed and Lakes* sketchbook. A small blue and grey wash drawing not by Turner but derived from this, TB XXXVI C (Pl. 213).

70 York Minster from the river opposite 'St Mary's Abbey' (Pl. 214).

71 York, St Mary's Abbey, west portal (Pl. 215). Resketched in 1816, cf. TB CXLVI 5–6, 1816.

72 York 'Ouse Br[idge]' and St William's Chapel, from immediately upstream (Pl. 209).

86 'York' Minster, south side from top of Minstergate (Pl. 217).

73 York Minster, south transept and crossing from north transept.

74 York Minster, crossing and choir screen from south transept.

75 York Minster, crossing, choir and choir screen from nave (Pl. 219). Cf. two small drawings of choir screen details TB LI E, F.

76 York Minster, crossing and choir screen from west aisle of south transept.

77 [Bound after f.19]

78 [Bound after f.19]

79 [Bound after f.46]

80 [Bound after f.7]

81 [Bound after f.7]

82 [Bound after f.19]

83 [Bound after f.23]

84 [Bound after f.27]

85 [Bound after f.19]

86 [Bound after f.72]

87 [Bound after f.33]

88 [Bound after f.23]

89 [Bound after f.15]

ABBREVIATIONS

NOE	*North of England* sketchbook
T&L	*Tweed and Lakes* sketchbook
TB	Tate Bequest
RA	Royal Academy
W.	Andrew Wilton, *The Life and Works of JMW Turner*, London, 1979
B&J	Martin Butlin and Evelyn Joll, *The Paintings of JMW Turner*, second (revised) edition, London, 1984
V&A	Victoria and Albert Museum
NT	National Trust
BM	British Museum
Birmingham CAG	Birmingham City Art Gallery
Boston MOA	Boston Museum of Art
G&L	T. Girtin and D. Loshak, *The Art of Thomas Girtin*, London, 1954
VF	*The Viewfinders: an Exhibition of Lake District Landscapes*, exhibition catalogue, Abbot Hall Art Gallery, Kendal, 1980.

NOTES AND REFERENCES

NOTES TO PART I

1 Thornbury, 1877, p.139.

2 J. Ruskin, *Modern Painters*, vol. V, part IX, chapter ix.

3 A watercolour, TB XXIII H, evidently not by Turner but rather the work of a pupil based on the pencil drawing TB XXIII G, is inscribed verso 'June 30, September 1st 1797'. There is no obvious explanation for the inscription, but it seems possible that it records the dates of the north of England tour.

4 Grant, 1797.

5 One of his 1798 R.A. exhibits (no. 640) was *Study in September of the fern house, Mr. Lock's Park, Mickleham, Surry*. See also note 3 above.

6 Leeds City Archives Department, Harewood Papers 189, 17 May 1797.

7 Hill, 1984/5, part I, p.26. The watercolour was exhibited at the R.A. 1796, no. 395 as 'St Erasmus in Bishop Islip's Chapel'. Presumably the intended title was St Erasmus's and Bishop Islip's chapels.

8 Farington Diary, 14 November 1795.

9 We have detailed knowledge of the tastes of Edward Lascelles from his personal account books preserved at Leeds City Archives Department. These are quoted in more detail in Hill, 1984/5, *passim*.

10 Lascelles's patronage is dealt with in more detail in Hill, 1995.

11 W.182–6.

12 Wilton, 1984, which contains a thorough review of the basic facts of Turner's association with Dr Monro.

13 The pencil drawings (TB CCCLXXVII) are attributed by Finberg to Girtin, but it seems obvious that there are several different hands present. Most give the impression of having been drawn direct from the motif rather than having been copied from other images. The group includes studies of Kirkstall Abbey (f.18), Barnard Castle (f.19), 'Horton' church (f.21), Middleham Castle (f.16), Lindisfarne Priory (f.33) and Lancaster (f.5). The watercolours (TB CCCLXXIX) are also given by Finberg to Girtin, and might possibly all be by the same artist except that three, f.1 Norham (repr. Wilton, 1984, pl.7), f.16 Lancaster, and f.18 Tynemouth) stand out as being rather superior in terms of handling, colour and dramatic impact. The same hand seems responsible for TB XXIX B a monochrome study of West Tanfield in Yorkshire, TB XXIX C a coastal scene, of similar size, and TB XXIX D a landscape with reapers (repr. Wilton, 1984, pl.9), all of which Finberg listed doubtfully as Turner. The latter is related to an oil painting called *Middleton Dale, Yorkshire* (repr. Wilton, 1984, pl.8 b/w as by Turner).

The rest of the watercolours TB CCCLXXIX form a weaker, but coherent group many of which are based on pencil studies from CCCLXXVII (f.13 Lancaster based on f.5; f.12 Kirkstall based on f.18; f.8 Middleham based on f.16; f.5 Walsingham based on f.2; f.11 Glasgow based on f.1; f.9 Kidwelly based on f.3; and f.20 Lake with Mountains based on f.10). Individually some of the weaker group compare with the stronger, and it seems possible that the whole group might be by the same hand. Since the weaker group could not possibly be Turner, my own feeling is that the whole series of watercolours is probably by Girtin, but the pencil drawings might be by a number of different hands, the principal contender being Edward Dayes.

The Turner Bequest also contains a number of other Monro circle works of north of England subjects which Finberg attributed to Turner. The first of these is a small blue and grey wash drawing of *York Minster from the south-west* (Pl. 213), which is certainly not by Turner even though it is clearly based on a sketch of 1797 (Pl. 212). This seems too weak to be by Girtin and is possibly by a pupil of Turner. Another is the larger watercolour study of *Knaresborough Castle from the High Bridge* (TB XXXIII C, Wilton, 1984, pl.12 where attributed to Turner), but this seems too weak to be by Turner, but equally unlikely to be Girtin. The authorship of this is complicated by the existence of a small watercolour by Girtin (Private Collection) which was sold at Sotheby's 8 November 1991, lot 102 as Turner. It is reproduced by Wilton, 1984, pl.11, where accepted as Turner, but it is perfectly commensurate in style with all the other small *c*.7.6 x 12 cm drawings and watercolours in this series. This has been thought to have been derived from the Turner Bequest watercolour (Wilton, 1984, p.12) but the two compositions are, however, more likely to be independent treatments of the same view. The situation is further complicated by the existence of a pencil sketch of the same subject attributed to Girtin, sold Christie's 13 July 1965 lot 165, where repr. b/w, which differs sufficiently in detail from each of the watercolours discussed here to be as independent of them as they are of each other. Turner sketched the view in 1816, cf. TB CXLIV 73a. It seems possible that the Turner Bequest watercolour is by Edward Dayes, and was again acquired by Turner from the Monro sale.

14 Leeds City Archives Department, Harewood Papers 191, 21 November 1798.

15 An example is illustrated in Hill, 1995, pl.5.

16 Farington Diary, 9 February 1799.

17 W. 370, at The Yale Center for British Art, New Haven, repr. and identification discussed in Hill, 1984/5, part 2, p.43.

18 W.280 as *Pembroke Castle, South Wales: thunder storm approaching*. Wilton confuses the exhibited titles, cf. discussion in Hill, 1984/5, part 2, p.41.

19 The *Wilson* sketchbook, TB XXXVII contains a list of north of England subjects on f.127. This is now almost impossible to read, but Andrew Wilton, *J.M.W.Turner, The Wilson Sketchbook*, Tate Gallery, 1988, p.36 managed to decipher 'Sta[m]ford, Lincoln, Mon Ch, Barrow Ch, Beverl[e]y, Howden, Ely, York, Knares[borough], Rippon, Selby, Dunstanborough, Richmond, Swale [and] Durham'. Although Turner did not visit all these sites in 1797, the list seems to record preliminary ideas for his itinerary.

20 W.102, York, 1980, no.5 repr. where dated to 1797. I now believe it to be c.1794–5 in style.

21 W.100, as untraced.

22 It is also possible, although no sketches have yet been identified, that he could have visited Wakefield and Sheffield in 1794 when his tour of the Midlands took him at least as far north as Derbyshire.

23 There are several of these in the Ashmolean Museum, Oxford.

24 Roget, 1891, i. 96.

25 Farington Diary, 14 December 1795.

26 Morris, 1989, and exhibition *Thomas Hearne 1744–1817*, Bolton Museum and Art Gallery, 1985.

27 See for example the windblown figures in his plate of St Mary's Abbey, York, published in the *Antiquities* on 1 September 1778, which might well have influenced the figures in Turner's watercolour of *Harewood Castle from the North* (Pl. 232).

28 Farington Diary, 15 November 1807.

29 Defoe, 1724–7, II 255.

30 Defoe, 1724–7, II 204–6.

31 Defoe, 1724–7, II 189–93.

32 Defoe, 1724–7, II 221.

33 Defoe, 1724–7, II 269–70.

34 Weinreb & Douwma, no. 121.

35 A copy of the print is at the Bowes Museum, Barnard Castle, repr. G. Grigson, *Britain Observed*, London, 1975, no.22 b/w.

36 Bicknell, 1990, no.3.

37 Bicknell, 1990, no.1.

38 Bicknell, 1990, no.77.

39 Roget, 1891, i 48.

40 Farington Diary, 22 April 1798.

41 Bicknell, 1990, no.2.

42 Bicknell, 1990, no.4.

43 Bicknell, 1990, no.10.

44 West, 1784, Addendum 1 p.192.

45 West, 1784, Addendum 1 p.219.

46 Bicknell, 1990, no.13. Extended passages of Brown and Dalton were quoted in William Hutchinson's *An Excursion to the Lakes in Westmoreland and Cumberland* 1774, 1776 (Bicknell, 1990 Nos 6, 7).

47 Bicknell, 1990, no.5.

48 Bicknell, 1990, no.8.

49 Cf. Gell, 1797.

50 Bicknell, 1990, no.18.

51 Gilpin, *Observations*, 1786, pp. 119–20, quoted A. Wilton, *Turner and the Sublime*, 1980, p.32.

NOTES TO PART II

1 For Sir George Beaumont in general see Brown and Owen, 1988. For Beaumont and Hearne *see* Morris, 1989. Beaumont usually appears in accounts of Turner as a vociferous critic, but this dates from after Turner was elected a full Royal Academician in 1802. Before this time Beaumont was an admirer of the young artist's work, cf. e.g. Finberg 1961, p.71. Beaumont seems to have given his encouragement to young artists freely, but I confess to having no information to connect Beaumont with Turner at this time. Nevertheless the route into Derbyshire is a huge detour, which requires some explanation along these lines, and whichever route Turner took to Wingfield must have taken him in the near vicinity of Coleorton. Whatever the case, two sketches of Wingfield, which was quite an obscure subject (*see* note 2) and one of Dronfield, even more so, cannot by themselves explain the route.

2 For Wingfield in general *see* Dixon, 1995. For a more detailed account of the building history see Emery, 1985. Wingfield seems to have been rarely depicted in the eighteenth century. Four plates were engraved and published by J. Nichols in Blore, 1793 (NW view from below, entrance porch from courtyard, great tower from courtyard, and NW view from an old painting), and although the first two of these are comparable with Turner's sketches, there does not seem to be any particular reason to believe that Turner had any knowledge of them.

3 Torrington Diaries, II 198. The print which Torrington mentions predates Blore, 1793, and perhaps might have been an earlier version of the view after an old painting published by Nichols. Emery, 1985, pl.X, reproduces a late seventeenth-century painting by Thomas Smith, evidently the basis of the engraving.

4 The name of Dronfield appears in a list on the back of a sketch of the interior of Beverley Minster, TB XXXVI N – *see* Part VII The Sketchbooks. The significance of the list is unclear.

5 *Universal British Directory*, 1793–8, pp. 243–4.

6 Torrington Diaries, II 22 ff.

7 Earlier views of Rotherham include a view of the chapel and bridge by C. Sparrow, 1775, engraved by J. Hooper in 1785, and a magnificent watercolour dated 1781 by Samuel Hieronymous Grimm, taken from a more distant viewpoint to include something of the industry at Masbrough, at Birmingham City Art Gallery (237'53).

8 Torrington Diaries, II 22.

9 For a detailed account of the history of Conisbrough Castle see Johnson, 1989. The keep has recently (1994) been restored with new roof and floors after standing for centuries as a hollow drum.

10 Dayes, 1805, p.25.

11 The viewpoint is not far from the King's Ferry. See Greathead, 1990, p.68 for a photograph of the site before dereliction, and p.11 for a photograph of the lock before removal in 1972. Cf. Torrington Diaries, III 27 for his visit to Walker's foundry in 1792.

12 Greathead, 1990, p.68.

13 The leaf could be from the *Tweed and Lakes* sketchbook. There is a similar subject in the *North of England* sketchbook, TB XXXIV 90. Gage, 1987, p.229 and n.78, on the other hand, suggests that this drawing might be related to a commission recorded on the fly-leaf of TB XXXVIII for '4 Drawings of the Iron Works of Richd Crawshay Esqre at Cyfaithfa, near Merthyr Tidvil'.

14 Defoe (1727), 1974, II 181-2.

15 Torrington Diaries, III 24 ff. (28-9).

16 A watercolour of Doncaster Church from the north, attributed to Turner, was sold at Sotheby's 10 October 1962. To judge from a back and white photograph, the attribution would appear to be doubtful.

17 For more detailed historical information see Miller, 1804 and Jackson, 1855.

18 That to the right is the tomb of Sir John Storey. The sarcophagus is engraved in Jackson, 1855, pl. viii. That to the left is perhaps the tomb of Lady Davenport. The positions of both are marked on a plan in Jackson, 1855, pl. ix.

19 Dayes, 1805, p.29.

20 Wakefield Museum and Art Galleries has a remarkable painting of Pontefract Castle attributed to Alexander Keirinx, dating to *c*.1625–30, recording it still fully intact.

21 Dayes, 1805, p.33.

22 *ibid*, p.33.

23 Grant, 1797, p.234.

24 Published on 1 June 1798. The original (W.101) is untraced.

25 It is possible that Turner might have visited Wakefield on his tour of the midlands in 1794, although the most northerly point that we know him to have visited is Matlock in Derbyshire. On balance, given the vagueness of detail in the engraving, I am inclined to think that he did not visit in 1794, and worked from someone else's sketch.

26 The entire frontage was replaced in 1847, and the original rebuilt at Kettlethorpe Hall.

27 From 1888.

28 It is not known when or for whom the watercolour was originally made, although in style it would seem to date from 1797–8. The sketch on which the watercolour was based, TB XXXIV 10 is inscribed on the back 'G.D'. It is tempting to speculate that this might be the architect George Dance RA, who took Turner's portrait in 1800 (cf. R.J.B.Walker, 'The Portraits of J.M.W.Turner: A Check-List', *Turner Studies*, 3 i, Summer 1983, p.23).

29 A pencil sketch at the Tate Gallery (TB XXXVI A) offers evidence that he conceived this pictorial strategy deliberately.

30 See e.g., Anon., *A history of the town and parish of Leeds, compiled from various authors. . . To which are added a history of Kirkstall Abbey and a Leeds directory, containing a list of the merchants, tradesmen &c in the town of Leeds.* Leeds, 1798, and *An Historical and Picturesque Account of Kirkstall Abbey*, Leeds and London, 1827. Cf. Brears, 1981.

31 See Bishop, 1977.

32 Quoted from *St James's Chronicle* for 20-3 May 1797 by Finberg, 1961, p. 43.

33 A watercolour showing the same view of the Chapter House as *NOE* 11 is listed (as *Kirkstall Abbey Refectory*) and repr. b/w by Wilton, 1979 as W.235. This was sold at Christie's 4 November 1975, lot 58. Wilton's reproduction is too small to permit any comment beyond this.

34 Based on a sepia study, TB CXVII O.

35 The relationship between the study and the sketch was brought to my attention by Ian Warrell, who suggests that the subject is a nativity. I am reminded somewhat of the studies of peasant distress and unrest in the *Hesperides (1)* sketchbook of 1805, TB XCIII 22a ff., cf. D.Hill, *Turner on the Thames*, 1993, p.141. The reversal of the composition suggests a context of engraving, and some likely connection with his thoughts for the *Liber Studiorum*.

36 1808 sketches, TB CVII, 1824 TB CCX, the latter the basis of a further watercolour for the 'Rivers of England' of *Kirkstall Lock*, cf. Shanes, 1990, p.114. Another sketchbook TB CLV, possibly dates to the latter visit.

37 Turner's route from Leeds to Knaresborough would have taken him past the gates of Harewood. It seems very likely that he would have called, and not impossible that some of his Harewood sketches on loose sheets were made at this time. The Harewood subjects in the sketchbooks, however, were clearly made on his return to Yorkshire after visiting the Lakes, so Harewood is treated at that point in this account.

38 For the history of Castle Mills, *see* Hargrove, (1775), 5th edition, 1798, pp. 38–9, who says 200 looms were in operation there in 1798. It would have interested Turner that the mill made paper 1770–91, cf. C. Giles and I. Goodall, *Yorkshire Textile Mills*, 1770–1930, HMSO, 1992, p.217. The origin of the mill does not seem to be known, but Giles and Goodall say that it formerly served as a corn mill, and it seems to have been adapted to industrial production after a large waterwheel was installed in 1764 for pumping water up to the town from the river (Hargrove, *ibid*.). Cf. also B. Jennings, *A History of Harrogate and Knaresborough*, 1970, pp. 263–4.

39 Torrington Diaries, III 42 ff.

40 Cf. TB CXLIV 56a, 57, 63a-64, 73a, 104a, 106, and CXLVI 31, 32. 56a equates most closely to the *England and Wales* composition.

41 Cf. York, 1985.

42 For further details of the history of the Minster see Wilkinson, 1974.

43 Finberg, 1961, p.44.

44 See Hill, 1984.

45 TB CXLIV 34a-36a, CXLVI 8 (revisiting the same view as XXXVI D) and 9 (cf. XXXVI E).

46 Cf. Gilyard-Beer, 1970 and Greeves & Mauchline, 1988.

47 York, 1985.

48 It might be significant that the passage from Thomson's *Seasons* (Summer ll 1647–53) that Turner quoted in relation to this composition is preceded by a passage in which the poet applauds 'the generous, still improving mind. . . To him the long review of ordered life Is inward rapture only to be felt.' It would be reasonable to describe Turner in such terms.

49 TB CXLIV 37–39, CXLVI 10, CXXXIV 42, 43, 63, 64. Finished watercolour, W.546, private collection, exh. York, 1980, no.35 where repr. b/w.

50 It is perhaps surprising that Turner did not go from Ripon to Richmond via (or at least did not record) Masham, Jervaulx and Middleham. He remedied the deficiency in 1816, when he made sketches in CXLIV and CXLVI.

51 For the history of the castle see Peers, 1953. Dayes, 1805, p.110 ff., and Torrington Diaries, III 62ff., both interesting on Richmond.

52 Girtin sketched exactly the same view, possibly in 1796 (G&L 252i where d. 1798), and completed a finished watercolour (G&L 252ii), now at the University of Liverpool.

53 Ian Warrell of the Tate Gallery has recently noted that the back of this sheet has a rough outline of the composition of a watercolour, W.277, now at the Whitworth Art Gallery, Manchester. The watercolour was formerly identified as Norham Castle, but this identification was abandoned in C. Hartley, *Turner Watercolours in the Whitworth Art Gallery*, 1984 no.19. The presence of the sketch raised the possibility that the subject might be one visited by Turner in 1797, perhaps near to Richmond, but no other subject from the tour can be related, and the possibility of Ellerton Priory on the Swale above Richmond has been discounted by the present author following a site visit in 1995. While the site does resemble that depicted in the watercolour in general terms, the remains of the priory itself cannot be reconciled with those depicted in the watercolour. It seems possible that the subject is one visited on some later tour, perhaps to Wales in 1798 or 1799.

54 Farington's Diary records that on 8 July 1799, Turner promised a finished watercolour of this subject to Robert Smirke. He was obviously trying to secure Smirke's support in the forthcoming election of Associates of the Royal Academy. There is no record of any finished watercolour ever being completed, perhaps this sheet records how far the intention progressed.

55 Cf. Hill, 1984, p.60 ff.

56 See Hamilton Thompson, 1936.

57 A watercolour attributed to Girtin (G&L 333, where d. 1799-1800) of exactly the same view is in the Metropolitan Museum, New York.

58 The sheet dimensions are very close, but it is not clear how, when or why this page should have become detached from the sketchbook. According to the provenance given by W.274, the earliest known owner is W.F.Morice, who is given as the owner by Armstrong, 1902, p. 238, but no previous owners are mentioned.

59 *See* Graham and Baillie Reynolds, 1958.

60 Turner resketched this view in 1816, cf. TB CXLVII 31.

61 This sketch is *NOE* 90 recto. The leaf has at some stage become detached from the main sequence of drawings in the *North of England* sketchbook. Now that we can identify the verso as Egglestone, it seems highly likely that it was originally located adjacent to ff. 27 and 28. The most obvious subject in these circumstances is Cooke's Mill.

62 Bower, 1990, no.40, where repr. b/w. For Turner's other work at Egglestone in 1816 see Hill, 1984, sketchbook listings p.29 ff. Turner also briefly revisited Egglestone in 1831, cf. TB CCLXVI 33a, 34.

63 Bower, 1990 gives the story of the Cooke family, nos 15, 40, 41.

64 For a full account see Saunders, 1971.

65 First published 1808.

66 A watercolour d.1778 by Thomas Hearne at the Bowes Museum, Barnard Castle, repr. in colour in Morris, 1989, p.83, makes interesting comparison.

67 Hearne also painted this view, engraved by Wm Byrne for the second series of his *Antiquities of England and Wales*, and published on 1 June 1799. Watercolours attributed to Thomas Girtin in the Bowes Museum (G&L 189ii), and British Museum (G&L 189i). The British Museum version is very weak, and seems to show the water flowing in the wrong direction.

68 TB CXLVII 32

69 TB CCLXVI 32-4.

70 A colour-beginning formerly in the collection of W.G.Rawlinson (W.890) is identified as Barnard Castle, but as Wilton notes 'the identification of the scene is doubtful'. I cannot see any grounds for identifying the subject as Barnard Castle.

71 Cf. TB XXXIV 32, a view from upstream, W bank, comparatively slight, but readily recognisable.

72 For Durham in general see Johnson, 1983. For the cathedral Stranks, 1970, and Andrew, 1993.

73 Girtin also painted this view. A slightly more distant view exists in G&L 159i (Private Collection), 159ii (V&A) and 237 (Birmingham CAG), all comparable with an 1801 sketch by Turner, TB LXX g. Exactly the same view as Turner's 1797 sketch and watercolour exists in G&L 158i (Boston MOA), 158ii (Private Collection) and 158iii (Manchester, Whitworth). 158ii (repr. Davies, pl.76 b/w) makes the closest comparison with Turner's finished watercolour, and has a very similar light effect. That in the Whitworth is more dramatic, but possibly sacrifices plausibility for effect, given that it sets the sun well to the north east. I have not had the opportunity to establish whether this effect is possible, but it could only occur if at all, near midsummer.

74 As reported by Farington Diary, 24 October 1798.

75 *ibid.*

76 TB XXXV 13a is inscr: '9 x 12 Mr Taylor', presumably J. Taylor, the publisher of Wharton's *Essays on Gothic Architecture*, 1800 (cf. Pl. 74).

77 There are interesting precedents for both views of Elvet bridge by Thomas Hearne, see Morris, 1989, pp.76, 80.

78 There are precedents for this by Hearne, cf. Morris, 1989, p.80, Dayes repr. Cormack, 1972, no.35 b/w, and also by Girtin, G&L 236i (at BM repr. b/w Hedley, 1982 no.81), although none attempts the composite treatment of Turner.

79 TB LIII 15a–28, 97, 98. In addition is a separate larger sheet, TB LXX g, measuring 260 x 413 mm, and possibly originating from the *Smaller Fonthill* sketchbook, TB XLVIII, which records Framwellgate bridge and the cathedral from a viewpoint further downstream from that of *T&L* 15. Other Durham subjects probably also from the *Smaller Fonthill* sketchbook are W.314-6. A sheet in the Ashmolean Museum, Oxford, cf. L. Herrmann, *Ruskin and Turner*, London, 1968, no. 65 repr. b/w., records the view of the castle looking across the south side of Framwellgate bridge. Exactly the same view is recorded in the *Helmsley* sketchbook of 1801, TB LIII 26a–27. Herrmann suggests that the sheet could have originated from the *Tweed and Lakes* sketchbook, but the drawing is insensitive for Turner, and I suspect that there is room to doubt that it is by Turner at all.

80 The idea of depiction and memory with respect to Durham is interestingly explored in Andrew, 1993, pp. 32–3.

NOTES TO PART III

1 Cf. Saunders, 1993.

2 A third sketch (*NOE* 34) of collier brigs at a small port is unidentified, but might show North Shields. Finberg, 1909 records a page missing after f. 33 which presumably contained a sketch of Tynemouth or North Shields.

3 Turner might have known the watercolour, now at the Laing Art Gallery, Newcastle, of the same subject at Tynemouth by Edward Dayes which uses a similar framing device. Exh. Hedley, 1982, no. 57 where repr. in colour.

4 In addition to the work described here there is a strange oil painting in the Turner Bequest (B&J 253, where dated *c.* 1820–5?) which takes the general form of the east end framed in the aisle doorway, and sets it in a cappriccio with an ogee doorway and urn on a pedestal. The intention of this remains obscure.

5 Wilton, 1979 lists this twice as nos 545 and 888.

6 William Finden, *The Ports and Harbours of Great Britain*, London, 1836, p.1, quoted in Shanes, 1990, p.204.

7 For information on Bothal see Bibby, 1973.

8 Images of Bothal prior to 1797 do not seem to be at all common. None have readily presented themselves to me.

9 First identified by Madgwick, 1993.

10 Cf. Hunter Blair and Honeyman, 1977, and Graham, 1971.

11 Wilton (W.257) lists and reproduces in b/w a watercolour of a similar view from the SE at the Beaverbrook Art Gallery, Fredericton, Canada. From Wilton's reproduction the attribution to Turner seems doubtful.

12 This view is close to that sketched by Girtin in 1796 and used as the basis of a subsequent watercolour, both now in the Yale Center for British Art, New Haven, see Morris, 1986, nos 48, 67 where both repr. b/w p.68, and likewise Hawes, 1982, p.42.

13 Madgwick, 1993, p.9.

14 Girtin made a similar view from the opposite side of the bridge which was published in the *Copper Plate Magazine*

on 1 May 1797 (repr. Graham, 1971, p. 11). The original is untraced, but the topographical detail of the engraving is so vague as to suggest that it was made from someone else's sketch before Girtin visited Warkworth in 1796.

15 There is a watercolour of this view d.1793 by Edward Dayes in the V&A (repr. Williams, 1952 pl. 170 b/w) and a related watercolour attributed to Girtin (G&L 34i) at Rochdale Art Gallery. A further watercolour in the Ashmolean Museum, Oxford, shows the same view with a different effect of light and lacks topographical knowledge of its subject, but is also attributed to Girtin (G&L 34ii).

16 Discussed in detail with regard to two watercolours of Pembroke Castle in Hill, 1984/5, pp.41–3.

17 Turner's first poetic quotations discussed in broader context by Ziff, 1982.

18 For further detail see Graham, 1994.

19 The sketches of the abbey gateway and the church were first identified by Madgwick, 1993.

20 Shanes, 1990, p.195 points out the clever visual simile between the deer's antlers and the pairs of sculpted figures on the battlements of the castle.

21 For history see Hunter Blair and Honeyman, 1982.

22 The most comprehensive account of Turner's work at Dunstanburgh is Joll, 1988. Girtin visited in 1796 and there is a pencil sketch of the ruins from the north at the Yale Center for British Art, New Haven (Morris, 1986 no.44 where repr. b/w). A dramatic composition of the view from the north east is at the Laing Art Gallery, Newcastle (G&L 183), and another at the Ashmolean Museum, Oxford, (G&L 72).

23 There is, however, beside the *North of England* sketchbook drawings, a number of Dunstanburgh studies or sketches, the exact status of which is hard to determine. The *Wilson* sketchbook, TB XXXVII 94–5 has a study apparently of the Lilburn tower against a lightning-rent sky, which recalls the watercolour of Dunstanburgh by Girtin in the Ashmolean Museum (G&L No 72). Ian Warrell has recently drawn to my attention a series of hurried sketches apparently showing Dunstanburgh in the *Dinevor Castle* sketchbook, TB XL 89–80a. This sketchbook was used mainly in Wales in 1798, and contains no other identified north of England subjects. Nevertheless it does seem possible that these sketches were made from the motif, although whether this was in 1797 or when he returned to Northumberland in 1801 it is hard to determine. If the former, one might wonder why he made no other sketches in what must then have been a new book. Besides these is a study in the *Studies for Pictures* sketchbook in use c.1800–2, TB LXIX 5. This shows a view from the north different from any of the others and was possibly made after a revisit in 1801.

24 A study in black chalk on rough paper is related to this, TB XXXVI R, although the topographical details are consistent enough to suggest that it could have been made from the motif.

25 It is worth noting that the clouds in the distance on the right of this study become cliffs in the colour study and the oil.

26 This watercolour has been largely overlooked by modern Turner scholarship, except for Joll. 1988 p.5. It is a pair to a watercolour of Brinkburn Priory, which has likewise escaped notice. They were both the property of Sir Charles

Trevelyan of Wallington Hall, Northumberland (NT) where they now hang, by 1929, when he lent them to the North East Coast exhibition, Palace of Arts, Newcastle upon Tyne, nos 483 (Dunstanburgh) and 492 (Brinkburn).

27 Cf. Shanes, 1990, p.191.

28 See Bamburgh guide, Jarrold, Norwich (n.d.).

29 Pennant, 1771, pp.33–4.

30 Catalogue of exhibition at Graphic Society, London, 1837. Ruskin was less enthusiastic, cf. *Modern Painters* i.144

31 See Cambridge, 1988 and Graham, 1975.

32 *NOE* 53 is comparable with the watercolour at the British Museum (G&L 184), and also a pencil sketch at the Whitworth Art Gallery, Manchester (G&L 164i) and a watercolour at the Fitzwilliam Museum, Cambridge (G&L 164ii).

33 *North of England* sketchbook, TBXXXIV, list inside cover.

34 The larger composition is possibly the watercolour sold from the estate of the late Mrs Moss of Otterspool, near Liverpool at Christie's 27 May 1873 lot 87 (£79.16.0). Wilton (W.236) also mentions a drawing *Off Holy Island* in the sale of Mrs Sara Austen, Christie's 11 April 1889, bought by Vokins, and suggests comparison with a watercolour recorded in Finberg's card index at the British Museum as being in the collection of J. Vavasseur. Since both measured approx 166 x 242 mm, these references might be identifiable with the smaller composition.

35 For more detailed historical background see Graham, 1980.

36 Turner revisited Berwick in 1831 in connection with his work for Sir Walter Scott, and made a number of sketches, see TB CCLXV, CCLXVII, and a finished watercolour (W. 1092). Cf. Finley, 1980, p.129ff.

37 Thornbury, 1877, p. 139 and cf. Finley, 1980, p. 129.

38 TB LIII 42a–50.

39 TB CXVIII D.

40 W. 1052, W. 1099

41 Lascelles paid twenty guineas for two drawings on 18 October 1798 (see Hill, 1984/5, p.38), which probably included Norham. One William Blake of Portland Place is recorded by Roget, 1891, i 121 as having been involved in the commission of one of the drawings, but as a result of a disagreement over the price cancelled his order (quoted Hill, 1984/5, p. 37).

42 There are views by Edward Dayes at Rhode Island School of Art and Design (Cormack, 1982 no.36, where repr. b/w), and the Yale Center for British Art, New Haven (White, 1977, no.91, repr. pl. xcvii b/w); Thomas Hearne at the V&A, 1778, repr. Morris, 1989, p.40 b/w, and followed by Girtin in a pencil sketch at the Ashmolean Museum, Oxford (G&L 170), and a watercolour by Dayes sold at Sotheby's 14 March 1985, lot 302. A watercolour by Girtin at the Whitworth Art Gallery, Manchester (G&L 199i), records a view of the west front comparable to Turner's sketch *NOE* 59.

43 For work dating from the 1831 visit see TB CCLXVII and watercolour W.1074. Cf. Finley, 1980, pp.126–9. TB CLIV (a) p.2a has a list of Scottish subjects including Jedburgh, Kelso, Melrose and Dryburgh, presumably preparatory to his 1818 visit to Scotland to gather material for illustrations to Sir Walter Scott's *Provincial Antiquities*. No sketches of

these subjects have yet been identified from that visit.

44 For a full account of the history of Melrose see Wood and Richardson, 1995.

45 Hearne published a similar view in the *Antiquities of Great Britain* in 1780 (repr. Morris, 1989, pl. 25), which was copied by Girtin in a watercolour at the British Museum (G&L 112).

46 There is a superb watercolour of a similar view by Girtin (not in G&L) now in the Pierpoint Morgan Library, New York, see *Gainsborough to Ruskin, British Landscape Drawings and Watercolours from the Morgan Library*, catalogue of the exhibition at the Musée Communal d'Ixelles, Brussels, 1994–5, where exh. no.46 and repr. in colour.

47 Thomas Hearne took a comparable view of Melrose, engr. *Antiquities of Great Britain*, 15 December 1779.

48 For 1831 sketches of Melrose cf. TB CCLXVII, CCLXVIII, and Finley, 1980, pp.120-1.

49 For the history of Dryburgh cf. Richardson and Tabraham, 1987.

50 For 1831 sketches of Dryburgh cf. TB CCLXVII. Finished watercolour W.1078 now at Tate Gallery, London. Cf. Finley, 1980, pp.119, 120.

51 For history of abbey see Fawcett, 1995.

52 Nos 423, *View of Jedborough Abbey, Scotland*, and 466, *View of Jedborough Abbey*.

53 Roget, 1891, i.120 describes a watercolour 19 x 27 ins (483 x 686 mm), of the abbey with the river in the foreground and figures washing linen on a sand bank, bought by Thomas Worthington for six guineas. This is perhaps identifiable with the watercolour now in the National Gallery of Ireland, Dublin (G&L 253).

54 For 1831 sketches see TB CCLXVII. Finished watercolour W.1072 in the Taft Museum, Cincinatti. It is tempting to see this as something of a homage to Girtin, cf. e.g. the watercolour by Girtin at the Cecil Higgins Art Gallery, Bedford (G&L 286). Cf. Finley, 1980, pp.125–8.

NOTES TO PART IV

1 At this point the *Tweed and Lakes* sketchbook was little more than a quarter full. Turner made fifty-four drawings in the Lake District.

2 It is perhaps odd that Turner did not, apparently, make any sketches of Carlisle. He was already familiar with it as a subject through having made a watercolour for an engraving in the *Copper Plate Magazine* published 2 October 1797. The watercolour, W.100, is presently untraced, but on the evidence of the engraving must almost certainly have been made before the tour of 1797, perhaps as early as c.1794, and based on sketches by another artist.

3 Gell, 1797, p.15 stayed at the Queens Head and was very satisfied, possibly taking the hint from Gray who put up there in 1769, cf. West, 1784, Addendum 3, p.201.

4 *T&L* 20. Turner revisited Cockermouth in 1809 (cf. TB CIX, CX) and made a painting for the Earl of Egremont (B&J 108), still at Petworth House in Sussex.

5 West, 1784, p.85. Despite the lack of enthusiasm, Keswick had considerable amenities for visitors, including two

museums, Gell, 1797, pp.13–4 has an entertaining description of one run by Peter Crosthwaite. Grant, 1797, pp. 269, 273 also visited that of Thomas Hutton.

6 West, 1784, Addendum 1, p.192.

7 West, 1784, Addendum 3, p.200.

8 Crow Park, near the boat landing seems to have been the most popular. It was the subject of a well-known print by Thomas Smith of Derby, plagiarised by Boswell, 1786, and described by Thomas Gray cf. West, 1784, Addendum 3, p.205, in which Gray mentions the print by Smith. The viewpoint was one of West's own stations (p.86ff.) in which he in turn quoted Gray.

9 Gell, 1797, pp. 16–7 visited on 28 June and was disappointed, likewise Grant, 1797, p.271 on 17 July. The latter remembered a phrase of poetry 'tumbling tide of dread Lodore', and John Dalton quoted in West, 1784, Addendum 2, p.195: 'Let other streams rejoice to roar/Down the rough rocks of dread *Lowdore*,/Rush raving on with boist'rous swep,/And foaming rend the frighted deep' and Mr Cumberland quoted in West, 1784, Addendum 4, p.222: 'I hear terrific *Lowdore* roar' were both guilty of inflaming expectations.

10 West, 1784, pp.ix–x.

11 Farington Diary, 24 October 1798 and July 6, 8 1799.

12 *T&L* 82a.

13 TB LVI Inside end cover inscribed: 'on the 5 of August finished this Book at Gretna Green'.

14 TB LX(a) and TB LXX. Cf. A. Wilton in *Turner Studies*, 8ii, p.28.

15 TB LXX B exh. Bower, 1990, no.27 where reproduced.

16 Friar's Crag is just south of the boat landing, and a popular viewpoint today. It was enjoyed by Gell, 1797, p. 16.

17 At this time Farington was at the opposite side of the country on his way to Scotland. He could not have received the gift until he returned to London early in 1802.

18 A mezzotint by Charles Mottram of *A Breakfast Party at Samuel Rogers's House, 1815*, (Tate Gallery, London, repr. C. Powell, *Turner in the South*, 1987, pl.138), gives some idea of the company kept by Rogers. Besides Turner and Southey it includes Wordsworth, Coleridge, Campbell and Byron.

19 W. 1182, 1183.

20 1831 sketches in CCLXVI.

21 W.1090.

22 Republished in *Turner Society News*, no.59, March 1991, p.12.

23 B&J 133.

24 Turner was at Keswick about 25 August 1831. C. C. Southey (ed.) *The Life and Correspondence of Robert Southey*, 6 vols, London, 1850, contains two letters written 15 July and 11 September from Keswick, which would seem to place Southey at home since neither mentions any intended or recently taken journey. The first letter expresses concern for Scott's health, which seems a coincidence, given that Turner was on his way to visit Scott at this time, and Scott's health was a major feature of the visit (see Finley, 1980 *passim*.).

25 Cf. Thomas De Quincey, *Recollections of the Lakes and the Lakes Poets*, London, 1970, p. 233, and Nicholson, 1995, p. 102ff.

26 Farington 1789 has an impressive view from near Ashness bridge which might have provoked Turner into looking for something similar, but generally it is the independence of Turner's view-finding which impresses. He certainly did not use (or at least did not follow) any of the best-known guides, such as Gray, West, Pennant or Gilpin.

27 The mine is above Seathwaite. It was described by Gilpin, 1786, p.205ff: 'Somewhat further . . . [down Borrowdale] rise those mountains, where the celebrated black-lead mine is wrought. I could not help feeling a friendly attachment to this place, which every lover of the pencil must feel, as deriving from this mineral one of the best instruments of his art; the freest and readiest expositor of his ideas. We saw the site of the mine at a distance, marked with a yellow stain, from the ochery mixtures thrown from its mouth, which shiver down the side of the mountain.' See also Adams, 1995, p.57.

28 John Knowles of the Theatre Manchester, had sales at Christie's, 7 April 1865 (W.794, W.1107), 19 May 1877 (W.585, W.796), and 5 June 1880 (W.554). The watercolour reproduced here was sold at Christie's, 8 July 1986, lot 150. Another, smaller (255 x 390 mm) version was sold at Sotheby's on 13 July 1989, lot 104. Neither is listed in Wilton, 1979, but the former is almost certainly identifiable with that listed by Armstrong 1902, p.275 as 'Rosthwaite, Borrowdale, *c*. 1807 [ex Canon Greenwell] Large Drawing. Stream passing under bridge, irregular masses of rock on either side. Roofs of village to left'. Finberg, 1909 under TB XXV 88 mentions 'A watercolour (painted about 1802) based on this sketch . . . now in the possession of Lord Joicey'.

29 See D. Hill, *Turner in the Alps*, London, 1992.

30 A large watercolour, TB XXXVIL (repr. A. Wilton, *Turner Watercolours in the Clore Gallery*, London, 1987 no.8 in colour) might possibly also record the view of Skiddaw from Brandlehow, but this would require some distortion of the profile of Skiddaw by the mist to sustain. It seems, however, to have been painted directly from the motif, and might more likely prove to be a Welsh subject dating from 1798.

31 Given that his first sketch is of Buttermere, and his last from the north end of Crummock Water, we might surmise that he went over Newlands, the route of approach described by West, 1784, p.125ff., and returned over Whinlatter. This is the round taken by Grant, 1797, p.274ff.

32 Hankinson, 1993, p.63.

33 Mary Robinson was noticed by both Grant, 1797, p. 275 and Gell, 1797, p. 18ff.

34 Hankinson, 1993, p.64ff. relates the full story.

35 From the road not far NW of the village, but now obscured by trees.

36 From the road near High Wood, grid ref. 158203, looking south to Rannerdale Knotts. The view is perfectly recognisable.

37 Ziff, 1982 suggests that Turner coloured TB XXXV 84 in the studio, and while doing so experimented with different positions for the rainbow. It seems to me, however, that the watercolour sketches on this tour were all coloured from nature – after all he told Hoppner that he had been colouring from nature to attend to the defect of his pictures tending to the brown (Farington Diary, 24 October 1798), and Farington himself reported from a visit to Turner's studio that the drawings had been 'tinted on the spot' (*see* p. 181). While the sketch seems therefore almost certainly to have been coloured on the spot, and the general effect observed from a passing shower backlit by the sun, it seems possible that he could have added or strengthened the streak of red in the studio, to develop the idea of the rainbow, which could not possibly have been observed in this position.

38 Turner's title, while not incorrect, could be the cause of some confusion. Crummock Water is in the foreground, and Buttermere in the distance.

39 The connection with Gilpin is made by Ziff, 1982, p.5. A reading of Gilpin as a whole does not convince that Turner actually used it in the Lakes. He might nevertheless have read it afterwards.

40 Two sketches after Crummock Water remain to be identified. The first *T&L* 30 is inscribed [perhaps] 'Basenwath', and shows a rather ramshackle overshot mill with what appears to be Skiddaw in the background. I have tried to identify this with the now disappeared corn mill at Braithwaite, but not entirely convincingly. Some mill in the area nevertheless seems likely. The second *T&L* 31 is inscribed 'Keswick', and shows a lake in the foreground with a hill to the left, possibly the north end of Derwentwater, but I have again been unable to find a thoroughly convincing location.

41 Plumptre's tours are unpublished, but the MSS are at Cambridge University Library. Cf. Bicknell, 1990, p.65.

42 Quoted Gell, 1797, p.49 n.17.

43 Dale End was known at this time as Tail End.

44 Gell, 1797, p.13.

45 See Adams, 1995, p.139.

46 It seems possible that this sketch influenced Turner's thinking in his development of the oil painting of *Morning amongst the Coniston Fells* (*see* p. 137), which also depicts a mining subject.

47 Gell, 1797, p.41.

48 *T&L* 37–43 & 78, *see* Pls 173–8 and Part VII The Sketchbooks.

49 Possibly with the aid of a local guide, see Gell, 1797, p.41.

50 Presumably no earlier than 1801 since Mawman also commissioned illustrations of Loch Lomond and Inveray, which Turner sketched on his tour to Scotland of that year.

51 Wordsworth, 1835, p.125.

52 Cf. *Journals of Dorothy Wordsworth*, Oxford, 1971, 16 April, 1802, p.111. The previous day Dorothy recorded her famous observation of daffodils growing by the shore of Ullswater.

53 Wordsworth, 1835, p.18.

54 West, 1784, p.157; Wordsworth, 1835, p.119.

55 Climbing to the fell tops was not unusual by 1797. Both Gell and Grant record climbs of Helvellyn and Skiddaw, the latter quite impulsively one evening to watch the sunset, very much enjoyed but not apparently thinking the climb particularly extraordinary. Anne Radcliffe made quite a meal of a horseback ascent of Skiddaw in 1794, but Joseph

Budworth charged up and down the hills with gusto in 1792. Thomas Hearne climbed Skiddaw in 1777, and made a watercolour of the view over Derwentwater from the summit (Morris, 1989, p.51.).

56 *Viewfinders*, no.80. Corn Mill established 1324, cf.Vf no.70.

57 Turner also revisited Rydal Water from Ambleside, and sketched the view from the lower end of the lake just to the left of the Rothay outflow (*T&L* 50). It is noteworthy that he did not (apparently) sketch the falls at Rydal Hall, since they were one of the most frequently depicted and described subjects in the whole of the Lake District.

58 no. 408.

59 *Discovery*, no.112.

60 West, 1784, p.72.

61 Exhibited, York, 1980, no.98. The picture is signed and dated 1821. A note of the commission, TB CCXI 10, records that Fawkes ordered six watercolours for one hundred and fifty guineas, i.e. twenty-five guineas each.

62 Or even in the sketch except for the twin peaks to the left. Quite what origin they had in reality is hard to determine in clear conditions.

63 Gell, 1797, p.11ff. describes hiring a boat from the White Lion at Bowness.

64 Belle Isle was begun soon after 1774 and completed by John and Isabella (hence Belle Isle) Curwen in the early 1780s. It caused controversy for years, but Gell's 1797 comment (p.11) was one of the most entertainingly apt: 'it wants only a little green paint and a label of Souchong or fine Hyson to make it exactly like a large shop tea cannister'. The house was gutted by a fire on Christmas Eve 1994, and is now being rebuilt.

65 Shanes, 1990, p.252 is mistaken in thinking that Turner looks south.

66 Many visitors noticed the boating activities around Belle Isle. Grant, 1797, p.257 describes a 'little fleet [owned by John Curwen] consisting of seventeen vessels. Groups of his men, who man them, form fine objects in scarlet uniforms, on the island'. Gell, 1797, p.45 watched from Bowness ferry landing 'Two boats deck't in their gayest colours . . . gliding gently towards the great island. They had each two or three sailors on board in red jackets, and the sun shone on the whole scene . . . Mr Curwen is said to take great pleasure in his little navy'. *Discovery*, no.115 is obviously wrong in saying that 'Turner would not have witnessed such a scene on his Lake District trip of 1797', but the connection made there to the vivid account given by J. G. Lockhart in his *Memoirs of the Life of Sir Walter Scott*, 1878, p.564, of the poet's visit to a grand regatta on Windermere in 1825 seems possible, given that Turner could have heard it direct from Scott himself, when he visited Abbotsford in 1831.

67 Coniston Old Hall was built in its present form by William Fleming in the late sixteenth century. The Flemings had lived on the site since at least the middle of the thirteenth century, and continued to do so until Sir Daniel Fleming (1633–1701) removed his household to Rydal Hall. The building is clearly derelict in Turner's sketches, but was refurbished about 1815. It was acquired by the National Trust in 1971 and restored, and is currently let as a farm and is not open to the public. I am indebted to Janet Martin,

archivist for the National Trust North West region, for these notes.

68 Coniston Copper Mine is reputed to have been worked in Roman times, and certainly from the late sixteenth century. It was worked up until about 1800 and then closed until 1823 when reopened by John Barrett. Production reached a peak in the 1850s when over 500 people worked in the valley. Production thereafter declined until the mine closed in 1915. Cf. Adams, 1995, p.146ff. and the leaflet produced by Philip Johnston, 1994, available on site. The site is now managed as a heritage trail and outdoor museum. Donations are always much appreciated. Slate quarrying has also been an important activity in the area.

69 Wilton, 1979 lists a watercolour (W.230) which was exhibited at Agnew's in 1982, lot 103, and sold at Christie's, 18 November 1983, lot 170 and Sotheby's, New York, 25 May 1990, lot 11. The subject is similar to the sketch and oil, but the relationship to both seems merely circumstantial. Agnew's 1982 catalogue argued: 'This watercolour is clearly a study for part of the oil', but this seems dubious. I am inclined to think that the watercolour is not by Turner. A watercolour by Edward Swinburne of the same subject as Turner, but recording the view from the north side of Church Beck, nearer to the falls, and looking more to the left, is in the Whitworth Art Gallery, Manchester, repr. Gage, 1987, fig. 236 b/w.

70 Book V, 185–8.

71 *Discovery*, p.45.

72 Turner might have been influenced in his memory by the sketch of the lead mine near Grasmere, made only a few pages previously (Pl. 174).

73 Or slate perhaps, but most of the slate would have been directly carted down to the lake on the south side of the back, not that on the north, as shown here, which leads directly to the Copper Mine. The bridge now connecting the two sides, just above the falls, was not built until 1858.

74 Turner seems to have revisited Coniston *c.* 1815, for about then he made a pair of watercolours of Tent Lodge, which stands on the eastern shore of the lake towards its northern end, W.552, 553, (and 554 which =553). A letter written by Turner on 1 August 1815 (cf. J. Gage (ed.), *Collected Correspondence of J. M. W. Turner*, Oxford, 1980, no.56), speaks of an intended visit to the Lakes that year, but no other evidence for the visit is known, except for the compositions of Tent Lodge.

NOTES TO PART V

1 Grant, 1797, p.245.

2 Nicholson, 1995 makes a similar point in a particularly vivid account of the sands crossing and quotes an entertaining variety of accounts. After 1816, the crossing became an important subject for Turner, see Hill, 1984, pp.84–5. Somewhere on the crossing Turner made a slight sketch (*T&L* 63) of a lime kiln by the shore. Limestone outcrops at various places around the northern shores of Morecambe Bay, and there were a number of kilns on the shores of Furness and elsewhere around the bay. The sketch contains little by way of landmarks that would help fix the location more exactly.

3 For detailed history and description cf. Dickenson, 1987.

4 Grant, 1797, p.249.

5 Grant, 1797, p.249 describes entering the abbey through 'a Gothic arched gateway, with a thick drapery of ivy hanging gracefully down one side.' This would seem to describe Turner's subject, and although a similar arch spans the road to the immediate north of the abbey, this is not exactly identifiable with that in the sketch, unless it has been substantially rebuilt and there have been considerable losses beyond.

6 Please do not be tempted to climb. This is good neither for one's own well-being, nor for that of the ruins.

7 Milner, 1990, no.25.

8 Milner, *ibid*, Hill, 1984, p.84.

9 I have developed this point in relation to Turner's later Thames subject in *Turner on the Thames*, 1993, Part III iii *passim*.

10 We cannot be sure of Turner's route from Lancaster to York, other than the fact that it took him past Bolton Abbey. The shortest route would be by the Lune valley to Kirkby Lonsdale or Ingleton and then via Settle to Skipton, but whether this would have been conveniently possible by coach is another matter. Another route, which is rather longer, but would certainly have been possible by coaching services, is via Preston, Clitheroe and Skipton. It has been suggested (cf. B&J 4) that he might have travelled via Wyresdale in the Trough of Bowland, but this would have been difficult and time-consuming, and not a regular coach route.

11 Bolton Priory founded 1154–5. For further details see Rhodes, 1990.

12 Turner returned to Bolton in 1808 and made a rather more leisurely survey, TB CLIV Q,R,S,T see York, 1980, p.28, nos 25, 26, which formed the basis of two finished watercolours painted for Walter Fawkes in 1809, W.531, 532, York, 1980, nos 32,33. He returned again in 1816 and made further sketches, TB CXXXIV 4, 54, 59, 73–6. 81a–82, the last of which formed the basis of a finished watercolour painted *c.*1825 for *Picturesque Views in England and Wales*, Shanes, 1990, no.135, Milner, 1990, no.11.

13 The date of the study is uncertain, but it was ascribed to *c.*1800 by Andrew Wilton in the catalogue of the exhibition *J. M. W. Turner: Dibujos y acuarelas del Museo Britanico*, Prado Museum, Madrid, 1983, no.10.

14 In the *North of England* sketchbook, the sketches of York clearly preceed those of Harewood.

15 TB CXLIX 290a–291 inscribed: 'Wrightson Kirby Black Horse Pavement'.

16 A watercolour d. 1802 by Thomas White exh. York, 1990, no. 81 where repr. b/w, shows that the Black Horse had by then been rebuilt.

17 York was a major subject for Girtin, and he had four exhibits of the subject in the 1797 exhibition at the Royal Academy.

18 This marks the first time that Turner had used the *North of England* sketchbook since Jedburgh. Possibly the *Tweed and Lakes* book was full.

19 Dayes, 1805, p.179.

20 A similar view of about 1803–5 by John Varley exh. York,

21 Turner returned to this subject in 1816, TB CXLIV 16a–17, and in 1818, TB CLIX 65as. The latter records a particularly interesting moment, for in this view taken from upstream, he has recorded the new bridge with the old still standing.

22 The leaf on which this is drawn is of such a size (238 x 365 mm) to have possibly originated from the Tweed and Lakes sketchbook (274 x 370 mm). The drawing, however, has been made within a ruled rectangle 194 x 289 mm. The reason for this is unclear, but determining a specific size would suggest him beginning a finished work. The sketch would nevertheless appear to have been made from the motif. The internal measurements of the mount inside the cover of the *Tweed and Lakes* sketchbook are such, 213 x 266 mm, as to preclude any connection.

23 Cf. York, 1990, no. 64.

24 Hill, 1995, p.37. A similar view by John Varley was sold at Sotheby's 11 July 1985, lot 134 repr.

25 York City Art Gallery has a view by Thomas Malton d.1778. One of the best views of the subject is by Thomas Hearne, engraved in *Antiquities of Great Brigain*, 1 September 1778. Turner would certainly have been attracted to Hearne's sense of the physical experience of the north, in his depiction of figures buffeted by the wind. A large watercolour attributed to Girtin at Birmingham City Art Gallery (G&L 384) seems to have a less than professional grasp of the architecture or the site. Turner resketched the site in 1816 TB CXLVI 5–6.

26 It is significant that Turner owned a copy of Joseph Halfpenny's *Gothic Ornament in the Cathedral Church of York*, 1795. Cf. Wilton, 1987, p.247. Unfortunately we do not know when he acquired it.

27 Cf. e.g. the watercolour attributed to Frederick Mackenzie, exh. York, 1990, no.104 where repr. in colour.

28 There is an extremely close comparison with a watercolour by Girtin (G&L 181). The comparison was drawn to my attention by Ian Warrell, and might offer another instance (cf. Part II Kirkstall) of Girtin perhaps working from a sketch by Turner.

29 In the sketches of the nave, it is noteworthy that the whole space is open. Benches and chairs were only introduced into the nave as a regular feature after 1863 (*Victoria County History, Yorkshire: York*, Oxford, 1961, p.354), up to which time the nave was a magnificent covered space which served the city as 'a place of fashionable promenade or gossip' (Aylmer, G. E. and Cant, R. (eds), *A History of York Minster*, Oxford, 1979, p.299). Although the building was never designed for them, the nave seats are now more-or-less a permanent feature of the nave. At the very least, this badly impairs the sense of scale, and the ordering of space that the building was intended to convey. On a different matter, the Turner Bequest contains two small sketches of the choir screen (TB LIE,F). The status of these is hard to determine. They compare well in style, though not in size, to Turner's other drawings in the *North of England* and *Tweed and Lakes* sketchbooks, but are made on a laminate of sheets glued together to form card similar to many of the small watercolours here attributed to Girtin, which were

bought at the Monro sale in 1833 (*see* p. 3). These drawings seem without doubt to be Turner's, but if made on the tour, it seems inexplicable that they were not made in the *Tweed and Lakes* sketchbook. Perhaps they were made later from some other source. The drawing of the figures on the choir screen (LIE) is interesting, however, in that it differs somewhat from the screen as we now find it in much superior condition. This is mostly the result of nineteenth-century restoration, but the figure on the far right is completely different. The screen when built had a figure of Henry VI, but this was early removed by Yorkists, and later replaced by a statue of James I, the figure depicted by Turner. In 1810 this was in turn removed and replaced by a new carving of Henry VI. The statue of James I is now at Ripon Cathedral, where the king was a major benefactor.

30 There is no obvious evidence that he called at Harewood on his way north, but it would seem likely in view of the fact that his route from Kirkstall to Knaresborough would have taken him right by the main gate. Perhaps some of the sketches of Harewood done on loose sheets, were made at this time.

31 For a fuller account of the Lascelles collection see Hill, 1995 and Hill, 1984/5.

32 Leeds City Archives Department, Harewood Papers, 189, 21 November 1797. The Lascelles accounts books are at Leeds City Archives Department, Harewood Papers, Calendar nos 189–192. Those of Edward's father, Lord Harewood also survive, nos 212, 211.

33 Leeds City Archives Department, Harewood Papers, 189, 15 March 1798.

34 TB L,R,S,T,Y,V,W,X,Y,Z cf. York, 1980 no. 11. Turner seems to have made a habit of running out of paper on his tours. Cf. D. Hill, *Turner in the Alps*, 1993, p.98ff.

35 TB LIR.

36 TB LIU.

37 It is perhaps a symptom of his reliance on LIU that there are a number of minor inaccuracies in the depiction of the house in the finished watercolour, for example the omission of the shallow bay which relieves the east wall of the pavilion, which is present in the sketch LIR.

38 There is a watercolour of exactly the same view by John Varley at Harewood, cf. Hill, 1995, p.47.

39 See essay by Ann Sumner in Hill, 1995, p.53ff.

40 Turner revisited Harewood Castle about 1808,. TB CVI 87a–83a, cf. Hill, 1995, p.26.

41 Farington Diary, 9 February 1799.

42 This is the only one of the series of large watercolours not in the Harewood collection today. The fourth Earl gave it to one of his sisters in 1858 and it has since descended to a private collection. There is a smaller version of the composition in the Harewood collection (Hill, 1995 p.27). An oil painting closely related to the small watercolour at Harewood was sold at Phillips, London, in 1988 as 'circle of J. M. W. Turner' and exhibited at the Northern Antiques Fair by Leger Galleries Ltd in 1993. Although the oil has been accepted by Andrew Wilton it does not seem likely to the present author that Turner himself would have repeated the composition so closely.

43 Leeds City Archives Department, Harewood Papers, 189.

44 Although Girtin's work of Harewood subjects is later in

date, cf. Hill, 1995, p.28ff.

45 He later sketched the Percy tomb in Beverley Minster (q.v.).

46 The castle was visited by Viscount Torrington on 6 June 1792 'where the day being delightful, I took my pencil for the first time on this journey' (Torrington Diaries, III 40). A pencil sketch attributed to Girtin, from a viewpoint a little to the right of Turner's, was sold Christie's 13 July 1965 lot 165, repr. Turner revisited the site in 1816 and made a number of sketches, TB CXLIV 1a–3, 6a–7a.

47 R. Buckle, *Harewood: A revised guide-book to the Yorkshire Seat of the Earls of Harewood*, Harewood, n.d. (1980), p.18. Robert Adam's design for the saloon, showing the original doors, and giving a hint of the original colour scheme, is at Sir John Soane's Museum, London (Adam series vol.35, no. 15).

48 Cf. Hargrove, 3rd ed., York, 1782, pp.90–1: 'Plumpton, Three miles from Harrogate, and two from Knaresborough, is much resorted to during the summer months, on account of its beautiful pleasure ground, which for its singularity of situation, and diversity of pleasing objects, has not its equal in Great Britain. It consists of about twelve acres of irregular ground, interspersed with a number of rocks, standing in detached pieces of various forms and magnitude, some whose hoary sides are fluted with the weather, others covered with grass and flowers. The walks are carried in different directions all over the place, sometimes leading up the rocky steep, then quickly descending into the gloomy vale. A fine lake of water washes the feet of these rocks, forming many curious inlets. Seats are placed in different parts from whence the spectator may have the most advantageous views of the different objects that compose this romantic scene. The striking contrast of the weather-beaten rock, with the blooming verdure that surrounds it, affords a pleasing instance of what nature, properly assisted by art, is capable of producing in the most rugged and barren soil.'

49 Watercolour study TB CXCXIII (repr. Bower, 1990, no.47), pencil sketch LIY recording the lake and rocks from the west. No study has yet been identified for the view from the south (Pl.237). Turner revisited the site in 1816, TB CXLIV 3a–6.

50 *See* Part VI, p. 184 for a discussion of the significance of the Plompton oils as a pair.

51 Farington Diary, 29 August 1801.

52 A point first made by John Gage, *Colour in Turner*, 1969, p.148.

53 Leeds City Archives Department, Harewood Papers, 211, 14 June 1798: 'Wm Turner for 2 Views of Plompton & Case for Do', presumably this worked out at fifteen guineas for each of the paintings, and nineteen shillings for the case.

54 His route presumably took him through Selby and it would be untypical of him not to have sketched its magnificent minster, particularly since he noted the subject, as also Howden and Beverley, in the list of northern subjects in the *Wilson* sketchbook, TB XXXVII p.127. Nevertheless, no sketches of Selby have yet been identified.

55 *The Minster Church of St Peter, Howden*, anon., n.d. c.1980. See also T. Clarke, *The History of the Church, Parish and Manor of Howden*, n.d.

56 Turner's sketches, and one by John Sell Cotman stemming from a visit to Howden in 1803 (Yale Center for British Art,

New Haven, B 1975.2.507, repr. Hawes, 1982, pl.35), are the earliest images of Howden that I am aware of. The Cotman records exactly the same view as Turner Pl.240.

57 The two sketches together would form a continuous view from the chapter house to the east end. It might seem odd that Turner did not take both subjects into the same sketch, but it is impossible to get back far enough today without the view being obscured by trees. Perhaps Turner had the same problem.

58 For further details see Rogerson, 1990.

59 This appears to be a leaf detached from the *North of England* sketchbook (*see* Part VII The Sketchbooks).

60 Farington Diaries, 24 October 1798. This has occasioned some dispute over the date of the visit to Brocklesby. Finberg, 1961, p.113 draws the obvious conclusion that the watercolours were made in October 1798, and Lyles, 1989, no. 29 takes the inference from Farington that Turner visited Brocklesby in October 1798. Wilton, 1987, p.47, however, speculates that a visit to Brocklesby might have been an integral part of the 1797 itinerary. This seems to me to be an inescapable conclusion, for the itinerary established by the sketchbook drawings takes him past the very gates of Brocklesby. In fact a visit to Brocklesby seems necessary to explain a huge detour at the end of an already exhausting itinerary. He seems on the basis of this to have gone twice. Perhaps he prospected the commission in 1797, and returned to make the finished drawings in 1798.

61 Finberg, 1909, TB LXXXIII identifies these sketches as constituting a sketchbook in their own right, but there is no sign of any covers.

62 TB LXXXIII 1–4.

63 TB LXXXIII 5.

64 TB LXXXIII 6.

65 TB LXXXIII 7.

66 N. Pevsner and J. Harris, *Buildings of England: Lincolnshire*, p.201.

67 Torrington Diaries, II 390–1, 12 July 1791.

68 TB CXXIU, cf. Lyles, 1989, no.29 where repr. b/w.

69 Finberg, 1961, p.113 says 'before 1909', but Pevsner, *op. cit.* gives a date of 1898 for a fire which gutted the main block.

70 See Maurice Davies, *Turner as Professor: The Artist and Linear Perspective*, catalogue of the exhibition at the Tate Gallery, London, 1992, where exh. no.13.

71 The date is usually given as *c*.1810, assuming that it was made specifically for the perspective lectures. Perhaps it could be earlier, although Turner is known to have had some connection with Wyatt (see e.g. W.333), and might well have had access to Wyatt's drawings. It is a remarkable exercise in accommodating an almost unmanageably large field of view. It is possible that this was one of the subjects of the three lost drawings that were mentioned by Farington (*see* p. 168) but even so there is no known pencil study of the subject.

72 Built *c*.1750 as the Corporation Mansion House, and later Louth Mechanics Institute, the facade was altered during the nineteenth century.

73 Given the narrowness of the street, its nature as a thoroughfare, and the fact that Louth has a proper market square not far away, such a scene seems highly improbable

in strict historical terms.

74 Shanes, 1990, p.190.

75 Given as Benjamin by Finberg, 1961, p.43, where it is suggested that he had commissioned some drawings for Turner to make on this tour. Turner had already made a watercolour of Grantham Church for him (q.v.), albeit from another artist's sketch.

76 *Louth Church*, G&L 149, publ. 1 October 1799, *Boston Church*, G&L 147, publ. 10 January 1799.

77 Boston church is visible from Keal, fourteen miles north, where the road from Louth drops from the wolds to the fens.

78 Molyneux and Wright, 1974, p.37.

79 Marsden, 1977, p.189.

80 White, 1856, p.281. The church contains a copy of Rubens's famous *Deposition* from Antwerp cathedral.

81 Thorold, 1989, p.37.

82 The wooden bridge recorded by Turner was replaced by an iron span designed by John Rennie in 1807 which in turn was replaced by the present bridge in 1913.

83 As recorded in the *North of England* sketchbook, inside cover 'Mr Howlett Boston Church VS' (*see* Part VII The Sketchbooks). Girtin made a watercolour which was published in 1799, *see* above note 76.

84 This colour-beginning was identified as Boston by Finberg, 1909. This was challenged by C. F. Bell in an annotated copy of Finberg at the British Museum, where he suggested St Mary Radcliffe, Bristol. The identification as Boston seems sound to me, however, and has been confirmed recently by Ian Warrell, *Watercolours and Drawings from the Turner Bequest*, Charleroi, 1994 no.64, and Eric Shanes in personal correspondence.

85 See Marsden, 1977, pp.137–40, White, 1856, p.430ff.

86 Cormack, 1972, no.48 questions the relationship of the watercolour to Howlett's engraving, but these doubts seem unnecessary.

87 Although it has to be said that he considerably magnified the apparent size of the market place.

88 I have discussed Turner's times of day elsewhere, see Hill, 1994.

89 W.232, where repr. b/w. Based on a sketch, according to the inscription on the plate, by Schenbbellie. The watercolour is now at the Yale Center for British Art, New Haven.

90 Though not, it has to be said for his tours in general. His tour of the midlands in 1794 is full of such subjects, and some of his best early watercolours such as Wolverhampton (W.139), are of subjects such as this.

91 Marsden, 1977, p.161. White, 1856, p.400 says Richard III lodged there on 16 October 1484. Turner must have passed through Grantham regularly on his frequent visits to Farnley Hall in Yorkshire between 1808 and 1824. His visit of 1816 is recorded in the *Yorkshire 2* sketchbook, TB CXLV p.186, when Turner noted that he paid 1s 6d there for brandy and water, see Hill, 1984, pp. 29 and 35.

92 I am not confident of my reading of one word as 'Laselles', but if correct, must have struck Turner, given his recent visit to the Lascelles family at Harewood.

93 Thorold, 1989, p.179.

94 Marsden, 1977, p.168.

95 Thornbury, 1877, p.391.

96 This might well be the cause of some confusion. Burghley was formerly in Northamptonshire, now in Cambridgeshire, but is usually thought of as being part of Stamford, which is in Lincolnshire.

97 *Guide to Burghley House, Stamford*, n.d., p.6.

98 TB XXIT (West front, basis of W. 126), U (SW spire), V (from north, basis of W.94).

99 W.94 (Peterborough City Museum and Art Gallery). A version of this was sold at Sotheby's 21 November 1984 (66 were repr.).

100 W.126 (Peterborough City Museum and Art Gallery). W.127 lists a version of this in a private collection (not repr.).

101 G&L (84iv) in the Ashmolean Museum, Oxford. C.f. Whitworth, 1975, no. 10, repr. b/w. There are versions of this in pencil at the Yale Center for British Art, New Haven, a pen and ink wash version at Birmingham City Art Gallery, and watercolour versions at the Courtauld Institute Galleries, and Whitworth Art Gallery, Manchester.

102 The gateway was built by Abbot Benedict 1177–93.

103 The porch built *c*.1380 is an extremely unusual feature. The sides are now closed in but the view is perfectly recognisable. The sculpture at the base of the slender *trumeau* column to the left of the centre is a lively carving in marble of Simon Magnus being cast into hell by devils, and the inscription noted by Turner in the foreground is a memorial to Anne Roberti Carrier who died in 1692, aged eight-two. I am indebted to Canon Higham, Librarian of Peterborough Cathedral for the historical notes on which this account is based.

NOTES TO PART VI

1 Leeds City Archives Department, Harewood Papers, 189: 'paid Mr Turner for two drawings . . . £21.0.0'.

2 Leeds City Archives Department, Harewood Papers, 189: 'paid Mr Turner for five drawings . . . £52.0.0'.

3 Cf. Hill, 1984/5, p.27ff. The two more distant views of Harewood House (Pls 224, 229) are dated 1798, so must have been among the group paid for in March 1798. The two nearer views of the house would have been the obvious place to start, and were probably therefore the two paid for in November 1797. The remaining three subjects (two larger version of Harewood Castle and one of Kirkstall Abbey) are listed together in the *North of England* sketchbook cover. Given that Lascelles paid for the pictures in two consignments, it seems possible that the initial commission was limited to two pictures, and that the remaining five were commissioned on the basis of the results achieved in these.

4 We do not know exactly when the list was made, nor indeed that everything in it was listed at the same time, but it seems probable that it records commissions to hand after November 1797, since it begins with the two Harewood Castle watercolours (*see* previous note), and before the April 1879 exhibition, since both Holy Island and Ambleside Mill were exhibited at the Academy.

5 Turner's spelling of Harewood is probably phonetic, recording the pronunciation as he had heard it. Har'wood is the pronunciation still properly given to the family name, and presumably was that current in 1797 for all uses. The name of the village is now more widely pronounced *Hare*wood.

6 For the two larger watercolours of Harewood Castle *see* Pls 232, 233.

7 Untraced, but *see* Pl.117.

8 Untraced, *see* p. 84.

9 This watercolour is now at Harewood, see Hill, 1995, p.27. Small in this case meant 222 x 305 mm.

10 *See* Pl. 188.

11 *See* Pl. 39. It is unclear why Turner differentiates Mr Lascelles, as in the two watercolours of Harewood Castle, from Hon Mr Lascelles as here. These watercolours were all owned by Edward Lascelles, and are listed in an inventory of his collection of 1814 (cf. Hill, 1995, pp 57–8 and Hill, 1984/5, p.33).

12 Untraced.

13 Untraced. Neither of the VS subjects of Louth or Boston seem to have been completed, *see* p. 171.

14 This is a little puzzling. Although Farington seems from the other subjects mentioned, to be describing the *Tweed and Lakes* sketchbook, it does not contain any sketches of Doncaster. These are in the *North of England* sketchbook, which contains all the subjects mentioned *except* the Lake District.

15 Farington Diary, 24 October 1798. Watercolour of Durham, Pl. 70.

16 The internal dimensions of the mount are 213 x 266 mm. What it contained remains a mystery.

17 We cannot be entirely sure that the two inscriptions are contemporary, but given that Ambleside occurs in the *North of England* sketchbook list, and that it was exhibited at the RA in 1798, it seems that Hoppner might have selected his Durham quite some while before Farington heard about it in October 1798.

18 TB XXXV 88 verso.

19 TB XXXV 13 verso, where dimensions of intended watercolour recorded as 9 by 12 ins (ie 229 x 305 mm).

20 TB XXXV 92 verso. The choice eventually had to be made for him by Robert Smirke, cf. Farington Diary, 8 July 1799 (quoted p.186).

21 TB XXXIV 67 verso. A William Blake of Portland Place is recorded as having had a disagreement with Turner over the price of Norham Castle (q.v.) cf. Roget, 1891, p.121, quoted Hill, 1984/5, part 2, p.37.

22 B&J 1

23 B&J 3.

24 B&J 2.

25 Quoted Finberg, 1961, p.41.

26 W.227.

27 Quoted Finberg, 1961, p.43.

28 The tenth being *Study in September of the fern house, Mr Lock's Park, Mickleham, Surry*. There appears to be no record of this composition beyond its exhibition.

29 Quoted Finberg, 1961, p.48.

30 Finberg, 1961, p.48.

31 Nor does he seem to have done so until 1816, see Hill, 1984, p.48ff. Given that Turner's subjects on the tour are mostly antiquarian, and the only 'pure' landscape subjects (i.e. those that do not feature some major architectural landmark) are those in the Lake District, a visit to Wensleydale for the purpose of landscape subjects as in 1816, would in any case seem unlikely for 1797.

32 The Ure being the river of Wensleydale.

33 Cf. B&J 4.

34 Or even Bolton Abbey (q.v.) but the brevity of that sketch would seem to make its use in this case unlikely.

35 B&J argues so, and Finberg, 1961, p.48 assumed so, but this does not seem to be absolutely certain.

36 Cf. Ziff, 1982, p.3 ff

37 Quoted B&J 5.

38 Quoted B&J 6.

39 Quoted B&J 5.

40 Quoted B&J 4.

41 Finberg, 1961, p.49.

42 *Ibid.*

43 Quoted B&J 5.

44 L. Gowing, *Turner: Imagination and Reality*, catalogue of the exhibition held at the Museum of Modern Art, New York, 1966, p.7.

45 A. Wilton, *Turner and the Sublime*, catalogue of the exhibition at Toronto, New Haven and London, 1980, pp.35–6. Although this is not quite the case with regard to the rainbow, cf. p.116.

46 The solidity of the cloud to the right is clearly an indication that the cloud has built up in that quarter of the sky. In the other painting it is still comparatively broken, although one can see a solid sheet of cloud advancing from the horizon in this direction.

47 Cf. discussion of figures in Harewood watercolours, p.154ff.

48 Turned used this same device in two watercolours of Pembroke Castle exhibited in 1801 and 1806. I have discussed this in Hill, 1984/5, pp. 41 ff.

49 Cf. the later watercolour of *St Agatha's Abbey* (Pl. 61), for yet another subtle effect of light. I went so far as to propose Turner's obtuseness as a deliberate strategem to invite and entrap uninformed criticism in Hill, 1994.

50 See Hill, 1984/5, part 1, p.24.

51 It is an irresistable temptation to observe that Turner well-timed the completion of Farington's watercolour. By the time it would have been delivered, that is after Farington's return to London early in 1802, Turner was pressing for election as full Royal Academician. He was successfully elected in February cf. Finberg, 1961, p.76.

52 That of Dunstanburgh was noticed by Joll, 1988. Turner's first visit to Brinkburn seems to have been 1801, and there are no indications of a visit in 1797. Since the watercolours are clearly a pair, they must both date from after 1801. The style might suggest a date of *c.*1802. It is perhaps also worth remarking here that the Laing Art Gallery, Newcastle has recently acquired an unrecorded pencil drawing of Brinkburn by Turner cf. *Turner Society News* no. 72, March 1996, p.2.

53 For 1808 sketches cf. TB CIX, CX. Lowther Castle oils B&J 111, 112.

54 Cf. York, 1980, and D. Hill, *Turner's Birds*, London, 1988.

55 Esp. W.535, *Grouse Shooting: Beamsley Beacon*, in the Wallace Collection, London, repr. in colour, Hill, 1984, p.102.

56 W.1052, 1056, the latter most recently sold at Sotheby's, 10 November 1992, lot 152.

57 W.1182 where repr. b/w.

58 W.183 where repr. b/w.

59 Shanes, 1990, frontispiece and p.6, where its inclusion is related to the Girtin plates in the same project.

60 Shanes, 1990, pp.13ff., and p.149.

61 Cf. Shanes, 1990, *passim*, and E. Shanes, *Turner's Picturesque Views in England and Wales*, London, 1979.

62 Cf. D. Hill, *Turner on the Thames*, 1993, p.152 and n.79.

63 Identified by Ian Warrell, *Watercolours and Drawings from the Turner Bequest*, Charleroi, 1994, n.65.

64 Lindsay, 1973, p.270.

65 Cf. B&J, pp. 298–9 and nos 509 ff.

66 K. Clark, *Landscape into Art*, London (1949) 1976, pp.194–5.

BIBLIOGRAPHY

ADAMS, J. *Mines of the Lake District Fells*, Skipton, 1995.

ANDREW, P. *Durham Cathedral, Artists and Images*, catalogue of the exhibition at Durham Art Gallery, 1993.

ANDREWS, M. *The Search for the Picturesque: Landscape, Aesthetics and Tourism in Britain, 1760–1800*, 1989.

ARMSTRONG, W. *Turner*, London, 1902.

BIBBY, R. *Bothal Revisited*, Frank Graham, Newcastle, 1973.

BICKNELL, P. *The Picturesque Scenery of the Lake District 1752–1855*, St Paul's Bibliographies, Winchester, 1990.

BISHOP, W. 'Views of Kirkstall Abbey', in *Leeds Arts Calendar*, no.81, 1977, pp.10–18, includes a list of 'Selected views of Kirkstall before 1830'.

BLORE, T. 'A History of the Manor and Manor House of South Wingfield in Derbyshire', in J. Nichols, *Bibliotheca Topographica Britannica*, Miscellaneous publications, 1793.

BOSWELL, H. *Historical Descriptions of. . . picturesque views of the antiquities of England and Wales*, London, 1786.

BOWER, P. *Turner's Papers: A Study of the Manufacture, Selection and Use of his Drawing Papers, 1789–1820*, catalogue of the exhibition at the Tate Gallery, London, 1990.

BOWERS, A. *A Study of the Prose and Poetry Descriptive of the Yorkshire Dales 1730–1830, with Special Reference to Materials in the Brotherton Library Collection*, Unpublished M.Phil. thesis, University of Leeds, 1986.

BREARS, P. *Kikstall Abbey, Leeds' Cistercian Monastery*, Leeds, n.d., (1981).

BUCK, S. and N. *Buck's Panoramic Views, 1774*, Sotheran Ltd, London, 1985.

BURKE, T. *Travel in England*, London, 1942.

BUTLIN, M. and JOLL, E. (B&J) *The Paintings of J.M.W. Turner*, New Haven and London (1977), 2nd edition, 1984.

CAMBRIDGE, E. *Lindisfarne Priory and Holy Island*, English Heritage, 1988.

CLARKE, M. *The Tempting Prospect*, London, 1981.

CORMACK, M. *British Watercolours and Drawings from the Museum of the Rhode Island School of Art and Design*, Bulletin of Rhode Island School of Art and Design, Rhode Providence, R.I., April, 1972.

DAYES, E. 'An Excursion through the principal parts of Derbyshire & Yorkshire', in *The Works of the Late Edward Dayes*, London, 1805, Facsimile reprint, Cornmarket Press, London, 1971.

DEFOE, D. *A Tour through the Whole Island of Great Britain, Divided into Circuits or Journies, Giving a particular and Diverting account of Whatever is curious and worth Observation, By a Gentleman*, London, in three parts 1724, 1725, 1727, the last treating the north of England, Everyman edition, 2 vols, 1962 incorporating *Tour to Scotland* (1723), reprinted in one vol. 1974.

DICKENSON, J. C. *Furness Abbey, Cumbria*, (1965), English Heritage, 1987.

Discovery. The Discovery of the Lake District, catalogue of the exhibition at the Victoria and Albert Museum, London, 1984–5.

DIXON, P. *Wingfield Manor*, English Heritage, 1995.

EMERY, A. 'Ralph, Lord Cromwell's Manor at Wingfield (1439–c.1450), its Construction, Design and Influence', *Archaeological Journal*, 142, 1985, pp. 276–339.

FARINGTON, J. *Views in the Lakes &c of Cumberland and Westmorland*, London, 1789.

FAWCETT, R. *Jedburgh Abbey*, (1990), Historic Scotland, 1995.

FINBERG, A.J. *A Complete Inventory of the Drawings of the Turner Bequest*, 2 vols, London, 1909.

FINBERG, A.J. *The Life of J.M.W. Turner*, (1939), 2nd ed. Oxford, 1961.

FINLEY, G. *Landscapes of Memory: Turner as Illustrator to Scott*, London, 1980.

GAGE, J. *Turner: A Wonderful Range of Mind*, New Haven and London, 1987.

GELL, W. *A Tour to the Lakes made in 1797*, ed. William Rollinson, Newcastle upon Tyne, 1968. MSS. at Barrow in Furness Public Library, inc. numerous watercolours, maps &c. not included in 1968 publication.

GILPIN, W. *Observations, Relative chiefly to Picturesque Beauty made in the year 1772 on several parts of England., particularly. . .the mountains and lakes of Cumberland and Westmorland.* 1st ed., 2 vols, 1786. Original extra-illustrated MSS. at Bodelian Library, Oxford.

GILYARD-BEER, R. *Fountains Abbey, North Yorkshire*, HMSO, 1970.

GIRTIN, T. and LOSHAK, D. (G&L) *The Art of Thomas Girtin*, London, 1954.

GRAHAM F. *Warkworth [&c]: A short History and Guide*, Newcastle, 1971.

GRAHAM, F. *Berwick, A short history and Guide*, Newcastle (1972), 1984.

GRAHAM, F. *Historic Holy Island*, Newcastle, 1975.

GRAHAM, F. *Northumbrian Castles: Aln, Tweed and Till*, Newcastle, 1993.

GRAHAM, F. *Alnwick, a short history and Guide*, Newcastle, 1994.

GRAHAM, R. and BAILLIE REYNOLDS, P. K. *Egglestone Abbey, Yorkshire*, HMSO, (1958), 1976.

GRANT, J. *Journal of a Three Weeks' tour in 1797 through Derbyshire to the Lakes*, published in William Mavor, *The British Tourists*, 1798, Vol.V, p.199, as by a Gentleman of the University of Oxford.

GREATHEAD, T. *Photographs of Old Conisbrough*, Doncaster, 1990.

GREEVES, L. and MAUCHLINE, M. *Fountains Abbey and Studley Royal*, National Trust, 1988.

HAMILTON THOMPSON, A. *Easby Abbey, Yorkshire*, English Heritage (1936) 2nd ed. 1948.

HANKINSON, A. *Coleridge walks the Fells*, London, (1991), 1993.

HARGROVE, E. *History of Knaresborough (&c)*, 1st ed. York, 1775, subsequent editions: 3rd, York,'1792; 4th much enlarged ,York, 1789; 5th, 1798; 6th, 1809; another 1832.

HAWES, L. *Presences of Nature: British Landscape 1780– 1830*, catalogue of the exhibition at the Yale Center for British Art, New Haven, 1982.

HEDLEY, G. *The Picturesque Tour in Northumberland and Durham, c.1720–1830*, catalogue of the exhibition at the Laing Art Gallery, Newcastle, 1982.

HILL, D. *In Turner's Footsteps through the hills and dales of Northern England*, London, 1984.

HILL, D. 'A Taste for the Arts: Turner and the patronage of Edward Lascelles of Harewood House', *Turner Studies*, Part 1, 4ii, Winter, 1984, pp. 24–33: Part 2, 5i, Spring 1985, pp. 30-46.

HILL, D. 'When Panting Art Toils after Truth in Vain', text of the 15th Kurt Pantzer Memorial Lecture, 1994, *Turner Society News*, 67, August 1994.

HILL, D. *Harewood Masterpieces: English Watercolours and Drawings*, Harewood House Trust, 1995.

HOWARD, P. *Landscapes: The Artists' Vision*, London, 1991.

HUNTER BLAIR, C. H. and HONEYMAN, H. L. *Warkworth Castle, Northumberland*, HMSO, (1954), 1977.

HUNTER BLAIR, C. H. and HONEYMAN, H. L. *Dunstanburgh Castle, Northumberland*, HMSO, (1936), 3rd ed, 1982.

HUNTER BLAIR, C. H. and HONEYMAN, H. L. *Norham Castle, Northumberland*, (1936), English Heritage, 1985.

JACKSON, J. E. *The History and Description of St George's Church at Doncaster*, London, 1855.

JOHNSON, M. *Durham: Historic and University City*, (1970), 4th ed., Durham, 1983.

JOHNSON, S. *Conisbrough Castle*, English Heritage, London, (1984), 2nd ed., 1989, reprinted 1995.

JOLL, E. 'Turner at Dunstanburgh', *Turner Studies*, 8ii, Winter 1988, pp. 3–7.

LEICESTER, 1970 *Sir George Beaumont of Coleorton, Leicestershire*, catalogue of the exhibition at Leicester Museum and Art Gallery, 1970.

LINDSAY, J. *Turner*, (1966) paperback edition, Granada publishing, 1973.

LYLES, A. *Young Turner: Early Work to 1800*, catalogue of the exhibition at the Tate Gallery, London, 1989.

MADGWICK, H. 'Turner in Northumberland in 1797', in *Turner Society News*, no. 63, March 1993, pp. 8–9.

MARSDEN, W. *Lincolnshire*, London, 1977.

MILLER, E. *History and Antiquities of Doncaster*, Doncaster, 1804.

MILNER, F. *Turner Paintings in Merseyside Collections*, Liverpool, 1990.

MOIR, E. *The Discovery of Britain: The English Tourists 1540–1840*, London, 1964.

MOLYNEUX, F. and WRIGHT, N. *An Atlas of Boston*, Boston, 1974.

MORRIS, D. *Thomas Hearne and his Landscape*, London, 1989.

MORRIS, S. *Thomas Girtin*, catalogue of the exhibition at the Yale Center for British Art, New Haven, 1986.

NICHOLS, J. *Bibliotheca Topographica Britannica*, 48 parts in 8 vols, London, 1780–90, plus Miscellanies, 1793 and 1819.

OWEN, F. and BROWN, D. B. *Collector of Genius – A Life of Sir George Beaumont*, London, 1988.

PEERS, C. *Richmond Castle, Yorkshire*, English Heritage (1953), 1977.

PENNANT, T. *Tour in Scotland in 1769*, Chester , 1771.

POCOCKE, R. *The Travels through England of Dr Richard Pococke, 1750–57*, ed. J.J. Cartwight in *Camden Society*, New Series, vols 42, 44, 1888–9.

RA, 1993 Andrew Wilton and Anne Lyles, *The Great Age of British Watercolours*, catalogue of the exhibition at the Royal Academy, London, 1993.

RHODES, K. *The Priory Church of St Mary and St Cuthbert, Bolton Abbey*, 1990.

RICHARDSON, J.S. and TABRAHAM, C.J. *Dryburgh Abbey*, (1937), fourth, revised edition, Historic Scotland, 1987.

ROGERSON, P. *Beverley Minster*, 1990.

ROGET, J.L. *History of the Old Watercolour Society*, 1891, reprinted 1972.

RUDD, M.D.C. *The Picturesque and Landscape Appreciation: The development of tourism in the Yorkshire Dales & County Durham*

1750–1860, unpublished M.A. thesis, University of Durham, 1990.

SAUNDERS, A. D. *Barnard Castle*, HMSO, 1971.

SAUNDERS, A. *Tynemouth Priory, Castle and Twentieth-Century Fortifications*, English Heritage, 1993.

SHANES, E. *Turner's England*, London, 1990.

STRANKS, C. J. *Durham Cathedral*, London, 1970.

THORNBURY, W. *The Life and Correspondence of J.M.W. Turner*, London, 1877.

THOROLD, H. *Lincolnshire Churches Revisited*, Salisbury, 1989.

Torrington Diaries, C. Bryun Andrews (ed), *The Torrington Diaries: Containing the tours through England and Wales of the Hon John Byng (later fifth Viscount Torrington) between the years 1781 and 1794*, 4 vols, London, 1934, reprinted 1970.

V&A, 1994 *Prospects, Thresholds and Interiors: Watercolours from the V&A* catalogue of the exhibition at the Victoria and Albert Museum, London, 1994.

Viewfinders (VF) *The Viewfinders: an exhibition of Lake District Landscapes*, catalogue of the exhibition at Abbot Hall, Kendal, 1980.

WEINREB and DOUWMA, 1977 *The British Isles, Part 1*, catalogue of an exhibition of books, prints and maps, London, 1977.

WEST, T. *Guide to the Lakes*, (1778), second, revised edition, with appendices, 1780, quoted here from third edition, 1784.

WHITE, C. *English Landscape, 1630–1850, Drawings, Prints & Books from the Paul Mellon Collection*, Yale Center for British Art, New Haven, 1977.

WHITE, W. *History, Gazetteer and Directory of Lincolnshire [&c]*, Sheffield, 1856, Facsimile reprint, David and Charles, 1969.

WHITWORTH, 1975, F. Hawcroft, *Thomas Girtin*, catalogue of the exhibition, Whitworth Art Gallery Manchester, and the V&A, London, 1975.

WHITWORTH, 1993, *From View to Vision: British Watercolours from Sandby to Turner*, catalogue of the exhibition, Whitworth Art Gallery, Manchester, 1993.

WILKINSON, W. E. *Ripon Cathedral*, London, 1974.

WILLIAMS, I. *Early English Watercolours*, (1954), reprinted Bath, 1970.

WILSON, M. I. *Early British Topography: A list of books and articles in the National Art Library, Victoria and Albert Museum*, V&A, 1977.

WILTON, A. (W.) *The Life and Work of J.M.W. Turner*, London, 1979.

WILTON, A. 'The Monro School Question: Some Answers', *Turner Studies*, 4ii, Winter, 1984, pp.8–23.

WILTON, A. *Turner in his Time*, London, 1987.

WOOD, M. and RICHARDSON, J. S. *Melrose Abbey*, (1932), revised edition, 1995.

WORDSWORTH, W. *Guide to the Lakes, 1835*, ed. Ernest de Selincourt, Oxford, 1977.

WROOT, H.E. 'Turner in Yorkshire; his Wanderings and Sketches', in *Publications of the Thoresby Society: Miscellanea*, Vol. XXVI, Part III, pp.221–42, 1921.

YORK, 1975 *A Yorkshire Tour*, catalogue of the exhibition at York City Art Gallery, 1975.

YORK, 1980 *Turner in Yorkshire*, catalogue of the exhibition at York City Art Gallery, by D. Hill, S. Warburton and M. Tussey, ed. R. Green, York, 1980.

YORK, 1985 *The Wonder of the North*, catalogue of the exhibition of images of Fountains Abbey and Studley Royal, York City Art Gallery, 1985.

ZIFF, J. 'Turner's First Poetic Quotations: an Examination of Intentions', *Turner Studies*, 2.i, Summer, 1982, pp.2–11.

INDEX

Principal sites are given in Capital Letters, picture titles in *italics*, page references in normal type, primary references to sites in **bold**, and plate numbers in *italics*. All works cited are by J.M.W. Turner unless otherwise stated.

PHOTOGRAPHIC ACKNOWLEDGEMENTS

2, 225, 226, 227, 228, 229, 232, 236, 240, 241: Reproduced by kind permission of the Earl and Countess of Harewood and the Trustees of the Harewood House Trust, photography Jim Kershaw; 25: By courtesy of the Trustees of Sir John Soane's Museum; 41: Gloucester City Museum; 80: Antonia Reeve Photography; 132, 184: Private Collection, courtesy of Agnew's London; 191: Bridgeman Art Library; 110: National Trust Photographic Library; 164: © Christie's Images; 171, 237: John Webb; 211, 255: Reproduced by courtesy of the Leger Galleries Ltd, London.